APPLIED KEYBOARDING

Includes commands and directions for
WordPerfect® 5.1, MS-DOS®
Microsoft® Works 2.0 and 3.0, MS-DOS®
Microsoft® Works 2.0, Macintosh®

Jerry W. Robinson, Ed.D.
Keyboarding Instructor
Moeller High School
Cincinnati

Jack P. Hoggatt, Ed.D.
Professor of Business Education
and Administrative Management
University of Wisconsin
Eau Claire

Jon A. Shank, Ed.D.
Professor of Administrative Management
and Business Education
Robert Morris College
Coraopolis (PA)

Arnola C. Ownby, Ed.D.
Professor of Office Administration
and Business Education
Southwest Missouri State University

Lee R. Beaumont, Ed.D.
Professor of Business, Emeritus
Indiana University of Pennsylvania

SOUTH-WESTERN PUBLISHING CO.

Executive Editor: Karen Schmohe
Developmental Editor II: Dorinda Clippinger
Coordinating Editor: Susan Richardson
Production Manager: Deborah Luebbe
Senior Production Editor: Alan Biondi
Production Editors: Timothy Bailey, Diane Bowdler
Associate Photo Editor/Stylist: Fred M. Middendorf
Production Artist: Sophia Renieris
Marketing Manager: Larry Qualls
Product Manager: Al Roane

ACKNOWLEDGMENTS

The authors and publisher acknowledge with thanks the work of six persons who thoroughly reviewed the manuscript and offered valuable suggestions for making a good textbook even better. Reviewers either teach keyboarding and/or word processing to high school students or have done so recently. Appreciation is expressed to:

Susan B. Boleware, Mississippi State University
Juliana Dellefave, Richardson High School, Dallas
Jeanette Kosiorek, Youngstown (OH) State University
Jennifer McDonald, Oak Hills High School, Cincinnati
Connie K. Morrison, Computer Education Consultant, Lexington, OH
Patricia M. Wathen, Formerly, Princeton High School, Cincinnati

HARDWARE/SOFTWARE CREDITS

IBM® is a registered trademark of International Business Machines Corporation.

Macintosh® is a trademark of McIntosh Laboratory, Inc., and is used by Apple Computer, Inc., with its express permission. References to MAC also refer to this note.

Microsoft® Works is a registered trademark of Microsoft Corporation. References to Works also refer to this note.

MS-DOS® is a registered trademark of Microsoft Corporation. References to DOS also refer to this note.

WordPerfect® is a registered trademark of WordPerfect Corporation.

PHOTO CREDITS

COVER PHOTO: © Bray Ficken
PHOTO, p. v: © Phillip A. Harrington
PHOTO, p. vii, photo 1: Photo courtesy of Apple Computer, Inc.
PHOTO, p. ix, photo 1: Photo courtesy of Epson America, Inc.
PHOTO, p. xv: © Phillip A. Harrington
PHOTO, p. 1: © Phillip A. Harrington
PHOTO, p. 49: © Phillip A. Harrington
PHOTO, p. 93: © Phillip A. Harrington
PHOTO, p. 159: © Phillip A. Harrington

ISBN: 0-538-62297-0 (TM37CA)
0-538-62298-9 (TM37CA1)

1 2 3 4 5 6 7 8 9 10 11 12 H 04 03 02 01 00 99 98 97 96 95 94 93

Printed in the United States of America

Library of Congress Cataloging-in-Publication Data

Applied Keyboarding / Jerry W. Robinson . . . [et al.].
p. cm.
Summary: Provides directions and exercises for basic skill building in keyboarding, for both typewriters and computers.
ISBN 0-538-62297-0. -- ISBN 0-538-62298-9
1. Electronic data processing--Keyboarding--Juvenile literature.
[1. Data processing--Keyboarding. 2. Computers. 3. Typewriting.]
I. Robinson, Jerry W.
QA76.9.K48A67 1994
652.5' 536--dc20 93-7454
CIP
AC

CONTENTS

CONTENTS

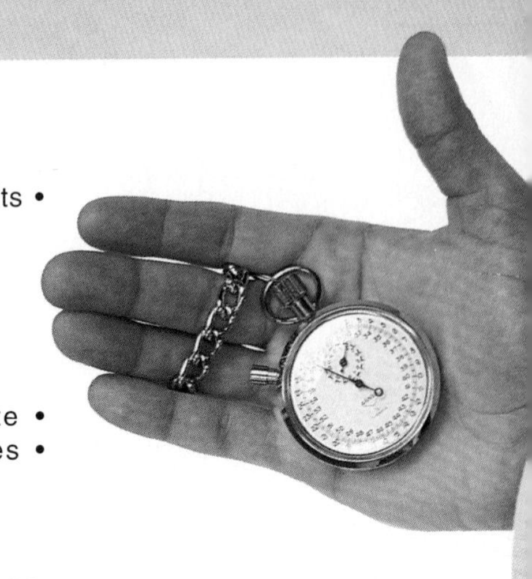

MODULE 3
MASTER DOCUMENT FORMATTING, 93

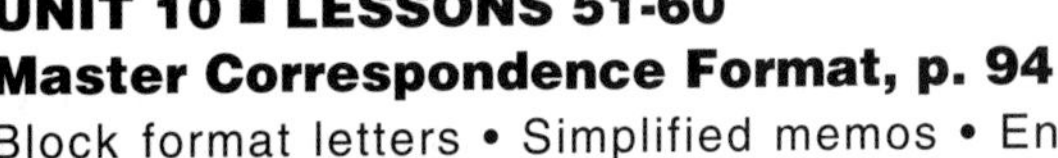

To Students

Changes in computer hardware and software have had a significant effect on the way we work, live, and learn. Many tasks that we used to do manually can now be performed by computers, many of which use a keyboard for entering or changing information. Likewise, keyboarding, document formatting, and word processing instruction have changed. Modern typewriters and computers, especially microcomputer hardware and software, have changed the way documents are prepared, improved the quality of documents, increased productivity, and afforded new methods for learning keyboarding skills. This third edition of this textbook integrates advances in technology into your applied keyboarding course so you can experience firsthand the impact of many of the changes.

The full-color text is appropriate for students using typewriters, those using stand-alone or networked microcomputers, and those studying in classrooms that have a mixture of typewriters and microcomputers. The text can be used by students using word processing software to process documents and by those learning about word processing operations without using software.

This lesson-planned textbook contains software-specific word processing commands for the features of three leading software packages: WordPerfect 5.1, Microsoft Works for IBM PCs and many compatibles, and Microsoft Works for the Apple Macintosh.

As your teacher leads you through the activities in the text, you will develop the following outcomes:

- mastery of the alphabetic keyboard
- mastery of the fourth-row numeric keyboard and the numeric keypad, if applicable
- ability to format documents in styles that take advantage of the advances in microcomputer hardware and word processing software
- ability to use the features that your equipment provides to perform various formatting and editing functions
- ability to prepare correspondence, reports, and tables that are acceptable in format, language usage, and error detection and correction

The textbook is organized into three carefully planned and written modules. A hardware/software overview follows this message to students. A glossary of key terms in the textbook is next. Special language skills activities, including a list of sound-alike words, follow the third module of lessons. A word processing command summary at the back of the textbook will be useful in the keyboarding course—or whenever you use one of the three software packages.

Module 1

Module 1 consists of Lessons 1-25 organized into three units.

At first your purpose will be to learn the standard key locations and to operate keys by touch (without looking). Only two new keys are presented in each lesson, and a review lesson occurs after every three lessons. Thus, you will learn the letter, punctuation, and basic service keys, such as the space bar and CAPS LOCK, at a comfortable pace.

Commands for some word processing features also are presented in Module 1. You will learn to adjust your equipment and to key words, sentences, even paragraphs, smoothly.

Becoming a skilled keyboard user requires that you intend to learn and that you practice intensively. Thus, you must become an active learner for these lessons to develop your skill to the level the lessons were designed to achieve.

Module 2

Module 2 consists of Lessons 26-50 organized into six units.

In these 25 lessons, you will learn to key figures and symbols by touch. By refining your technique, you will improve the speed and accuracy of your keying. Besides straight (printed) copy, you will build skill on handwritten and rough-draft copy and copy containing numbers.

More word processing features are presented in Module 2, and you will become more adept at adjusting your equipment. The numeric keypad is presented in these lessons, along with drills for learning to enter data rapidly and accurately by touch.

Preface, continued

Module 3

Module 3 consists of Lessons 51-80 organized into four units.

In the lessons of this module, you will learn to arrange (format) copy. You will apply your keyboarding skill to these kinds of documents: letters and memos, reports, and tables (information in columns).

Along with formatting guidelines, still more word processing features are presented. Thus, you will be able to prepare letters, reports (with references and title page), and tables for your needs in school or at home.

These same documents also are often prepared by business employees. In fact, Module 3 gives you an opportunity to use what you learn as a part-time "employee" of a real-estate company.

Throughout these lessons, you will work to improve your speed and accuracy at the keyboard. Your performance on basic keyboarding skill and formatting will be evaluated and assessed in some lessons of Module 3.

Hardware and Software Review

Beginning on page vii is a thorough section that will help you to learn the various parts of the equipment that you will use in this course and tell you how to take care of your equipment. Computer users will learn the basics of taking care of software; "powering up" and "powering down" computers; naming, saving, and retrieving a word processing file; and printing a document. Typewriter users will learn how to adjust the paper guide, insert paper, select line spacing, and plan and set margins.

Glossary

Beginning on page xv is a two-page glossary that lists the word processing operations presented in the text. Each operation is described briefly in general terms. You should refer to this glossary whenever you encounter an unfamiliar word processing term. The glossary also contains the special two-letter abbreviations used in textbook directions.

Language Skills

Beginning on page 147 is a series of language skills improvement activities. Using the popular Rule/Learn/Apply sequence, you have the opportunity to review and apply the rules of capitalization, number expression, subject/verb agreement, and punctuation. This section of the textbook also includes word lists to improve your ability to use and spell words that are often confused with other words and to divide words at the end of lines.

The language skills may be made a formal part of your applied keyboarding course, or your teacher may have you complete them by yourself or as a member of a group of classmates.

Command Summary

Following page 79 is a command summary that lists the keystrokes needed to use features of the three software packages included in this textbook. You should use the command summary as a reference when you need to perform an operation and you are unsure of the keystrokes required.

If more information about a specific operation is needed, you should refer to the textbook page on which a description of the operation is given, use the on-line Help feature of your word processing software package, or refer to the user's guide for the software you are using.

Applied Keyboarding, Third Edition, is a textbook that will help you and your teacher develop your keyboarding, document formatting, and word processing skills to a high level. It includes all of the following and more:

- properly spaced learning and application materials and activities
- up-to-date formatting procedures for documents that you will use for school, work, and/or home
- the main features of three word processing software packages often used in schools, offices, and homes

You, however, will ultimately determine the extent to which you develop your skills in these areas. Remember: You can improve your performance if you become an active learner who practices according to your teacher's directions as you proceed through the textbook activities.

J. W. R.
J. P. H.
J. A. S.

KNOW YOUR MACINTOSH

The illustrations below show the major parts of a Macintosh. The following copy identifies each numbered part. These parts are found on almost all computers, but their location may vary. If you are using a Macintosh computer other than the model illustrated, see the manufacturer's booklet for the exact location of each part.

1. **Keyboard:** an arrangement of letter, figure, symbol, and other keys used to input characters, commands, and functions to the computer
2. **CPU (Central Processing Unit):** the internal operating unit or "brain" of a computer
3. **Disk drive:** a unit, connected to or situated inside the computer, that reads and writes onto disks
4. **Monitor:** TV-like device used to display text and graphic images on a screen
5. **Printer:** a unit attached to a computer that produces text on paper (hard copy)
6. **Numeric keypad:** a calculator-type keyboard used when large amounts of numeric data are to be keyed (not available on all keyboards)
7. **Function (F) keys:** special keys used alone or in combination with other keys to perform special functions
8. **Space bar:** a long bar at the bottom of the keyboard used to insert a space between words or characters
9. **Caps lock:** a key that when locked down causes all letters to be capitalized without affecting any other keys
10. **Shift keys:** keys used to make capital letters and certain symbols
11. **Control (Ctrl):** a key depressed as another key is struck to perform a special function
12. **Tab:** a key that when struck causes the cursor (enter point) to move to a preset position, as in indenting paragraphs
13. **Escape (Esc):** a general purpose key that is often used to transfer to another section of the application software and to "back out" of commands
14. **Delete:** a key that when struck moves the cursor one position to the left, deleting any character occupying that space
15. **Return:** a key that when struck causes the cursor to move to the left margin and down to the next line
16. **Arrow keys:** keys that move the cursor in the direction indicated by the arrow on the key; serve as an alternative to using a mouse to move the cursor
17. **⌘ (Command):** a key that when depressed at the same time another key is struck causes that key to serve as an alternative to choosing a menu command
18. **Num Lock:** a key used to switch the numeric keypad back and forth between numeric entry and editing
19. **Mouse:** a device that is rolled across desk surface to control movements of an indicator on screen

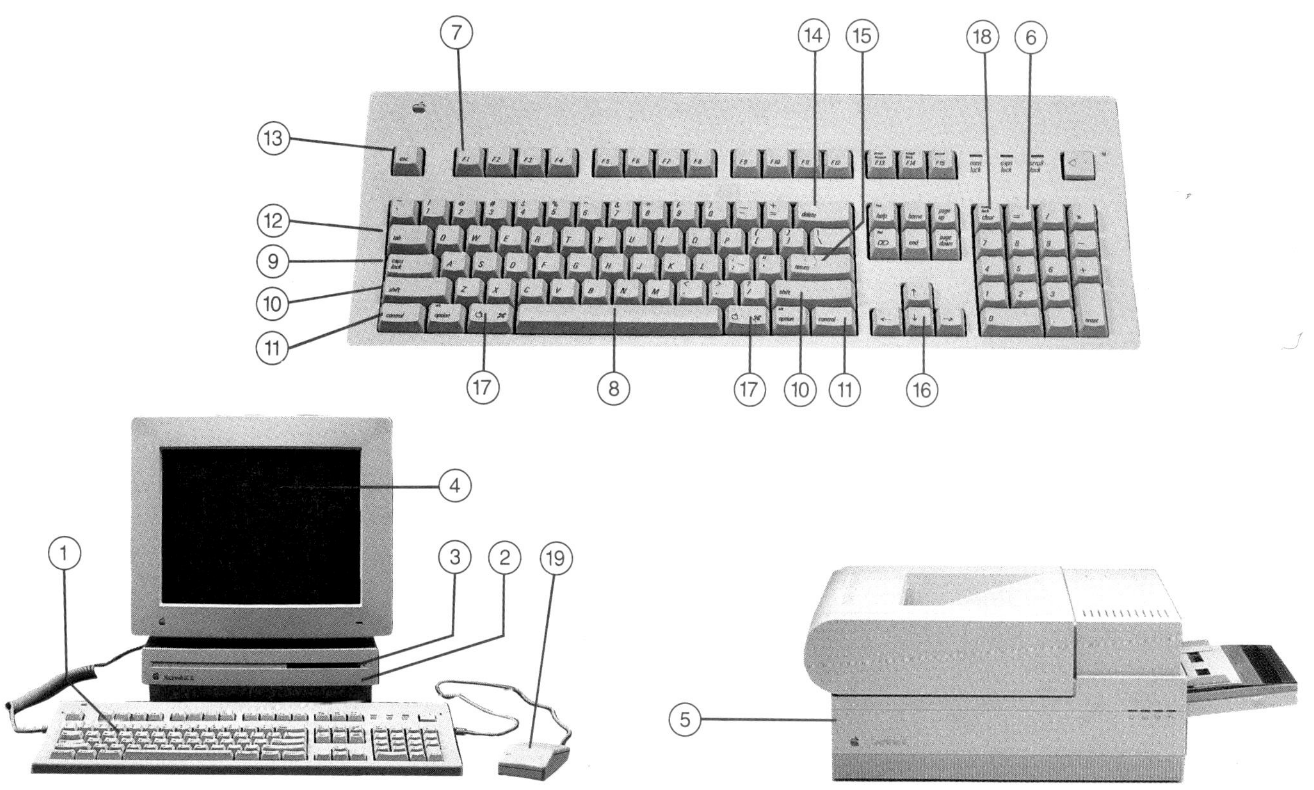

Know Your Macintosh, continued

Open

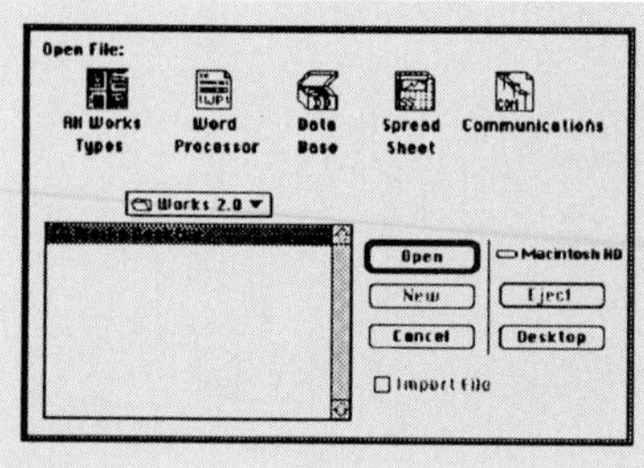

New

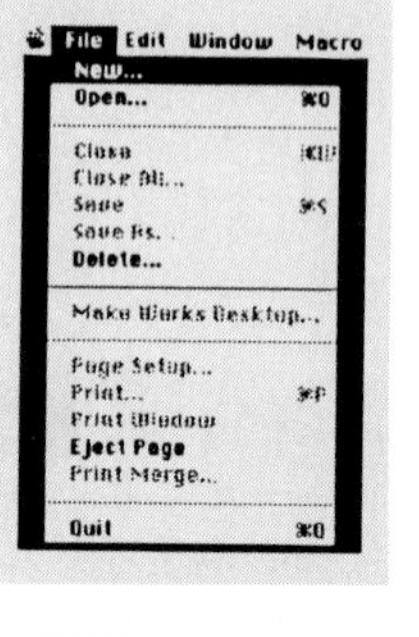

Close

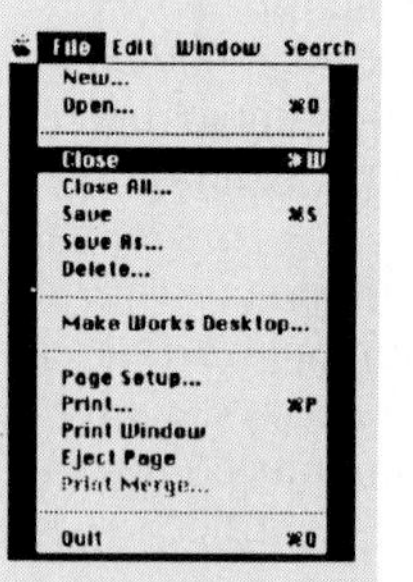

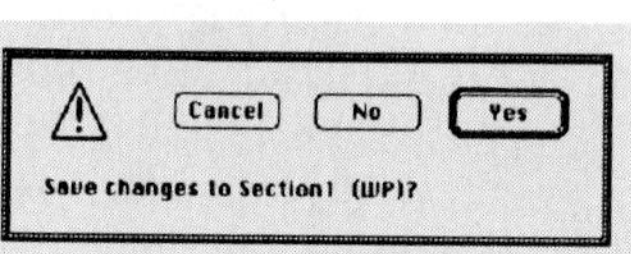

Powering Up a Macintosh

Power up (turn on) your Macintosh computer as follows:

1. Turn on any external devices connected to your Macintosh.
2. **Macintosh Classic or LC models:** Press the on/off switch on the back of the computer. If the Macintosh LC monitor does not turn on, make sure that the monitor's on/off switch is on. **Macintosh II models:** Press the Power On key (upper-right corner on extended keyboards; above the 4, 5, and 6 number keys on standard keyboards).
3. When your computer is powered up, a "desktop" will appear on the screen. The desktop is a field with a bar of menu names and icons across the top. Once the desktop is displayed, the computer is ready to accept instructions from you.
4. If your Macintosh doesn't power up, it will display an icon representing a 3.5" disk with a ? (question mark). If this mark is displayed, ask your teacher for assistance.

Powering Down a Macintosh

Power down (turn off) your Macintosh computer as follows:

1. Use the mouse to point to the Special menu in the menu bar.
2. Press and hold down the mouse button.
3. Drag through the items in the Special menu until the Shut Down command is highlighted, then release the mouse button.
4. **Macintosh LC and Classic models:** Press the on/off switch on the back of the computer when a message on the screen indicates that it is safe to do so. If you have a Macintosh LC, switch off the monitor. **Macintosh II models:** The computer and monitor turn off by themselves when the Shut Down Command is selected.

Retrieving a File on Your Macintosh with Microsoft Works Software

To retrieve (or open) an existing file (document) stored on your hard disk or internal or external disk drives:

1. Choose Open from the File menu.
2. Select (highlight) the name of the file you want to retrieve.
3. Click the Open button.

Creating a New File on Your Macintosh with Microsoft Works Software

To create (open) a new file (document), you can use the New command or the Open command. To use the New command:

1. Choose New from the File menu (displays the Create New Document dialog box).
2. Click the icon for the type of document you want to create.
3. Click the OK button (a new window is opened for you to create the document).

To create a new document from the Open dialog box, which is displayed when you start Works or when you choose the Open command from the File menu:

1. With the Open dialog box displayed, click the icon for the type of document you want to create.
2. Click the New button.

Closing a Document on Your Macintosh with Microsoft Works Software

When you want to remove a document from the desktop, you close the file. During the close process, Works will save or delete this copy of the document, or cancel the command. If you want to save this copy of the document on a disk, you should elect to save the changes. To use the Close command and save the copy:

1. Choose Close from the File menu.
2. Click the Yes button to save the changes.

Printing a Document on Your Macintosh with Microsoft Works Software

To print a document using the default page setups:

1. Make certain the printer is turned on and ready for printing.
2. Choose Print from the File menu.
3. Click the OK button.

KNOW YOUR IBM PC OR COMPATIBLE COMPUTER

The illustrations below show the major parts of an IBM PC. The following copy identifies each numbered part. These parts are found on almost all computers, but their location may vary. If you are using an IBM PC or compatible computer other than the model illustrated, see the manufacturer's booklet for the exact location of each part.

1. **Keyboard:** an arrangement of letter, figure, symbol, and other keys used to input characters, commands, and functions to the computer
2. **CPU (Central Processing Unit):** the internal operating unit or "brain" of a computer
3. **Disk drive:** a unit, connected to or situated inside the computer, that reads and writes onto disks
4. **Monitor:** TV-like device used to display text and graphic images on a screen
5. **Printer:** a unit attached to a computer that produces text on paper (hard copy)
6. **Numeric keypad:** a calculator-type keyboard used when large amounts of numeric data are to be keyed (not available on all keyboards)
7. **Function (F) keys:** special keys used alone or in combination with other keys to perform special functions, such as setting margins and centering copy
8. **Space bar:** a long bar at the bottom of the keyboard used to insert a space between words
9. **Caps Lock:** a key that when locked down causes all letters to be capitalized
10. **Shift keys:** keys used to make capital letters and certain symbols
11. **Control (Ctrl):** a key depressed as another key is struck, causing that key to perform a special function
12. **Tab:** a key that when struck causes the cursor (enter point) to move to a preset position, as in indenting paragraphs
13. **Escape (Esc):** a key used to transfer to another section of the software and to "back out" of commands
14. **Delete:** a key that when struck moves the cursor one position to the left, deleting any character occupying that space
15. **Return (Enter):** a key that when struck causes the cursor to move to the left margin and down to the next line
16. **Arrow keys:** keys that move the cursor in the direction indicated by the arrow on the key
17. **Alternate (Alt):** a key that when depressed immediately before or as another key is struck causes that key to perform a special function
18. **Num Lock:** a key used to switch the numeric keypad between numeric entry and editing

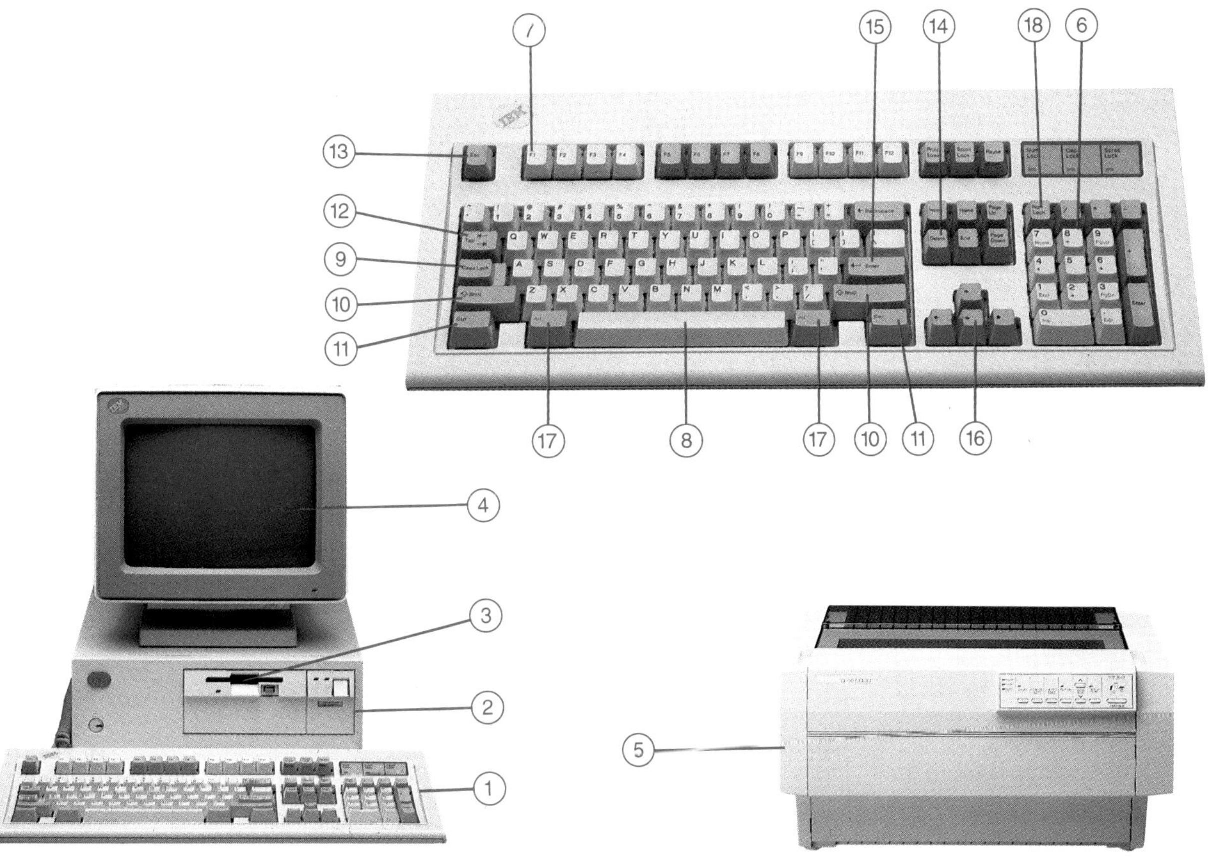

Know Your IBM PC or Compatible Computer, continued

Open:
Works DOS

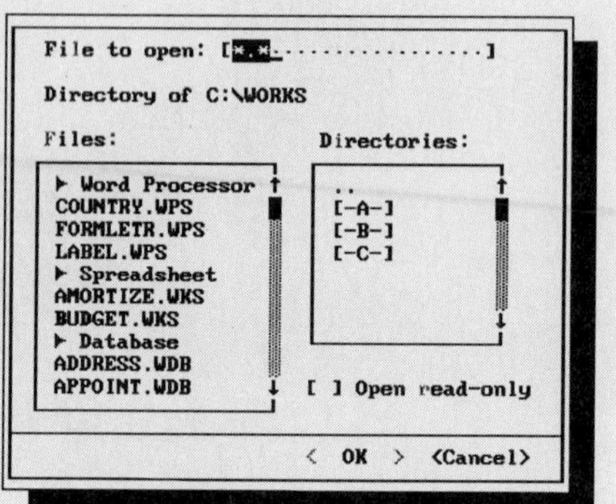

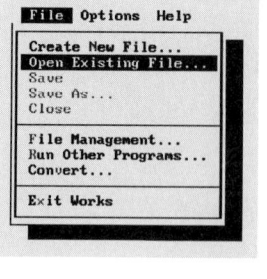

Create:
Works DOS

The following information applies to IBM PCs and most compatibles that have a hard disk drive (named the C drive) with one or two other disk drives (one named A and one named B). If your computer has a different configuration, your teacher will give you the information you need; or you should refer to the user's manual for your equipment.

Powering Up an IBM PC or Compatible Computer

Power up (turn on) your IBM PC or compatible computer as follows:

1. If there is a disk inserted into either drive A or B, remove it by turning the lever on the drive door so the disk can be removed from the disk drive (5.25" disks) or by pressing the button to eject the disk from the drive (3.5" disks).
2. Turn the computer's power switch or button on.
3. If the monitor still is not on, turn the monitor's power switch or button on.
4. If a printer will be used, turn on the printer's power switch or button.
5. The computer will display C> to tell you that it is turned on (powered up) and ready to accept instructions from you.

Powering Down an IBM PC or Compatible Computer

Power down (turn off) your IBM PC or compatible computer as follows: (Some systems require the hard drive to be "parked" before powering down; see booklet from manufacturer.)

1. Prepare to remove each disk from its drive by turning the lever (5.25" disks) or by pressing the button to eject the disk (3.5" disks).
2. Gently remove each disk from the disk drive and store it safely.
3. Turn off the power switch or button for each piece of equipment that you are using.

Retrieving a File on Your IBM PC or Compatible Computer

Microsoft Works Software

Microsoft Works lets you retrieve (or open) existing files (documents) stored on your hard disk (C) or in internal or external disk drives (A, B):

1. Depress the Alt key; hold it down as you strike F. Release the keys; strike O (chooses Open Existing File from the File menu and displays the Files dialog box, listing all files and folders on the current disk).
2. Select (highlight) the name of the file you want to retrieve.
3. Strike Enter (Works displays a copy of the file you selected).

WordPerfect 5.1 Software

To retrieve an existing file (document) stored in the current directory (disk):

1. Strike F5; strike Enter (displays a listing of files in the current directory).
2. Select (highlight) the name of the file you want to retrieve.
3. Strike 1 or R (displays a copy of the file you selected).

Creating a New File on Your IBM PC or Compatible Computer

Microsoft Works Software

When you create a new file (document), Works displays an empty window in the tool you choose. To create a new file:

1. Depress Alt and hold it as you strike F; release; then strike N (chooses the Create New File option from the File menu).
2. Key the underlined letter of the tool you want to use (a new window is opened for you to create the document).

WordPerfect 5.1 Software

To create a new file (document) from a directory listing, strike F7 to display a clear screen and then begin keying the document.

To create a new file when there is a document on the screen, strike F7, then key Y (to save the document) or N (to not save the document).

1. If N is keyed, strike Enter at the *Exit WP* prompt (displays a clear screen) and begin keying the new document.
2. If Y is keyed, key the file name at the *Document to be saved* prompt; strike Enter; and key Y at the *Replace*

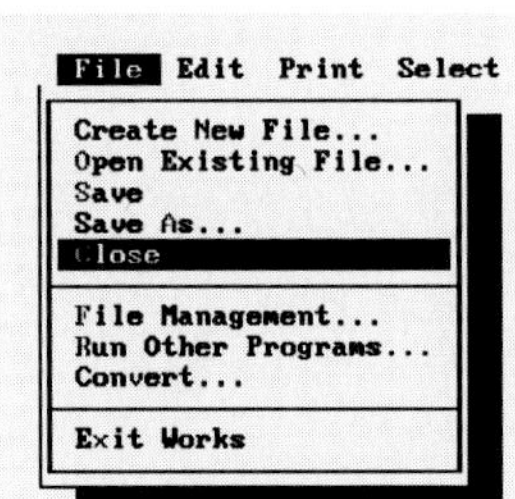

Close:
Works DOS

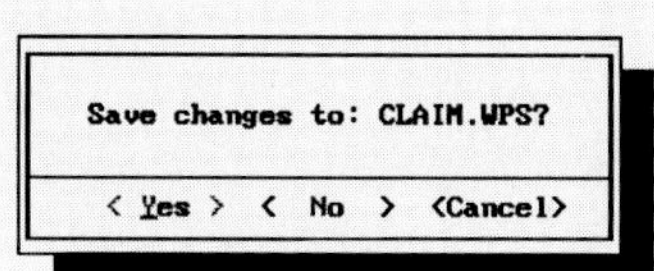

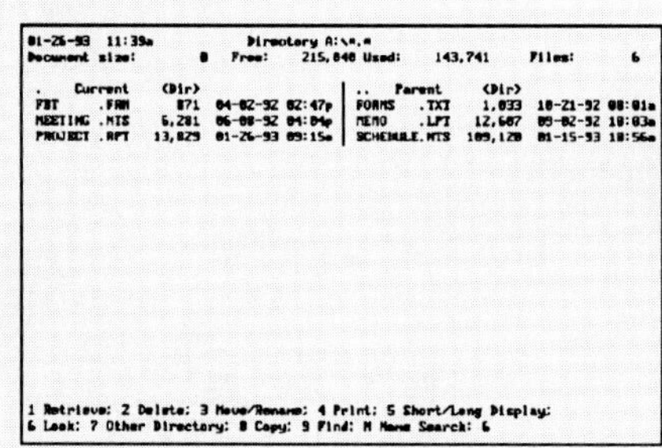

List Directory: WordPerfect

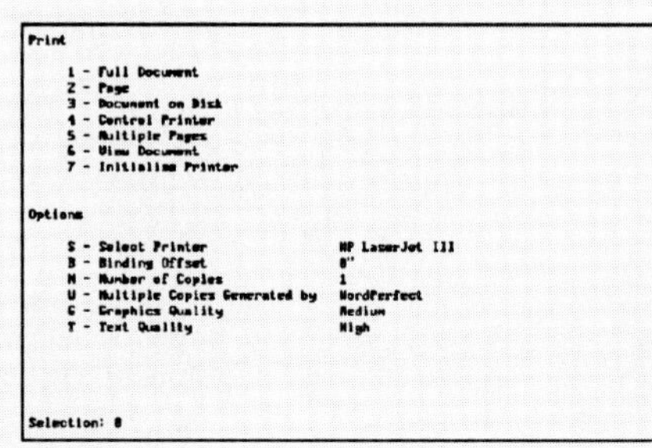

Print Screen: WordPerfect

prompt, if needed; key N at the *Exit WP* prompt; (displays a clear screen); and begin keying the new document.

Closing (Saving) a File with Your IBM PC or Compatible Computer

Microsoft Works Software

When you want to remove a document from the desktop, close the document. During the close process, Works will let you save or delete this copy of the document or cancel the Close command if you have not saved the file or have made changes since you last saved the file. If you want to save this copy of the document on a disk, you should elect to save the changes. To use the Close command:

1. Depress and hold Alt; strike F. Release; strike C (chooses Close from the File menu).
2. Strike Enter (selects the Yes option and Works closes the document and removes it from the desktop; the copy of the document on the current disk, if any, will be replaced by this copy).

WordPerfect 5.1 Software

When you want to remove a document from the desktop, save (or close) the document. During the save process, WordPerfect will let you save or delete this copy of the document or cancel the Save command. If you want to save this copy of the document on a disk, you should elect to save the changes. To use the Save command:

1. Strike F7; then choose Yes (selects the option to save the copy of the document)
2. At the *Document to be saved* prompt,
   a. Key the file name for the document if the document is being saved for the first time or if you want to change the file name.
   b. Strike Enter if the document is not being saved for the first time or you do not want to change the file name; then at the *Replace* prompt, key Y (replaces the copy of the document that is on the disk with this copy).
3. Select the desired option at the *Exit WP* prompt.

Printing a Document on Your IBM PC or Compatible Computer

Microsoft Works Software

To print a document using the default (preset) page setups:

1. Make certain the printer is turned on and ready for printing.
2. Depress and hold Alt and strike P; release, strike P again (chooses Print from the Print menu).
3. Strike Enter (prints the document using the default print specifications).

WordPerfect 5.1 Software

To print a document using the default (preset) page setups:

1. Make certain that the printer is on and ready for printing.
2. Strike Shift F7 (displays the print menu).
3. Key 1 (selects Option 1—entire document is to be printed).
4. Strike Enter (executes the Print command).

CARE FOR AND MAINTAIN YOUR COMPUTER SAFELY

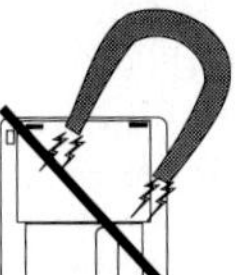

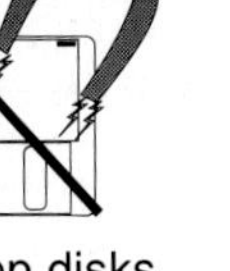

Keep disks away from magnets

Keep disks dry

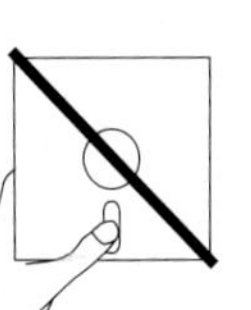

Do not touch the exposed part of the disk

Avoid exposing disks to direct sunlight

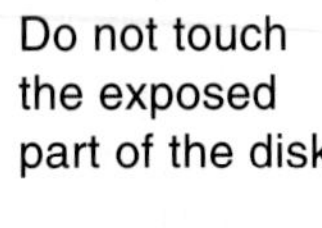

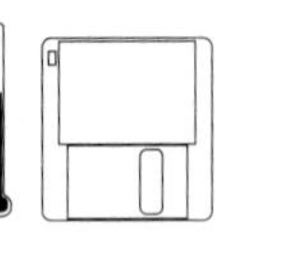

Store disks at temperatures between 50°F and 125°F.

Do not use an eraser on a disk label.

Follow these guidelines when working with your computer to ensure your safety and to protect the computer from harm:

Computer Equipment

- Place all computer components on a sturdy, flat surface in a dust-free area that is not in direct sunlight.
- Do not remove or insert computer cables without proper supervision or without turning off the equipment.
- Take care not to spill any food or liquid on or in any computer component. If you do, turn off the computer immediately, unplug it, and notify your teacher before cleaning up the spill or turning on the equipment.
- Do not attempt to open or service the computer's high-voltage power supply—call an authorized service provider.
- Make sure the ventilation openings on the computer and monitor are not obstructed so the equipment does not overheat.
- Don't use aerosol sprays, solvents, or abrasives near your computer equipment.
- Before moving an IBM PC or compatible, determine if the hard drive needs to be "parked." If so, consult your teacher for the "parking" procedure.
- Avoid jolting or jostling your computer if it becomes necessary to move it.
- Do not drop books or other objects on or near computer equipment.

Floppy Disks and Drives

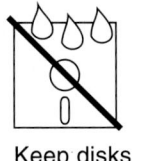

- Avoid exposing disks to extremely hot or cold temperatures.
- Do not use an eraser on a disk label; use a felt-tip pen when writing on disk labels.
- Keep disks dry and free of dust.
- Do not touch the exposed part of a disk.
- Keep disks away from magnets, x-ray devices, and direct sunlight.
- Do not bend or fold a disk or attach a paper clip to it.
- Carefully insert disks into and remove them from the disk drive and replace each disk in its envelope when it is not being used.
- Use a disk only on the computer system for which it is formatted.

KNOW YOUR ELECTRONIC TYPEWRITER

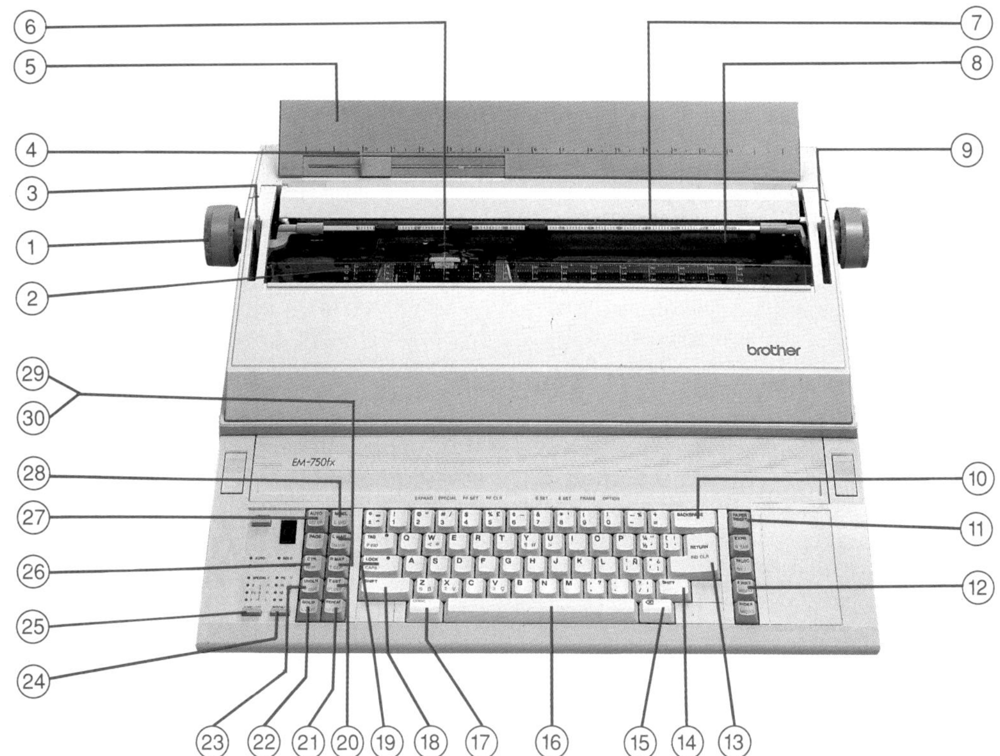

The diagram above illustrates the major parts of an electronic typewriter. If you have the manufacturer's booklet, use it to identify the exact location of each major part, including special parts that may be on one machine but not on another.

1. **Left platen knob:** used to turn platen manually (not on some models)
2. **Line-of-writing (margin) scale:** indicates pitch scales (10, 12, and 15); may indicate margin positions and the printing point
3. **Paper-bail release lever:** used to pull paper bail away from platen
4. **Paper guide:** used to position paper for insertion
5. **Paper support:** supports paper when it is in the machine
6. **Print carrier:** includes ribbon cassette, daisy wheel, correction tape, carrier adjust lever, and printing mechanism
7. **Paper bail:** used to hold paper against platen
8. **Platen (cylinder):** provides a hard surface against which the type element strikes
9. **Paper release lever:** used to allow paper to be removed or aligned
10. **Backspace key:** used to move printing point to left one space
11. **Paper insert:** use to feed paper to specified loading position
12. **Relocate (RELOC) key*:** used to return printing point to previous position after corrections are made
13. **Return key:** used to return printing point to left margin and to move paper up
14. **Right shift key:** used to key capitals of letter keys controlled by the left hand
15. **Correction key:** used to erase a character
16. **Space bar:** used to move printing point to the right one space at a time
17. **Code key:** used simultaneously with another key to cause that key to perform a special function
18. **Left shift key:** used to key capitals of letter keys controlled by the right hand
19. **Caps Lock key:** used to key text in ALL CAPS (capital letters)
20. **Tab set*:** used to set tabulator stops (tabs); tab clear may be same key on some models
21. **Repeat:** used to repeat a previously struck key or function
22. **Bold key:** used to print boldface characters
23. **Underline (UNDLN) key:** used to print underlined characters
24. **Pitch select key:** used to set type size (10-, 12-, or 15-pitch) to correspond to the daisy wheel being used
25. **Line-space select key:** sets machine to advance the paper 1, 1.5, 2, or 3 lines when return key is used
26. **Centering key:** used to center text automatically between the left and right margins
27. **Auto*:** set to return the printing point automatically to the left margin, next line when it reaches the right margin
28. **Margin release*:** used to move printing point beyond the margin stops
29. **Left margin (L MAR):** used to set left margin
30. **Right margin (R MAR):** used to set right margin
31. **Tabulator (Tab)*:** used to move printing point to tab locations

* Key that performs special functions when depressed together with the CODE key

Adjust paper guide

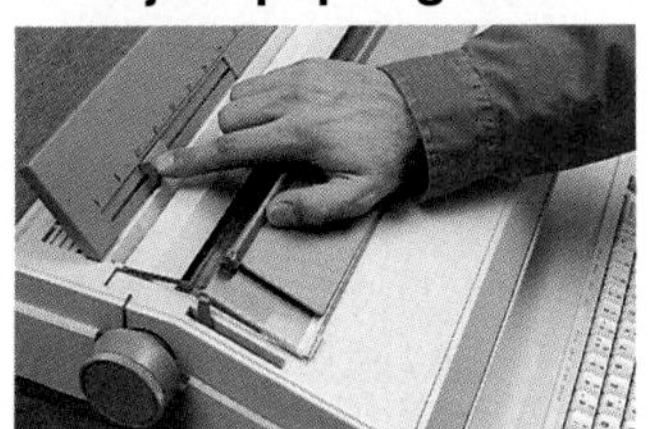

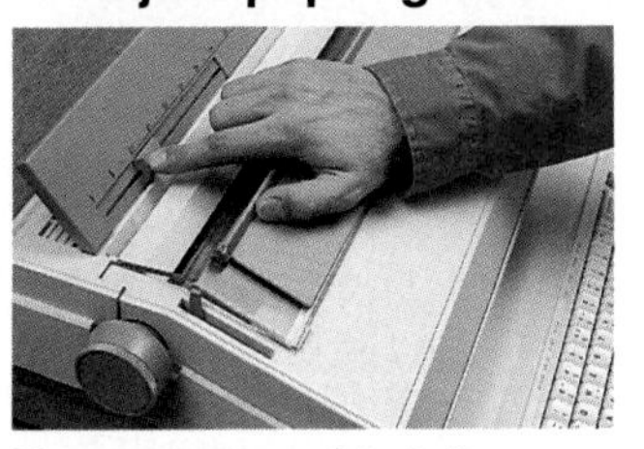

Move **paper guide** left or right so that it lines up with 0 (zero) on the **paper guide scale** or the **line-of-writing** or **(margin) scale**.

Insert paper

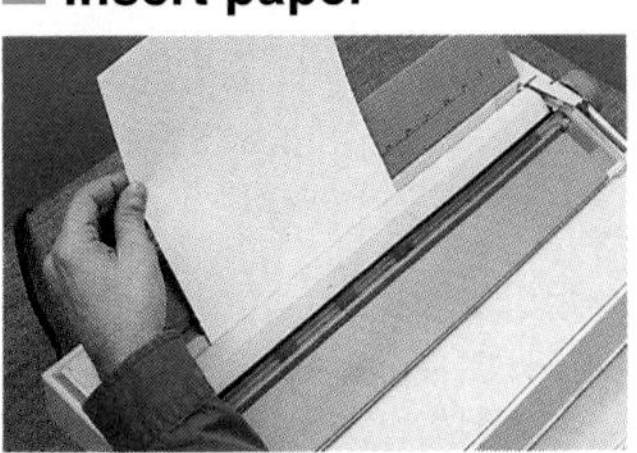

1. Place paper against **paper guide**, behind the **platen**.

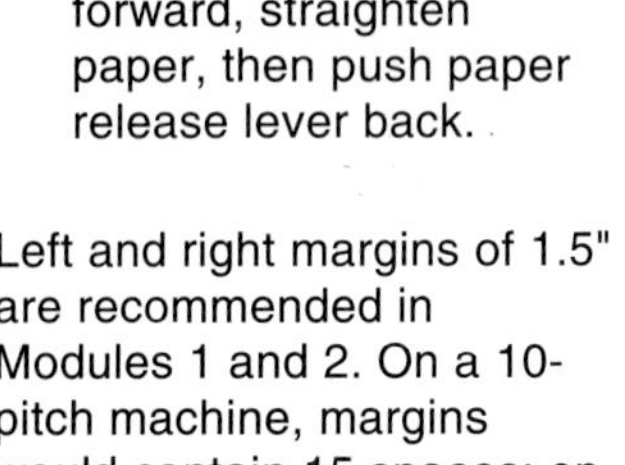

2. Strike **paper insert key**.

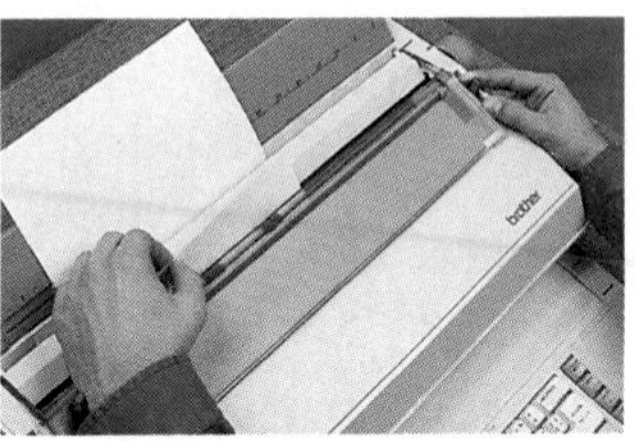

3. If paper is not straight, pull **paper release lever** forward, straighten paper, then push paper release lever back.

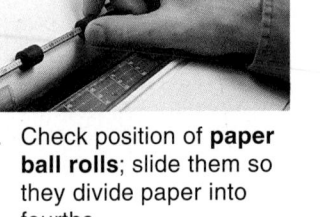

4. Check position of **paper ball rolls**; slide them so they divide paper into fourths.

Set line-space select key

Many machines offer three choices for line spacing—1, 1.5, and 2 indicated by bars or numbers on the **line-space select key**.

Set the line-space select key on (–) or 1 to single-space (SS) or on (=) or 2 to double-space (DS).

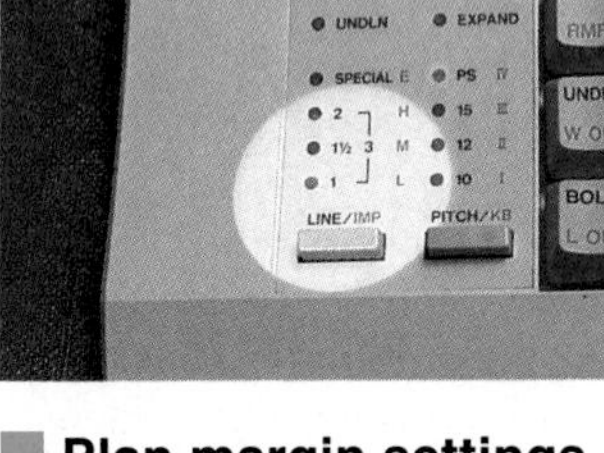

Plan margin settings

A typewriter may have 10-pitch (pica) type—10 spaces to a horizontal inch—or 12-pitch (elite) type—12 spaces to a horizontal inch.

Machines have at least one **line-of-writing** scale that reads from 0 to 90 or more for machines with 10-pitch type, from 0 to at least 110 for machines with 12-pitch type.

Left and right margins of 1.5" are recommended in Modules 1 and 2. On a 10-pitch machine, margins would contain 15 spaces; on a 12-pitch machine, 18 spaces.

When 8.5" x 11" paper is inserted into the typewriter (short side at top) with left edge of paper at 0 on the line-of-writing scale, the left margin would be set at 15 (10-pitch) or 18 (12-pitch). Also, the right margin would be set 15 or 18 spaces from the right edge of the sheet—70 (10-pitch) or 84 (12-pitch). The exact center point is 42.5 (10-pitch) or 51 (12-pitch) when 8.5" paper is inserted with left edge at 0. Use 42 for 10-pitch center or 51 for 12-pitch center.

To center lines of text, set left and right margins the same number of spaces left and right of the center point. When you begin to use the warning bell, 5 or 6 spaces may be added to the right margin.

Set margins

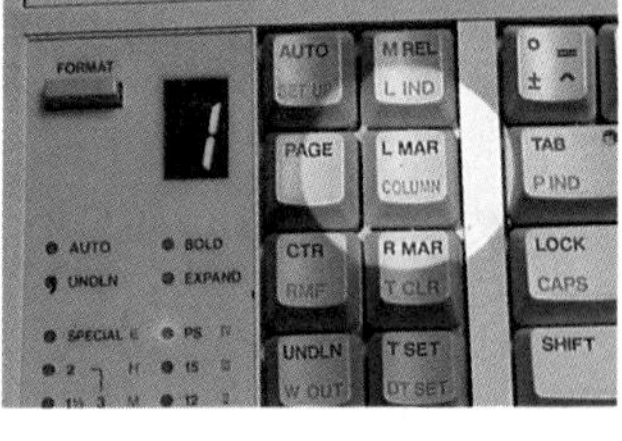

Electronic set

To set the left margin on the Brother EN-750 space to the desired margin; strike the L MAR key.

To set the right margin, space to the desired margin; strike the CODE key <u>and</u> the R MAR key.

On some models of IBM, space to the desired margin; strike the CODE key <u>and</u> the margin key.

To set margins on Xerox and Silver-Reed, space to the desired margin; strike the margin key.

Push-lever set

Single element typewriters, such as Adler, Olivetti,

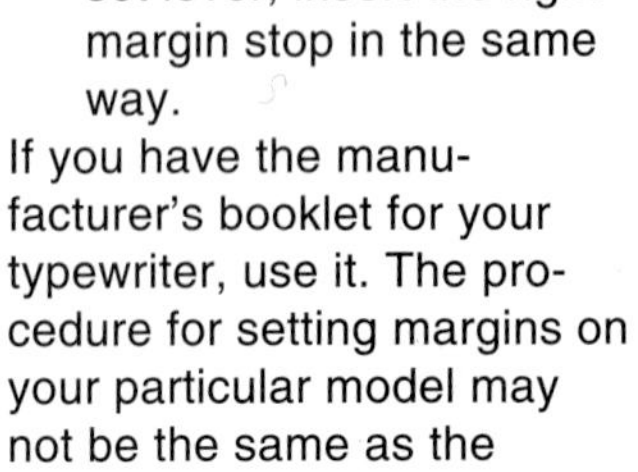

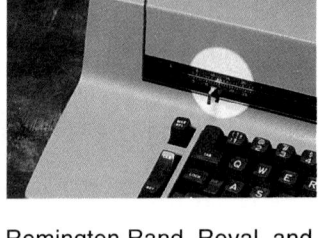

Remington Rand, Royal, and IBM Selectric

1. Push in on the left margin set lever.
2. Slide it to desired position on the line-of-writing (margin) scale.
3. Release the margin set lever.
4. Using the right margin set lever, insert the right margin stop in the same way.

If you have the manufacturer's booklet for your typewriter, use it. The procedure for setting margins on your particular model may not be the same as the procedure given here.

Common word processing terms are defined below and on page xvi. Each term represents a feature of word processing software. Whether you use a typewriter or computer in this course, you would be wise to learn these terms.

For Macintosh users, this symbol (~) is introduced to represent the word(s) *click* and *click on*. *Click* and *click on* refer to using a mouse.

Block—p. 80 Defines a specific portion of text (word, phrase, sentence, paragraph) to be bolded, centered horizontally, copied, deleted, moved, or underlined (*see* Bold, Center, Copy, Delete, Undelete, Move, Underline)

Bold—p. 42 Prints designated text darker than the rest of the copy to add emphasis; may be used as text is keyed or afterwards (*see* Block)

Center—p. 42 Centers text horizontally; may be used as text is keyed or on existing text (*see* Block)

Center Page—p. 128 Centers documents vertically on a page (WordPerfect only)

Copy—p. 83 Duplicates text from one location and places the duplicated text at another location

Cursor—p. 2 A light on the screen that shows where the next keystroke will be entered

Decimal tab—p. 124 Aligns numbers at the decimal point (*see* Tab)

Default—pp. 6, 35 Preset conditions in software for word processing features such as Margins, Line Spacing, Tabs, and Insert Mode; the operator may override these settings as part of formatting and keying a document

Delete (File)—p. 107 Removes a document (file) from a disk to free up disk space and make management of the remaining files easier

Delete (Text)—p. 80 Removes a segment of text (character, space, or word) by means of the Backspace or Delete key or (line, sentence, or paragraph) by means of the Block feature (*see* Block)

Document Retrieval—p. 98 Displays a document for the purpose of editing and/or printing after it has been saved or stored

Document View—p. 95 Displays a page or pages of a document so you may see the format before printing the document; also called Print Preview

Hard Return—p. 5 Moves the cursor to the left margin of the next line.

Indent—p. 119 Sets a tab that serves as a temporary left margin (*see* Tab)

Insert Mode—p. 40 Allows new text to be keyed into existing text; the default software mode (*see* Typeover Mode)

Left Tab—p. 124 Aligns text to the right of the tab (*see* Tab)

Line Spacing—p. 44 Allows you to set the number of blank lines left between lines of text; usually single spacing (no blank lines) or double spacing (one blank line)

Margins—p. 44 Specification of the number of spaces (or inches) at the left and right of printed lines; also, at the top and bottom of printed pages

Move—p. 83 Takes a designated block of text from one location and places it in another location (*see* Block)

Page Break—p. 98 Ends a page and begins a new page; inserted automatically (soft) when text exceeds a page; inserted manually (hard) to force the software to start a new page

Print Preview—p. 95 *See* Document View

Glossary, continued

Rename File—p. 109 Allows operator to assign a new file name to a file that has been saved or stored

Reveal Codes—p. 82 Displays text along with formatting codes for features such as Bold, Center, and Underline that were used in the text (WordPerfect only)

Right Tab—p. 124 Aligns text to the left of the tab (*see* Tab)

Ruler Line—p. 44 Line across top or bottom of screen that shows the position of the cursor in relation to the edges of a printed page; used to set left and right margins, tabs, and line spacing

Sort—p. 136 Arranges text in a specific order, such as alphabetically or numerically (WordPerfect only)

Spell Check—p. 100 Checks text for misspelled words against a dictionary included in the software

Status Line—p. 44 Shows the location of the cursor, the number of the document in use, the page of the document in process, the line on the page being keyed, and the position of the cursor; indicates whether bold, underline, and ALL CAPS features are activated (WordPerfect only)

Tab—p. 124 Causes the cursor to skip across the screen to a point set by the operator or to the tabs preset every five spaces (*see* Default, Decimal tab, Left tab, and Right tab)

Typeover Mode—p. 40 Replaces existing text with newly keyed text (*see* Insert Mode)

Undelete—p. 80 Restores deleted text (*see* Delete (Text))

Underline—p. 42 Underlines text as it is keyed or existing text (*see* Block)

KEY TO ABBREVIATIONS USED IN APPLIED KEYBOARDING

CS
Columnar spacing; space between columns of a table

DS
Double-space; double spacing

GWAM (*gwam*)
Gross words a minute; keyboarding rate in terms of standard (5-keystroke) words/minute

LM
Left margin

LS
Line spacing

PB
Page beginning

PI
Paragraph indent

QS
Quadruple-space; quadruple spacing

RM
Right margin

SM
Side margins

SS
Single-space; single spacing

MODULE 1
Master Alphabetic Keyboarding Technique

All professional and business offices in the modern workplace use a typewriter-like keyboard to enter data, retrieve information, and communicate facts and ideas. To achieve success in most careers today, you must be able to operate a keyboard with skill — on an electric or electronic typewriter or computer.

Fortunately, the alphabetic keyboards on these kinds of equipment have standard key locations. As a result, if you learn to key on one kind of machine, you can readily adapt to other keyboarding machines.

Your primary goal during the next few weeks is to learn to operate a letter keyboard with proper technique (good form) and at a reasonable level of keyboarding speed.

Module 1 (Lessons 1-25) will help you learn to:

1. Operate the letter keyboard by touch (without looking at the keyboard).
2. Adjust equipment for correct margins and vertical line spacing.
3. Use basic service keys with skill: Space Bar, Return/Enter key, Shift keys, caps lock, and tabulator.
4. Key words, sentences, and paragraphs with proper technique and without time-wasting pauses between letters and words.
5. Learn basic word processing features.

Confusing Words, continued

their (pron) belongs to them
there (adv/pron) in or at that place; word used to introduce a sentence or clause
they're (contr) they are

threw (vb) past tense of throw; to fling; toss
through (prep) passage from one end to another; indicated a period of time

to (prep/adv) used to indicate action, relation, distance, direction
too (adv) besides; also; to excessive degree
two (pron/adj) one plus one in number

vary (vb) change; make different; diverge
very (adv/adj) truly; to high degree

wait (vb/n) to stay in place or to pause; to serve as a waiter; act of waiting
weight (n/vb) amount something weighs; give relative importance to something

weak (adj) lacking strength, skill, or proficiency
week (n) a series of seven days; a series of regular days within a seven-day period

wear (vb/n) to bear or have on the person; diminish by use; clothing
where (adv/conj/n) at, in, or to what degree; what place, source, or cause

weather (n) state of the atmosphere
whether (conj) if

whose (adj/pron) of or to whom something belongs
who's (cont) who is

your (adj) of or relating to you or yourself as possessor
you're (contr) you are

Word-Division Guides

1 Divide words between syllables only; therefore, do not divide one-syllable words. When in doubt, consult a dictionary or a word-division manual.

through-out pref-er-ence em-ploy-ees
reached toward thought

2 Do not divide words of five or fewer letters even if they have two or more syllables.

into also about union radio ideas

3 Do not separate a one-letter syllable at the beginning of a word or a one- or two-letter syllable at the end of a word.

across enough steady highly ended

4 Divide a word between double consonants, except when adding a syllable to a word that ends in double letters. In that case, divide after the double letters of the root word.

writ-ten sum-mer expres-sion excel-lence
will-ing win-ner process-ing fulfill-ment

5 When the final consonant is doubled in adding a suffix, divide between the double letters.

run-ning begin-ning fit-ting submit-ted

6 Divide after a one-letter syllable within a word; but when two single-letter syllables occur together, divide between them.

sepa-rate regu-late gradu-ation evalu-ation

7 When the single-letter syllable a, i, or u is followed by the ending *ly*, *ble*, *bly*, *cle*, or *cal*, divide before the single-letter syllable.

stead-ily siz-able vis-ible mir-acle
cler-ical but musi-cal practi-cal

8 Divide only between the two words that make up a hyphenated word.

self-contained well-developed

9 Do not divide a contraction or a single group of figures.

doesn't $350,000 Policy F238975

10 Avoid dividing proper names and dates. If necessary, divide as follows.

Mary J./Pembroke not Mary J. Pem-/broke
November 15,/1995 not November/15, 1995

SPECIAL SERVICE KEYS

Arrow (Cursor) Keys

1. Read the copy at the right.
2. Study the pictures beneath the copy which show what the arrow keys do.
3. Locate the left/right and up/down arrows in the picture below and then on your own computer keyboard.
4. You will use these keys to move the cursor around the screen.

A cursor is a light on the screen that shows where the next keystroke will be entered. Arrow keys are used to move the cursor up/down or left/right on the screen to choose items from a menu (as in this *Alphabetic Keyboarding* example) or to proofread and edit text. These four keys are often clustered at the right of the letter keys.

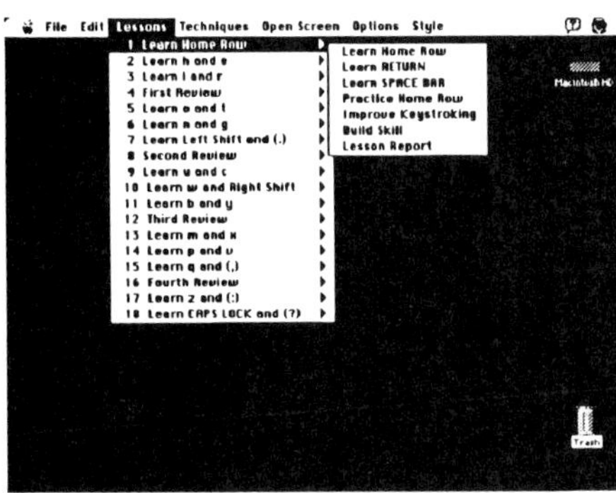

Left and Right Arrow Keys

The left-arrow key moves the cursor one space at a time to the left. The right-arrow key moves the cursor one space at a time to the right.

Up and Down Arrow Keys

The up-arrow key moves the cursor up one line at a time. The down-arrow key moves the cursor down one line at a time.

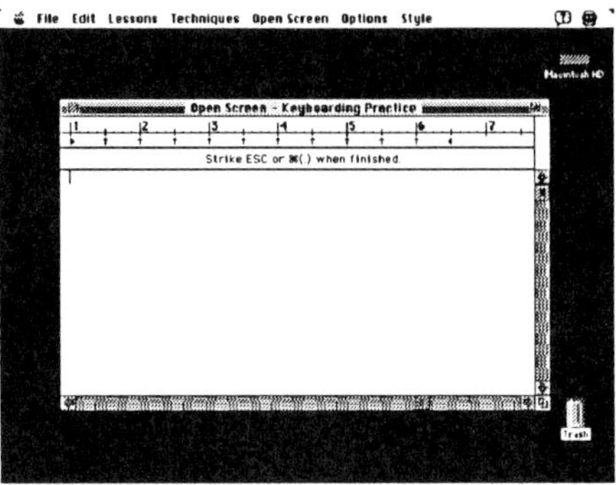

Backspace/Delete Key (Also on typewriters)

1. Read the copy at the right.
2. Study the pictures below the copy which show the screen before and after the Backspace/Delete key is used.
3. Find the Backspace/Delete key on your own keyboard (often at the right end of the number/symbol row of the keyboard).
4. Use this key only when directed by your teacher to take out (delete) errors you make as you key.

The Backspace/Delete key lets you backspace and take out (delete) a letter or a series of characters you have keyed.

Each time you strike the Backspace/Delete key, the letter or character to the left of the cursor is taken out (deleted).

ESC (Escape) Key

1. Read the copy at the right.
2. Find the Esc key on your own keyboard (usually at the left end of the number/symbol row).
3. See your software user's guide. What does it say about use of the Esc key?

The Esc (escape) key permits you to "escape from" a situation within a program such as *Alphabetic Keyboarding.* For example, if you are working on one part of a lesson, you can strike the Esc key which will take you back to the lesson menu where you can choose another lesson part.

By striking the Esc key a second time, you may also move from a lesson menu back to the main menu to choose a different lesson. In word processing software, use of the Esc key varies from one program to another. For example, Esc does not work as described on Macintosh computers.

CONFUSING WORDS

accept (vb) to receive; to approve; to take
except (prep, vb) with the exclusion of; leave out

advice (n) recommendation; information
advise (vb) to give counsel; to recommend

affect (vb) to produce a change in or have an effect on
effect (n) result; something produced by an agent or a cause

buy (n/vb) a bargain; to purchase; to acquire
by (prep/adv) close to; via; according to; close at hand; at/in another's home or workplace

cents (n) specified portion of a dollar
sense (n/vb) meaning intended or conveyed; to perceive by sense organs; ability to judge
since (adv/conj) after a definite time in the past; in view of the fact; because

cite (vb) use as support; commend; summon
sight (n/vb) ability to see; something seen; a device to improve aim; to observe or examine by taking a sight
site (n) the place something is, was, or will be located

complement (n) something that fills up, completes, or makes perfect
compliment (n,vb) a formal expression of respect or admiration; to pay respect or admiration

fair (adj/n) just, equitable, visually beautiful or admirable; a competitive exhibition
fare (n) a charge for personal transportation

farther (adv) greater distance
further (adv) additional; in greater depth or extent

hear (vb) to gain knowledge of by the ear
here (adv) in or at this place; at this point; in this case; on this point

its (adj) of or relating to itself as the possessor
it's (contr) it is; it has

knew (vb) past tense of know; to have understood; to have recognized the truth or nature of
new (adj) novel; fresh; having existing for a short time; created in recent past

know (vb) to be aware of the truth of; to have an understanding of
no (adv/adj/n) in no respect or degree; not so; indicates denial or refusal

lead (vb) to guide or direct; to be first
led (vb) past tense of lead

leased (vb/adj) granted use or occupancy or under contract in exchange for rent; something so used or occupied
least (adj) lowest in rank, size, or importance

lessen (vb) to cause to decrease; to make less
lesson (n) something to be learned; a period of instruction; a class period

loan (n/vb) a sum of money lent at interest; to lend something of value
lone (adj) solitary; single; companionless

passed (vb) past tense of pass; already occurred; gave an item to someone
past (adv/adj/prep/n) gone or elapsed; time gone by; moved by

personal (adj) of, relating to, or affecting a person; done in person
personnel (n) a staff of persons making up a workforce in an organization

plain (adj/n) with little ornamentation or decoration; a large flat area of land
plane (n) an airplane or hydroplane

poor (adj) having little wealth or value
pore (vb/n) to study carefully; a tiny opening in a surface, as in skin
pour (vb) to make flow or stream; to rain hard

principal (n/adj) a chief or head person; a sum of money that draws interest; of or relating to the most important thing or matter
principle (n) a central rule, law, or doctrine

real (adj/n) genuine; not artificial; anything that actually exists
reel (n/vb) revolving device on which to wind lines; to turn round and round

right (adj) factual; true; correct
rite (n) customary form of ceremony; ritual
write (v) to form letters or symbols; to compose and set down in words, numbers, or symbols

sew (vb) to fasten by stitches
so (adj/conj) in the same manner or way; in order that; with the result that
sow (vb) to plant seed; scatter; dispense

some (n/adv) unknown or unspecified unit or thing; to a degree or extent
sum (n/vb) the whole amount; the total; summary of points; to find a total

stationary (adj) fixed in a position, course, or mode; unchanging in condition
stationery (n) paper and envelopes used for processing personal/business documents

than (conj/prep) used in comparisons to show differences between items
then (n/adv) that time; at that time

UNIT 1

LESSONS 1-20

Master Letter Keyboarding Technique

Learning Outcomes: After completing this unit, you will be able to

1. Operate the letter, punctuation, and service keys by touch (without looking) and with correct technique.
2. Key sentences and paragraphs, using all letters of the alphabet, with correct technique and acceptable speed.

LESSON 1 HOME KEYS (ASDF JKL;)

Side margins (SM): 1.5" or defaults; Line spacing (LS): single (SS)

1A ◆ GET READY TO KEY

1. Arrange work area as shown at right.

Typewriter

- front frame of machine even with front edge of desk
- book at right of machine, top raised for easy reading
- paper at left of machine
- unneeded books and supplies placed out of the way

Computer

- alphanumeric (main) keyboard directly in front of chair; front edge of keyboard even with edge of table or desk
- monitor placed for easy viewing; disk drives placed for easy access
- *Alphabetic Keyboarding* software and/or your word processing diskettes within easy reach
- book behind or at right of keyboard; top raised for easy reading
- unneeded books and supplies placed out of the way

2. Turn on equipment (ON/OFF control of typewriter or computer/monitor).
3. Insert paper into typewriter (see p. xiv).

Properly arranged work area: typewriter

Properly arranged work area: computer

Punctuation, continued

OTHER MARKS

SM: 1.5" inches or defaults

LS: SS; DS between sets of related sentences

1. Read the first rule highlighted in color at the right.
2. Key the **Learn** sentences (omit the line number) below it, noting how the rule has been applied.
3. Key the **Apply** sentences, supplying the needed mark of punctuation.
4. Repeat Steps 1-3 for each of the other rules.
5. If time permits, key the **Apply** sentences again to increase decision-making speed.

COLON

Use a colon to introduce an enumeration or a listing.

Learn 1 Bring these three items: a textbook, a notebook, and a pen.
Apply 2 Lunch includes these items a sandwich, an apple, and milk.

Use a colon to introduce a question or a long direct quotation.

Learn 3 My concern is this: Does the end justify such extreme means?
Apply 4 Here is my question Who are we to make this moral judgement?

Use a colon between hours and minutes expressed in figures.

Learn 5 The student rally will begin promptly at 7:00 p.m.
Apply 6 My 1116 a.m. flight to Boston did not depart until 130 p.m.

HYPHEN

Use a hyphen to join compound numbers written as words from twenty-one to ninety-nine.

Learn 7 The age range is twenty-one to thirty-four.
Apply 8 Spell each number as you key it: 46 and 71.

Use a hyphen to join compound adjectives preceding a noun they modify as a unit.

Learn 9 The CD-of-the-Month Club lists this album.
Apply 10 The out of bounds pass stopped our first half run.

Use a hyphen after each word or figure in a series that modifies the same noun (suspended hyphenation).

Learn 11 I have used all the 1-, 3-, and 25-cent stamps I had.
Apply 12 All first and second string players were used in the game.

QUESTION MARK

Use a question mark at the end of a sentence that is a direct question; however, use a period after a request that appears in the form of a question.

Learn 13 Can you write a simple computer program?
Learn 14 Will you please let me know if you have this item in stock.
Apply 15 How soon do you believe you will finish all the documents.
Apply 16 Will you help me verify the data in this report.

EXCLAMATION MARK

Use an exclamation mark after emphatic exclamations and after phrases and sentences that are clearly exclamatory.

Learn 17 Wow! What a great game!
Apply 18 This view is really spectacular.

1B ◆

TAKE PROPER POSITION

Proper position is the same for typewriters and computers. The essential features of proper position are illustrated at right and listed below:

- fingers curved and upright over home keys
- wrists low, but not touching frame of keyboard
- forearms parallel to slant of keyboard
- body erect, sitting back in chair
- feet on floor for balance

Proper position at computer

Proper position at typewriter

1C ◆

HOME-KEY POSITION

1. Locate the home keys on the chart: **f d s a** for left hand and **j k l ;** for right hand.
2. Locate the home keys on your keyboard. Place left-hand fingers on **f d s a** and right-hand fingers on **j k l ;** *with your fingers well curved and upright (not slanting).*
3. Remove your fingers from the keyboard; then place them in home-key position again, curving and holding them *lightly* on the keys.

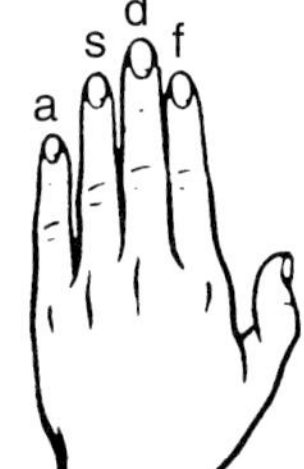

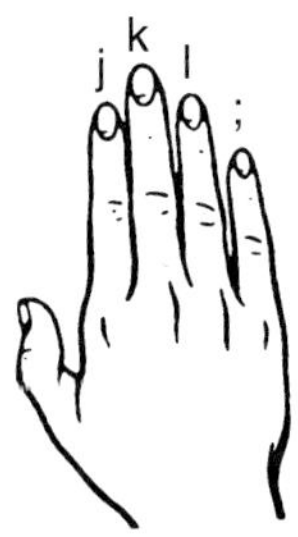

1D ◆

STRIKE HOME KEYS AND SPACE BAR

1. Read the statement and study the illustrations at right.
2. Place your fingers in home-key position as directed in 1C, above.
3. Strike each letter key for the first group of letters in the line of type below the technique illustrations.
4. After striking ; (semicolon), strike the Space Bar once.
5. Continue to key the line; strike the Space Bar once at the point of each arrow.

Keystroking technique
Strike each key with a light tap with the tip of the finger, snapping the fingertip toward the palm of the hand.

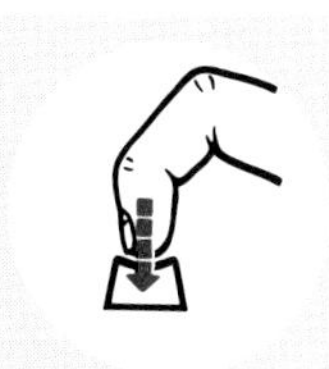

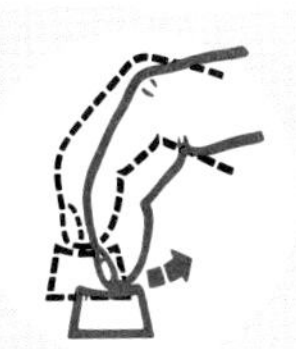

Spacing technique
Strike the Space Bar with the right thumb; use a quick down-and-in motion (toward the palm). Avoid pauses before or after spacing.

Space once

```
fdsajkl; f d s a j k l ; ff jj dd kk ss ll aa ;;
```

Punctuation, continued

APOSTROPHE

SM: 1.5" inches or defaults

LS: SS; DS between sets of related sentences

1. Read the first rule highlighted in color at the right.
2. Key the **Learn** sentence (omit the line number) below it, noting how the rule has been applied.
3. Key the **Apply** sentence, supplying the needed apostrophes.
4. Repeat Steps 1-3 for each of the other rules.
5. If time permits, key the **Apply** sentences again to increase decision-making speed.

Use an apostrophe *plus s* to form the plural of most figures, letters, and words (6's, A's, five's). In market quotatons, form the plural of figures by the addition of *s only*.

Learn 1 Your f's look like 7's. Boston Fund 4s are due in 2005.
Apply 2 Cross your ts and dot your is. Sell United 6's this week.

To *show possession*, use an apostrophe *plus s* after a (a) singular noun and (b) a plural noun which does not end in s.

Learn 3 The boy's bicycle was found, but the women's shoes were not.
Apply 4 Childrens toys are on sale; buy the girls bicycle.

To *show possession*, use an apostrophe *plus s* after a proper name of one syllable that ends in s.

Learn 5 Please pay Jones's bill for $675 today.
Apply 6 Is it Bess' hat, Ross' shoes, or Chris' watch that is lost?

To *show possession*, use *only* an apostrophe after (a) plural nouns ending in s and (b) a proper name of more than one syllable which ends in s or z.

Learn 7 The girls' counselor will visit the Adams' home.
Apply 8 The ladies handbags were found near Douglas Restaurant.

Use an apostrophe as a *symbol* for *feet* in billings or tabulations or as a *symbol* for *minutes*. (The quotation mark may be used as a *symbol* for *inches* or *seconds*.)

Learn 9 Please deliver ten 2" x 4" x 10' pine boards to my address.
Apply 10 He ran the mile in 3 min. 54 sec. The room is 12 ft. 6 in. x 18 ft.

Use an apostrophe as a symbol to indicate the omission of letters or figures (as in contractions).

Learn 11 Each July 4th, we try to renew the "Spirit of '76."
Apply 12 Use the apostrophe in contractions: isnt, cant, youll.

UNDERLINE

Follow the directions given above, *except* that you will supply underlines as needed in the **Apply** lines.

Use an underline to indicate titles of books and names of magazines and newspapers. (Titles may be keyed in ALL CAPS without the underline.)

Learn 1 The book Learning to Think was condensed in Reader's Digest.
Apply 2 I read the review of Anyone Can Write in the New York Times.

Use an underline to call attention to special words or phrases (or use quotations marks). **Note**: Use a continuous underline (see preceding rule) unless each word is to be considered separately a shown below.

Learn 3 She asked us to spell separate, privilege, and stationery.
Apply 4 He misspelled supersede, concede, and proceed.

1E ◆

RETURN AT LINE ENDINGS

Return the *printing point indicator* of a typewriter or the *cursor* of a computer to the left margin and move down to the next line as follows:

- Strike the Return key (hard return). The key may be labeled Enter on your computer.

Study the illustrations at right and return 4 times (quadruple-space) below the line you completed in 1D, p. 4.

Hard Return

Reach the little finger of the right hand to the Return key or Enter key, tap the key, and return the finger quickly to home-key position.

Striking the Return/Enter key is called a "hard return." You will use a hard return at the end of all drill lines in this lesson and those that follow in this unit.

1F ◆

PRACTICE HOME-KEYS/SPACING

1. Place your hands in home-key position (left-hand fingers on **f d s a** and right-hand fingers on **j k l ;**).
2. Key the lines once: single-spaced (SS) with a double space (DS) between 2-line groups. Do not key line numbers.

Fingers curved and upright

Down-and-in spacing motion

Strike the Return/Enter key twice at the end of a line to double-space (DS).

Strike Space Bar once to space

```
1 j jj f ff k kk d dd l ll s ss ; ;; a aa jkl; fdsa
2 j jj f ff k kk d dd l ll s ss ; ;; a aa jkl; fdsa
```
Strike the Return/Enter key twice to double-space (DS)
```
3 a aa ; ;; s ss l ll d dd k kk f ff j jj fdsa jkl;
4 a aa ; ;; s ss l ll d dd k kk f ff j jj fdsa jkl;
```
DS
```
5 jf jf kd kd ls ls ;a ;a fj fj dk dk sl sl a; a; f
6 jf jf kd kd ls ls ;a ;a fj fj dk dk sl sl a; a; f
```
DS
```
7 a;fj a;sldkfj a;sldkfj a;sldkfj a;sldkfj a;sldkfj
8 a;fj a;sldkfj a;sldkfj a;sldkfj a;sldkfj a;sldkfj
```
Strike the Return/Enter key 4 times to quadruple-space (QS)

1G ◆

PRACTICE RETURN

each line twice single-spaced (SS); double-space (DS) between 2-line groups

Each time you strike the Return/Enter key to space down one line, you insert a "hard return."

```
1 a;sldkfj a;sldkfj
```
DS
```
2 ff jj dd kk ss ll aa ;;
```
DS
```
3 fj fj dk dk sl sl a; a; asdf ;lkj
```
DS
```
4 fj dk sl a; jf kd ls ;a fdsa jkl; a;sldkfj
```
QS

Reach out with little finger; tap Return/Enter key quickly; return finger to home key.

Punctuation, continued

PARENTHESES

SM: 1.5" inches or defaults

LS: SS; DS between sets of related sentences

1. Read the first rule highlighted in color at the right.
2. Key the **Learn** sentence (omit the line number) below it, noting how the rule has been applied.
3. Key the **Apply** sentence, supplying parentheses where needed.
4. Repeat Steps 1-3 for each of the other rules.
5. Key the **Apply** sentences again to increase decision-making speed.

Use parentheses to enclose parenthetical or explanatory matter and added information.

Learn 1 Mai-ling's article (published by Newsweek) is astonishing.
Apply 2 Here are the inspection reports Exhibits C and D.

Use parentheses to enclose identifying letters or figures in lists.

Learn 2 The test covers: (1) keying skill and (2) word processing.
Apply 3 Emphasize in order: 1 technique, 2 speed, and 3 accuracy.

Use parentheses to enclose figures that follow spelled-out amounts when added clarity or emphasis is needed.

Learn 4 His account balance of two hundred dollars ($200) is overdue.
Apply 5 My condo fee was raised to one hundred ninety dollars $190.

Use parentheses to enclose a name and date used as a reference.

Learn 6 A new job means new learning (Oliverio et al., 1993).
Apply 7 Efficiency is not a negative word Wilson and Clark, 1993!

QUOTATION MARKS

Follow the directions given above, *except* that you will supply quotation marks as needed in the **Apply** lines.

Use quotation marks to enclose direct quotations. (When a question mark applies to the entire sentence, it is placed *outside* the quotation marks.)

Learn 1 My supervisor asked, "Have you finished the monthly report?"
Learn 2 Was it Emerson who said, "To have a friend is to be one"?
Apply 3 Zinsser said, Writing is the logical arrangement of thought.
Apply 4 Did Shakespeare say, All the world is a stage?

Use quotation marks to enclose titles of articles, poems, songs, television programs, and unpublished works such as dissertations and theses.

Learn 5 Have you heard the song "From a Distance" by Bette Midler?
Apply 6 We have enjoyed watching the long-running TV series Cheers.

Use quotation marks to enclose special words or phrases used for emphasis or for coined words (words not in dictionary usage).

Learn 7 Many of us have "limited resources" but "unlimited wants."
Apply 8 Dan's oral report was generously sprinkled with "you knows.

Use a single quotation mark (the apostrophe) to indicate a quotation within a quotation.

Learn 9 I said, "We must take, as Frost suggests, a 'different road.' "
Apply 10 I wrote, "We must have, as Tillich said, the courage to be."

1H ◆
KEY LETTERS, WORDS, AND PHRASES

1. Key the lines once (without the numbers); strike the Return/Enter key twice to double-space (DS).
2. Rekey the drill at a faster pace.

Technique hint
Keep fingers curved and upright over home keys with right thumb just barely touching the Space Bar.

Spacing hint
Space once after ; used as punctuation.

```
1 aa ;; ss ll dd kk ff jj a; sl dk fj jf kd ls ;a jf
                                                  DS
2 a a as as ad ad ask ask lad lad fad fad jak jak la
                                                  DS
3 all all fad fad jak jak add add ask ask ads ads as
                                                  DS
4 a lad; a jak; a lass; all ads; add all; ask a lass
                                                  DS
5 as a lad; a fall fad; ask all dads; as a fall fad;
```

1I ◆
END OF LESSON

Electronic typewriter

1. Press the PAPER UP (or EJECT) key to remove paper.
2. Turn machine off.

Electric typewriter

1. Raise PAPER BAIL or pull it toward you and pull PAPER RELEASE LEVER toward you.
2. Remove paper; push PAPER RELEASE LEVER to its normal position.
3. Turn machine off.

Computer

1. Exit the software according to procedure in *User's Guide.*
2. Remove diskette from disk drive and store it.
3. If directed to do so, turn equipment off.

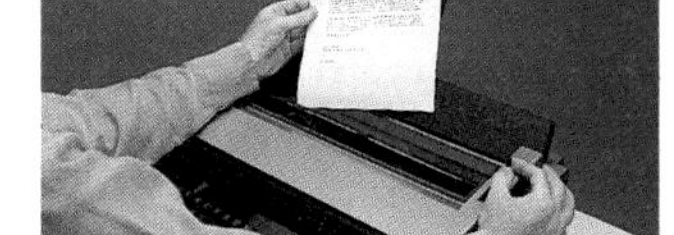

REVIEW LESSON 1 HOME KEYS (ASDF JKL;)

Side margins (SM): 1.5" or defaults; Line spacing (LS): single (SS)

R1A ◆
GET READY TO KEY

Typewriters

1. Arrange your work area (see p. 3).
2. Get to know your equipment (see p. xiii).
3. Make machine adjustments and insert paper into machine (see p. xiv).
4. Take keyboarding position shown at right.

Computers

1. Arrange your work area (see p. 3).
2. Get to know your equipment (see pp. vii-xi).
3. Make adjustments unless you are using the built-in (default) margins and line spacing.
4. Take keyboarding position shown at right.

Punctuation, continued

Follow the directions given on page 152.

Use a comma to separate the day from the year and the city from the state. (In dates, use a comma following the year.)

Learn 21 On July 4, 1776, the Declaration of Independence was signed.
Learn 22 The next convention will be held in New Orleans, Louisiana.
Apply 23 Kingsborough Community College is located in Brooklyn New York.
Apply 24 Abraham Lincoln was born on February 12 1809 in Kentucky.

Use a comma to separate two or more parallel adjectives (adjectives that could be separated by the word "and" instead of the comma).

Learn 25 The angry, discouraged teacher felt she had been betrayed.
Learn 26 Sara opened the door and found a small brown box. (comma cannot be used)
Apply 27 Karen purchased a large antique desk at the auction on Friday.
Apply 28 Ms. Sawyer was an industrious dedicated worker for our company.

Use a comma to separate (a) unrelated groups of figures that appear together and (b) whole numbers into groups of three digits each. (Policy, year, page, room, telephone, and most serial numbers are keyed without commas.)

Learn 29 Before 1998, 1200 more employees will be hired by our firm.
Apply 30 The serial number on the television in Room 1338 is Z83251.
Apply 31 The telephone number listed on Policy #39445 is 834-8822.
Apply 32 During the summer of 1993 32980 policyholders submitted claims.

SEMICOLON

Follow the directions given on page 152, *except* that you will supply semicolons where needed in the **Apply** lines.

Use a semicolon to separate two or more independent clauses in a compound sentence when the conjuction is omitted.

Learn 1 I cannot live on past achievements; I must strive to improve.
Apply 2 To be merely good is easy to be excellent may be difficult.

Use a semicolon to separate independent clauses when they are joined by a conjunctive adverb (however, therefore, consequently, etc.).

Learn 3 Max is a top singer; therefore, he receives many invitations.
Apply 4 You ran the red light consequently, you were pulled over.

Use a semicolon to separate a series of phrases or clause (especially if they contain commas) that are introduced by a colon.

Learn 5 Here are figures: 1992, $6,387,490; 1993, $7,582,460.
Apply 6 Group leaders are: Jan Motz, Group A Juan Peron, Group B.

Place the semicolon *outside* the closing quotation mark; the period, *inside* the quotation mark.

Learn 7 Ms. Uhl wrote on "Building Speed"; Mr. Sanchez on "Accuracy."
Apply 8 Coach Riggs said, "Just relax;" Bobby said, "I'll try".

R1B ◆

REVIEW HOME-KEY POSITION

1. Locate the home keys on the chart: **f d s a** for left hand and **j k l ;** for right hand.
2. Locate the home keys on your keyboard. Place left-hand fingers on **f d s a** and right-hand fingers on **j k l ;** *with fingers well curved and upright (not slanting).*
3. Remove fingers from the keyboard; then place them in home-key position.

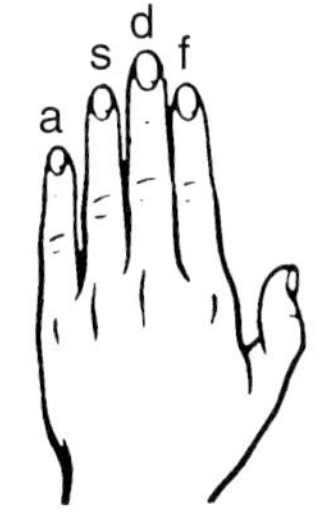

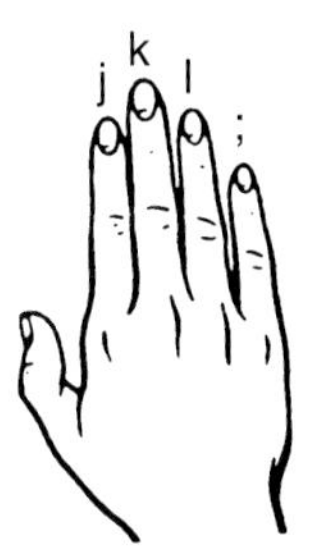

R1C ◆

REVIEW TECHNIQUES

Keystroke

Curve fingers over home keys. Strike each key with a quick-snap stroke; release key quickly.

Space

Strike the Space Bar with a quick down-and-in motion of the right thumb. Do not pause before or after spacing stroke.

Hard Return

Reach the right little finger to the Return/Enter key, tap it, and return the finger quickly to home key.

Remember to use a hard return at the end of all drill lines. To double-space (DS), use two hard returns.

Key the lines once as shown: single-spaced (SS) with a double space (DS) between 2-line groups. Do not key the line numbers.

Strike Space Bar once to space

1 f ff j jj d dd k kk s ss l ll a aa ; ;; fdsa jkl;
2 f ff j jj d dd k kk s ss l ll a aa ; ;; fdsa jkl;

Strike the Return key twice to double-space (DS)

3 j jj f ff k kk d dd l ll s ss ; ;; a aa asdf ;lkj
4 j jj f ff k kk d dd l ll s ss ; ;; a aa asdf ;lkj

DS

5 a;a sls dkd fjf ;a; lsl kdk jfj a;sldkfj a;sldkfj
6 a;a sls dkd fjf ;a; lsl kdk jfj a;sldkfj a;sldkfj

Strike the Return key 4 times to quadruple-space (QS)

R1D ◆

IMPROVE HOME-KEY STROKING

1. Review the technique illustrations in R1C above.
2. Key the lines once as shown: single-spaced (SS) with a double space (DS) between 2-line groups.

Goal: To improve keystroking, spacing, and return technique.

1 f f ff j j jj d d dd k k kk s s ss l l ll a a aa;
2 f f ff j j jj d d dd k k kk s s ss l l ll a a aa;

DS

3 fj dk sl a; jf kd ls ;a ds kl df kj sd lk sa ;l j
4 fj dk sl a; jf kd ls ;a ds kl df kj sd lk sa ;l j

DS

5 sa as ld dl af fa ls sl fl lf al la ja aj sk ks j
6 sa as ld dl af fa ls sl fl lf al la ja aj sk ks j

QS

May be used after completing Unit 6.

COMMA USAGE

SM: 1.5" inches or defaults

LS: SS; DS between sets of related sentences

1. Read the first rule highlighted in color at the right.
2. Key the **Learn** sentences (omit the line number) below it, noting how the rule has been applied.
3. Key the **Apply** sentences, supplying the needed commas.
4. Repeat Steps 1-3 for each of the other rules.
5. Key the **Apply** sentences again to increase decision-making speed.

Use a comma after (a) introductory words, phrases, or clauses and (b) words in a series.

Learn 1 If you finish your homework, you may go to the play with Mary.
Learn 2 We will play the Tigers, Yankees, and Indians on our next home stand.
Apply 3 The next exam will cover memos simple tables and unbound reports.
Apply 4 When she came to visit Jo brought Dave Rob and Juanita with her.

Do not use a comma to separate two items treated as a single unit within a series.

Learn 5 Her favorite breakfast was bacon and eggs, muffins, and juice.
Apply 6 My choices are peaches and cream brownies and strawberry shortcake.
Apply 7 She ordered macaroni and cheese ice cream and a soft drink.

Use a comma before short direct quotations.

Learn 8 The announcer said, "Please stand and welcome our next guest."
Apply 9 The woman asked "What time does the play begin?"
Apply 10 Sachi answered "I'll be in Chicago."

Use a comma before and after word(s) in apposition.

Learn 11 Jan, the new reporter, has started working on the next newsletter.
Apply 12 Our branch manager Carmen Jackson will be here tomorrow.
Apply 13 The editor Jason Maxwell said several changes should be made.

Use a coma to set off words of direct address.

Learn 14 If I can be of further assistance, Mario, please let me know.
Apply 15 Finish this assignment Martin before you start on the next one.
Apply 16 I would recommend Mr. Clinton that we cancel the order.

Use a comma or commas to set off nonrestrictive clauses (not necessary to the meaning of the sentence); however, do not set off restrictive clauses (necessary to the meaning of the sentence).

Learn 17 The manuscript, which I prepared, needs to be revised.
Learn 18 The manuscript that presents banking alternatives is now available.
Apply 19 The movie which was on the top ten list was very entertaining.
Apply 20 The student who scores highest on the exam will win the scholarship.

(continued)

R1E ◆

IMPROVE RETURN TECHNIQUE

each line twice single-spaced (SS); double-space (DS) between 2-line groups

Goals

- curved, upright fingers
- quick-snap keystrokes
- down-and-in spacing
- quick return without spacing at line ending

Return without moving your eyes from the copy.

Technique hint

Reach out with the little finger, not the hand; tap Return/Enter key quickly; return finger to home key.

```
1 a;sldkfj a;sldkfj
                    DS
2 a ad ad a as as ask ask
                          DS
3 as as jak jak ads ads all all
                                DS
4 a jak; a lass; all fall; ask all dads
                                        DS
5 as a fad; add a jak; all fall ads; a sad lass
                                                QS
```

R1F ◆

KEY WORDS/ PHRASES

each line twice single-spaced (SS); double-space (DS) between 2-line groups

Goals

- curved, upright fingers
- eyes on copy in book or on screen
- quick-snap keystrokes
- steady pace

Correct finger curvature

Correct finger alignment

Down-and-in spacing motion

```
1 a jak; a jak; ask dad; ask dad; as all; as all ads
                                    Return twice to DS
2 a fad; a fad; as a lad; as a lad; all ads; all ads
                                                  DS
3 as a fad; as a fad; a sad lass; a sad lass; a fall
                                                  DS
4 ask a lad; ask a lad; all jaks fall; all jaks fall
                                                  DS
5 a sad fall; a sad fall; all fall ads; all fall ads
                                                  DS
6 add a jak; a lad asks a lass; as a jak ad all fall
```

R1G ◆

END OF LESSON

Electronic typewriter

1. Press the PAPER UP (or EJECT) key to remove paper.
2. Turn machine off.

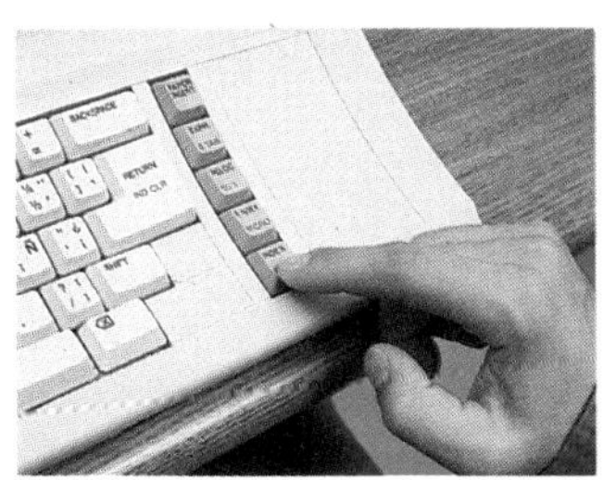

Electric typewriter

1. Raise PAPER BAIL or pull it toward you and pull PAPER RELEASE LEVER toward you.
2. Remove paper; push PAPER RELEASE LEVER to its normal position.
3. Turn machine off.

Computer

1. Exit the software according to procedure in *User's Guide.*
2. Remove diskette from disk drive and store it.
3. If directed to do so, turn equipment off.

Grammar, continued

Follow the directions given on page 150.

Use a singular verb when *number* is used as the subject and is preceded by *the*; however, use a plural verb if *number* is preceded by *a*.

Learn 23 The number of students who pass the CPA exam has increased.
Learn 24 A number of women have volunteered to assist with the project.
Apply 25 A number of clients (has, have) complained about our service.
Apply 26 The number of students in our district (is, are) increasing.

PLURAL VERBS

Use a plural verb with a plural subject (noun or pronoun).

Learn 1 The three pictures have been framed.
Learn 2 They are going to ask you to present the award.
Apply 3 The napkins (is, are) on the counter.
Apply 4 New desks (has, have) been ordered.

Use plural verbs with compound subjects joined by *and*.

Learn 5 Tom and Sue are in charge of the program.
Apply 6 Mr. Miller and his wife are registered to vote on Tuesday.
Apply 7 My dog and your cat (has, have) been fighting in the garden.
Apply 8 The treasurer and the secretary (is, are) planning to attend.

OTHER VERB GUIDES

If there is confusion whether a subject is singular or plural, consult a dictionary.

Learn 1 The data presented in your report are confusing.
Learn 2 A few alumni are to speak at graduation this year.
Learn 3 The analyses completed by Mrs. Carter are excellent.
Apply 4 The same criteria (has, have) been used in the past.
Apply 5 The analysis (is, are) very extensive.

When used as the subject, the pronouns, I, we, you, and they, as well as plural nouns, require the plural verb *do not* or the contraction *don't*.

Learn 6 They do not want to become involved with the project.
Learn 7 The plans don't include a private office for the manager.
Apply 8 I (don't, doesn't) agree with the report you submitted.
Apply 9 The reviews (don't, doesn't) look very promising.

When used as the subject, the pronouns, he, she, it, as well as singular nouns, require the singular verb *does not* or the contraction *doesn't*.

Learn 10 She doesn't want the office layout changed.
Learn 11 The price does not include the software.
Apply 12 It (don't, doesn't) concern me; you take care of it.
Apply 13 The job (don't, doesn't) require voice transcription.

LESSON 2 H AND E

SM: 1.5" or defaults; LS: SS

2A ◆ GET READY TO KEY

1. Arrange work area (see p. 3).
2. Adjust equipment. (For typewriters, see p. xiv.)
3. Insert paper if necessary (see p. xiv) or check paper supply in printer.

Your teacher may guide you through the appropriate steps for your equipment.

2B ◆ REVIEW HOME KEYS

each line twice single-spaced (SS): once slowly; again, at a faster pace; double-space (DS) between 2-line groups

all keystrokes learned

```
1 a;sldkfj a; sl dk fj ff jj dd kk ss ll aa ;; fj a;
2 as as ad ad all all jak jak fad fad fall fall lass
3 a jak; a fad; as a lad; ask dad; a lass; a fall ad
```

Return 4 times to quadruple-space (QS) between lesson parts

2C ◆ LEARN H AND E

h *Right pointer* finger

e *Left middle* finger

Learn h

```
1 j j hj hj ah ah ha ha had had has has ash ash hash
2 hj hj ha ha ah ah hah hah had had ash ash has hash
3 ah ha; had ash; has had; a hall; has a hall; ah ha
```

Return twice to double-space (DS) after you complete the set of lines

Learn e

```
4 d d ed ed el el led led eel eel eke eke ed fed fed
5 ed ed el el lee lee fed fed eke eke led led ale ed
6 a lake; a leek; a jade; a desk; a jade eel; a deed
```

Combine h and e

Do not attempt to key the vertical lines separating word groups in line 7.

```
7 he he he|she she she|shed shed|heed heed|held held
8 a lash; a shed; he held; she has jade; held a sash
9 has fled; he has ash; she had jade; she had a sale
```

Return 4 times to quadruple-space (QS) between lesson parts

May be used after completing Unit 6.

SUBJECT-VERB AGREEMENT

SM: 1.5" inches or defaults

LS: SS; DS between sets of related sentences

1. Read the first rule highlighted in color at the right.
2. Key the **Learn** sentences (omit the line number) below it, noting how the rule has been applied.
3. Key the **Apply** sentences, using the correct verb in the parentheses.
4. Repeat Steps 1-3 for each of the other rules.
5. Key the **Apply** lines again to speed up selection of the correct verb.

SINGULAR VERBS

Use a singular verb with a singular subject (noun or pronoun).

Learn 1 The mail carrier has not delivered today's mail.
Learn 2 She has already completed her solo.
Apply 3 An outstanding executive assistant (is, are) difficult to find.
Apply 4 He (has, have) been accepted at Harvard.

Use singular verbs with indefinite pronouns (each, every, any, either, neither, one, etc.) used as subjects.

Learn 5 Every employee is expected to attend the awards banquet.
Learn 6 Everyone has been given permission to attend the game.
Apply 7 Each person (has, have) his or her own ideas on the subject.
Apply 8 Neither one of the gymnasts (is, are) very good.

Use a singular verb with singular subjects linked by *or* or *nor*. Exception: If one subject is singular and the other is plural, the verb agrees with the closer subject.

Learn 9 Either my mother or father is invited to the opening ceremony.
Learn 10 Neither Mr. Neal nor the computer operators have the manual.
Apply 11 Either Eric or Marsha (has, have) the blueprints.
Apply 12 Neither the editor nor the authors (was, were) to be present.

Use a singular verb with a singular subject that is separated from the verb by phrases beginning with *as well as* and *in addition to*.

Learn 13 The report as well as the letters has to be finished by noon.
Apply 14 The advisor as well as two students (is, are) to go with us.

Use singular verbs with collective nouns (committee, team, class, jury, etc.) if the collective noun acts as a unit.

Learn 15 The finance committee has the April budget.
Learn 16 A parliamentary procedure team is going to perform on Friday.
Apply 17 The board (is, are) going to discuss that issue next week.
Apply 18 The staff (wants, want) to be in charge of the banquet.

Use singular verbs with the pronouns *all* and *some* (as well as fractions and percentages) when used as subjects *if* their modifiers are singular. Use plural verbs *if* their modifiers are plural.

Learn 19 Some of the research is finished.
Learn 20 All of the girls were planning to attend the banquet.
Apply 21 All of the wood (is, are) stacked behind the garage.
Apply 22 Some of the clothes (was, were) purchased in Paris.

(continued)

2D ◆

IMPROVE KEYBOARDING TECHNIQUE

1. Key the lines once as shown: SS with a DS between 2-line groups.
2. Key the lines again at a faster pace.

Do not attempt to key the labels (home row, h/e), line numbers, or vertical lines separating word groups.

Space once after ; used as punctuation.

Fingers curved

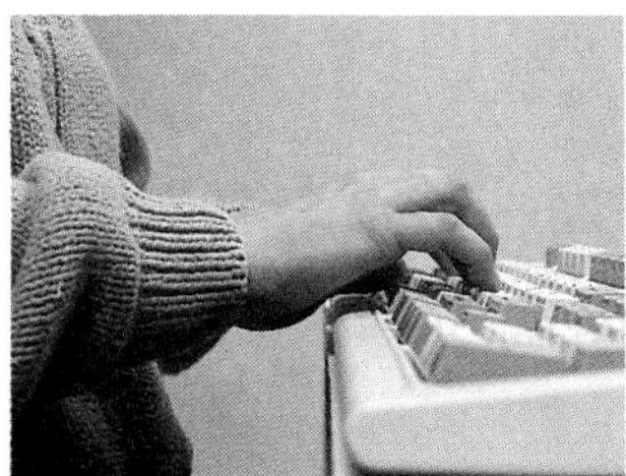

Fingers upright

home row
1 ask ask | has has | lad lad | all all | jak jak | fall falls
2 a jak; a lad; a sash; had all; has a jak; all fall
DS

h/e
3 he he | she she | led led | held held | jell jell | she shed
4 he led; she had; she fell; a jade ad; a desk shelf
DS

all keys learned
5 elf elf | all all | ask ask | led led | jak jak | hall halls
6 ask dad; he has jell; she has jade; he sells leeks
DS

all keys learned
7 he led; she has; a jak ad; a jade eel; a sled fell
8 she asked a lad; he led all fall; she has a jak ad

LESSON 3 I AND R

SM: 1.5" or defaults; LS: SS

A time schedule for the parts of this lesson and lessons that follow is given as a guide for pacing your practice. If you key a drill in less than this amount of time, rekey selected lines.

3A ◆ 5'

GET READY TO KEY

Follow the steps on p. 3.

3B ◆ 7'

CONDITIONING PRACTICE

each line twice SS; DS between 2-line groups

Goals

First time: Slow, easy pace, but strike and release each key quickly.

Second time: Faster pace, move from key to key quickly; keep element or cursor moving steadily.

Technique hints

1. Keep fingers upright and well curved.
2. Try to make each reach without moving hand or other fingers forward or downward.

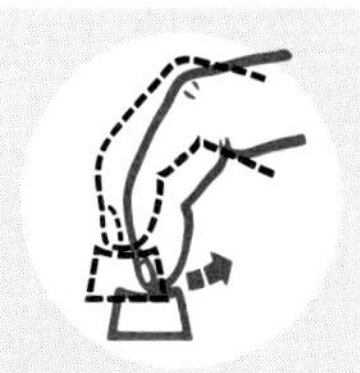

home keys
1 a;sldkfj a;sldkfj as jak ask fad all dad lads fall
Return twice to DS

h/e
2 hj hah has had sash hash ed led fed fled sled fell
DS

all keys learned
3 as he fled; ask a lass; she had jade; sell all jak
Return 4 times to quadruple-space (QS) between lesson parts

NUMBER EXPRESSION

May be used after completing Unit 5.

IMPROVE SKILLS

1. Read the first rule highlighted in color at the right.
2. Key the **Learn** sentence (omit the line number) below it, noting how the rule has been applied.
3. Key the **Apply** sentence, supplying the appropriate number expression.
4. Repeat Steps 1-3 for each of the other rules.
5. If time permits, key the eight **Apply** sentences again to improve number control.

Use figures for house numbers except house number One.

Learn 1 My home is at 9 Vernon Drive; my office, at One Weber Plaza.
Apply 2 The Nelsons moved from 4037 Pyle Avenue to 1 Maple Circle.

Use figures to express measures and weights.

Learn 3 Gladys Randoph is 5 ft. 6 in. tall and weighs 119 lbs. 6 oz.
Apply 4 This carton measures one ft. by six in. and weighs five lbs.

Use figures for numbers following nouns.

Learn 5 Review Rules 1 to 22 in Chapter 6, pages 126 and 127, today.
Apply 6 Case 2659 is reviewed in Volume five, pages eight and nine.

Spell a number that begins a sentence even when other numbers in the sentence are shown in figures.

Learn 7 Twelve of the new shrubs have died; 38 are doing quite well.
Apply 8 40 members have paid their dues, but 15 have not done so.

Use figures for numbers above ten, and for numbers one to ten when they are used with numbers above ten.

Learn 9 She ordered 2 word processors, 15 computers, and 3 printers.
Apply 10 Did he say they need ten or 12 sets of Z11 and Z13 diskettes?

Use figures to express dates and times.

Learn 11 He will arrive on Paygo Flight 62 at 10:28 a.m. on March 21.
Apply 12 Candidates must be in Ivy Hall at eight ten a.m. on May one.

Use figures for a series of fractions, but spell isolated fractions and indefinite numbers.

Learn 13 Rhonda has a 1/3 interest in Plat A, 1/2 in B, and 3/4 in C.
Learn 14 More than twenty workers voted; that is about three fourths.
Apply 15 Guide calls: one fourth, 1/2, 3/4, and one—each 15 seconds.
Apply 16 Over 90 parents saw the game; isn't that about 1/2?

3C ◆ 18'

LEARN I AND R

1. Key each line twice SS (slowly, then faster); DS between 2-line groups.
2. Key each line once more.

Goals

- curved, upright fingers
- finger-action keystrokes
- quick return, eyes on textbook copy

i *Up* with *right middle* finger

r *Up* with *left pointer* finger

Learn i

```
1 k k ik ik is is if if did did aid aid kid kid hail
2 ik ik if if is is kid kid his his lie lie aid aide
3 a kid; a lie; if he; he did; his aide; if a kid is
```

DS

Learn r

```
4 f f rf rf jar jar her her are are ark ark jar jars
5 rf rf re re fr fr jar jar red red her her far fare
6 a jar; a rake; a lark; red jar; hear her; are dark
```

DS

Combine i and r

```
7 fir fir|rid rid|sir sir|ire ire|fire fire|air airs
8 a fir; if her; a fire; is fair; his ire; if she is
9 he is; if her; is far; red jar; his heir; her aide
```

Quadruple-space (QS) between lesson parts

3D ◆ 20'

IMPROVE TECHNIQUE

1. Key the lines once as shown: SS with a DS between 2-line groups.
2. Key the lines again at a faster pace.

Goals

- curved, upright fingers
- finger-action keystrokes
- down-and-in spacing
- quick return, eyes on textbook copy

reach review

```
1 hj ed ik rf hj de ik fr hj ed ik rf jh de ki fr hj
2 he he if if all all fir fir jar jar rid rid as ask
```

DS

h/e

```
3 she she|elf elf|her her|hah hah|eel eel|shed shelf
4 he has; had jak; her jar; had a shed; she has fled
```

DS

i/r

```
5 fir fir|rid rid|sir sir|kid kid|ire ire|fire fired
6 a fir; is rid; is red; his ire; her kid; has a fir
```

DS

all keys learned

```
7 if if|is is|he he|did did|fir fir|jak jak|all fall
8 a jak; he did; ask her; red jar; she fell; he fled
```

DS

all keys learned

```
9 if she is; he did ask; he led her; he is her aide;
10 she has had a jak sale; she said he had a red fir;
```

Capitalization, continued

Follow the directions given on page 147.

Capitalize names of clubs, organizations, and companies.

Learn 15 The Beau Monde Singers will perform at Music Hall.
Apply 16 lennox corp. now owns the hyde park athletic club.

Capitalize geographic names, regions, and locations.

Learn 17 Val drove through the Black Hills in South Dakota.
Apply 18 we canoed down the missouri river near sioux city.

Capitalize names of streets, avenues, and buildings.

Learn 19 Jemel lives at Bay Towers near Golden Gate Bridge.
Apply 20 our store is now in midtown plaza on kenwood road.

Capitalize an official title when it precedes a name and elsewhere if it is a title of high distinction.

Learn 21 In what year did Juan Carlos become King of Spain?
Learn 22 Masami Chou, our class president, made the awards.
Apply 23 will the president speak to us in the Rose Garden?
Apply 24 mr. koch, our company president, chairs the group.

Capitalize initials; also letters in abbreviations if the letters would be capitalized when the words were spelled out.

Learn 25 Does Dr. R. J. Anderson have an Ed.D. or a Ph.D.?
Learn 26 He said the UPS stands for United Parcel Service.
Apply 27 we have a letter for ms. anna m. bucks of boston.
Apply 28 m.d. means Doctor of Medicine, not medical doctor.

Capitalize the first word after a colon only if that word begins a complete sentence; space twice after the colon.

Learn 29 My motto: Only my best effort will be enough now.
Learn 30 Add to list: detergent, bleach, fabric softener.
Apply 31 Daily reminder: set your goal high and go for it.
Apply 32 New features: reveal codes, spell check, sort.

Capitalize first and last words and all other words in titles of books, articles, periodicals, plays, and poems and in headings, except words of four or fewer letters used as articles, prepositions, and conjunctions.

Learn 33 Suzanne read the book As the Crow Flies by Archer.
Learn 34 Review the article "The Computer Age" by Ian Hart.
Apply 35 Joe's report was on line of duty by Michael Grant.
Apply 36 Wilda may use "the will to win" as her talk title.

LESSON 4 REVIEW

SM: 1.5" or defaults; LS: SS

4A ◆ 3'

REVIEW GET-READY PROCEDURES

1. Review the steps for arranging your work area (see p. 3).
2. Review the steps required to ready your equipment.
3. If using a typewriter, review the steps for inserting paper (see p. xiv).
4. Take good keyboarding position:
   - fingers curved and upright
   - wrists low, but not touching frame of machine
   - forearms parallel to slant of keyboard
   - body erect, sitting back in chair
   - feet on floor for balance

4B ◆ 5'

CONDITIONING PRACTICE

each line twice SS; DS between 2-line groups; if time permits, rekey selected lines

all keystrokes learned

1 a;sldkfj fj dk sl a; jh de ki fr hj ed ik rf fj a;
2 a if is el he la as re led fir did she has jak jar
3 he has fir; she had a jak; a jade jar; a leek sale

QS

4C ◆ 10'

IMPROVE SPACE-BAR TECHNIQUE

1. Key each line twice SS; DS between 2-line groups. Space *immediately* after keying a word; make the space a part of the word it follows.
2. Rekey lines 1-3.

Use down-and-in motion

Short, easy words

1 if is ha la ah el as re id did sir fir die rid lie
2 ad lad lei rah jak had ask lid her led his kid has
3 hah all ire add iris hall fire keel sell jeer fall

DS

Short-word phrases

4 if he|he is|if he is|if she|she is|if she is|as is
5 as he is|if he led|if she has|if she did|had a jak
6 as if|a jar lid|all her ads|as he said|a jade fish

QS

4D ◆ 10'

IMPROVE RETURN TECHNIQUE

1. See the illustration at far right. (The Return/Enter key will be called simply *Return* in the remaining lessons.)
2. Key each line twice SS; DS between 2-line groups. Keep up your pace at the end of the line, return quickly, and begin the new line immediately.
3. Rekey the drill.

1 if he is;
2 as if she is;
3 he had a fir desk;
4 she has a red jell jar;
5 he has had a lead all fall;
6 she asked if he reads fall ads;
7 she said she reads all ads she sees;
8 his dad has had a sales lead as he said;

QS

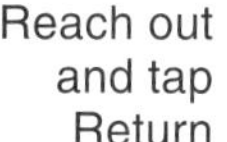

Reach out and tap Return

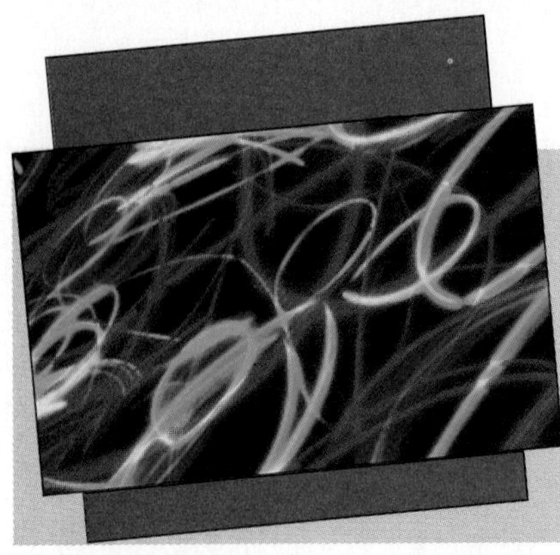

Language Skills

Learning Outcomes: After completing this review, you will be better able to

1. Capitalize words and express numbers appropriately.
2. Match subjects and verbs and punctuate sentences correctly.
3. Use confusing words correctly and divide words acceptably at line endings.
4. Use sound-alike words correctly.
5. Divide words properly at line endings.

CAPITALIZATION

May be used after completing Unit 5.

IMPROVE SKILLS

SM: 1.5" inches or defaults

LS: SS; DS between sets of related sentences

1. Read the first rule highlighted in color at the right.
2. Key the **Learn** sentence (omit the line number) below it, noting how the rule has been applied.
3. Key the **Apply** sentence, supplying the needed capital letters.
4. Repeat Steps 1-3 for each of the other rules.
5. Key the **Apply** sentences again to increase decision-making speed.

Capitalize the first word in a sentence.

Learn 1 Mindy left her coat here. Can she stop by for it?
Apply 2 do you plan to go today? the game begins at four.

Capitalize personal titles and names of people.

Learn 3 I wrote to Mr. Katz, but Miss Dixon sent the form.
Apply 4 do you know if luci and lex bauer are with dr. tu?

Capitalize names of cities, states, and other important places.

Learn 5 When you were in Nevada, did you visit Hoover Dam?
Apply 6 did he see paris from the top of the eiffel tower?

Capitalize the days of the week.

Learn 7 Did you ask if the OEA contest is to be on Friday?
Apply 8 does FBLA meet on wednesday, thursday, and friday?

Capitalize the months of the year.

Learn 9 August was very hot, but September is rather cool.
Apply 10 they are to spend july and august at myrtle beach.

Capitalize names of holidays.

Learn 11 Kacy and Zoe may visit their parents on Labor Day.
Apply 12 gus asked if memorial day comes at the end of may.

Capitalize the names of historic periods and events and special events.

Learn 13 The Fourth of July honors the American Revolution.
Apply 14 bastille day is in honor of the french revolution.

(continued)

4E ◆ 10'

BUILD SPEED BY REPEATING WORDS

Each word in each line is shown twice. Practice a word the first time at an easy speed; repeat it at a faster speed.

1. Key each line once SS; DS after the third line. Use the plan suggested above.
2. Key each line again. Try to keep the printing point or cursor moving at a steady speed. QS (4 hard returns) at the end of the drill.

Technique hint
Think and say the word; key it with quick-snap strokes using the finger-tips.

Goal: to speed up the combining of letters

```
1 is is|if if|ah ah|he he|el el|irk irk|aid aid|aide
2 as as|ask ask|ad ad|had had|re re|ire ire|are hare
3 if if|fir fir|id id|did did|el el|eel eel|jak jaks
                                                  QS
```

4F ◆ 12'

BUILD SPEED BY REPEATING PHRASES

1. Key each line once SS. Speed up the second keying of each phrase.
2. Key the lines once more to improve your speed.

Space with right thumb

Use down-and-in motion

Goal: to speed up spacing between words

```
1 ah ha|ah ha|if he|if he|as if|as if|as he|as he is
2 if a|if a|a fir|a fir|a jar|a jar|irk her|irks her
3 he did|he did|if all|if all|if she led|if she fled
4 a lad|a lad|if her|if her|as his aide|as his aides
```

LESSON 5 O AND T

SM: 1.5" or defaults; LS: SS

5A ◆ 8'

CONDITIONING PRACTICE

each line twice SS (slowly, then faster); DS between 2-line groups

In this lesson and the remaining lessons in this unit, the time for the *Conditioning Practice* is changed to 8 minutes. During this time you are to arrange your work area, ready your equipment for keying, and practice the lines of the *Conditioning Practice*.

Fingers curved

Fingers upright

```
home row      1 a sad fall; had a hall; a jak falls; as a fall ad;
3d row        2 if her aid; all he sees; he irks her; a jade fish;
all keys
learned       3 as he fell; he sells fir desks; she had half a jar
                                                                QS
```

Document 14

Message from JESSICA SAMPSON

Changes have been made to the PARADE OF HOMES table that you prepared. These changes are shown on the attached sheet. Check to see if these changes will make revisions necessary to any of the other documents created for the Parade of Homes.

JS 5/17

PARADE OF HOMES

June 7-21, 19--

Location	Builder	Price
3885 Wimbledon Lane	Brock Construction	$~~133,000~~ 139,500
3892 Glencliffe Lane	Murphy Homes, Inc.	95,000
114 Fernbrook Lane	J & P Construction	215,000
803 Ashmore Drive	Berry & Sons Construction	149,000
5574 Blue Hills Road	Homes by Makely [transpose: Makley]	99,000
4348 Mossridge Drive	Valleyview Home Builders	10~~5~~8,000
3872 Glencliffe Lane	Dalton & James Realty	91,000
1~~2~~30 Fernbrook Lane	Your Home Builders	175,000

Document 15

Message from JESSICA SAMPSON

Send the attached letter with the changes shown to

Ms. Katelin Andalusia
461 Brantwood Avenue
Green Bay, WI 54303-6624

JS 5/17

RITTER
REALTY ▲ COMPANY
410 BRADLEY STREET ■ HOUSTON, TX ▲ 77009-3658 ■ 713-555-2758

May 15, 19--

~~Mr. Charles L. Atkins~~
~~1241 Warren Drive~~
~~Denver, CO 80221-7463~~ Katelin Andalusia

Dear ~~Mr. Atkins~~

It appears as though you would fit in very nicely with the "Ritter Realty Team." Your resume looks very impressive, and your references all speak very highly of you.

As you know from speaking with ~~John Morgan about two weeks ago at the convention in Miami~~ Mark Grayson, we are looking for a person from outside the area who can bring in new ideas and who has been successful in the promotion and sales area. Your background shows a strength in both of these areas.

Would you be available to spend a day with us in Houston during the week of ~~May 26-30~~ June 2-6 to discuss the position? I will call next week to determine your availability and to make arrangements for your visit.

Sincerely

Jessica A. Sampson

Ms. Jessica A. Sampson
Branch Manager

xx

Document 16

Message from JESSICA SAMPSON

Mr. Jerry Sawyer has cancelled his appointment on June 6 with Roxanne Davis. I've scheduled Mr. and Mrs. Clayton Barns in place of Mr. Sawyer. Please revise Roxanne's schedule with this change and print a new copy for her. Also, send the form letter to Mr. and Mrs. Barns confirming their appointment. Their address is 929 Spring Creek Lane, Houston, Texas 77017-2600; their telephone number is 555-1955.

JS 5/17

5B ◆ 20'

LEARN O AND T

each line twice SS (slowly, then faster); DS between 2-line groups; key lines 7-9 again

o *Right ring* finger

t *Left pointer* finger

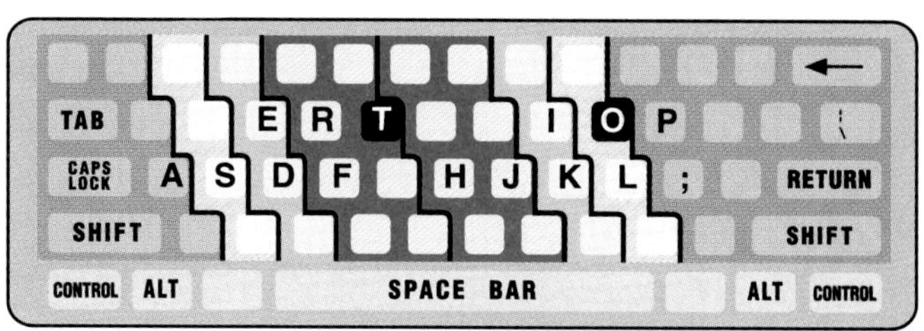

Learn o

1 l l ol ol do do of of so so lo lo old old for fore
2 ol ol of of or or for for oak oak off off sol sole
3 do so; a doe; of old; of oak; old foe; of old oak;

DS

Learn t

4 f f tf tf it it at at tie tie the the fit fit lift
5 tf tf ft ft it it sit sit fit fit hit hit kit kite
6 if it; a fit; it fit; tie it; the fit; at the site

DS

Combine o and t

7 to to | too too | toe toe | dot dot | lot lot | hot hot | tort
8 a lot; to jot; too hot; odd lot; a fort; for a lot
9 of the; to rot; dot it; the lot; for the; for this

QS

5C ◆ 22'

IMPROVE TECHNIQUE

1. Key the lines once as shown: SS with a DS between 2-line groups.
2. Key the lines again at a faster pace.

Goals

- curved, upright fingers
- quick-snap keystrokes
- down-and-in spacing
- quick return, eyes on textbook copy

reach review

1 hj ed ik rf ol tf jh de ki fr lo ft hj ed ol rf tf
2 is led fro hit old fit let kit rod kid dot jak sit

DS

h/e

3 he he | she she | led led | had had | see see | has has | seek
4 he led | ask her | she held | has fled | had jade | he leads

DS

i/t

5 it it | fit fit | tie tie | sit sit | kit kit | its its | fits
6 a kit | a fit | a tie | lit it | it fits | it sits | it is fit

DS

o/r

7 or or | for for | ore ore | fro fro | oar oar | roe roe | rode
8 a rod | a door | a rose | or for | her or | he rode | or a rod

DS

space bar

9 of he or it is to if do el odd off too for she the
10 it is | if it | do so | if he | to do | or the | she is | of all

DS

all keys learned

11 if she is; ask a lad; to the lake; off the old jet
12 he or she; for a fit; if she left the; a jak salad

74B-80B ◆ (cont.)

Document 12

Message from JESSICA SAMPSON

Three more clients have accepted invitations to the private showing. Send a copy of the attached letter using the information provided below.

Mr. and Mrs. Mark O'Mara
1583 Nassau Bay Drive
Houston, TX 77058-2196

Ms. Kathy S. Ristow
1418 Rainwood Drive
Houston, TX 77079-3170

Mr. and Mrs. Juan Cruz
4573 Red Maple Drive
Houston, TX 77064-4407

Mark Grayson will show Mr. and Mrs. O'Mara and Ms. Ristow the homes on Saturday, June 6, at 7 p.m. Matthew Sparks will show Mr. and Mrs. Cruz the homes on Friday, June 5, at 1 p.m. JS 5/16

May 16, 19--

Mr. and Mrs. Jason R. Walton
1825 Victoria Drive
Houston, TX 77022-1903

Dear Mr. and Mrs. Walton

We are pleased to have you take part in our private showing of the homes that will be in this year's Parade of Homes. The eight homes you will see combine quality construction, professional decorating, and exclusive landscaping to make this year's show the best ever.

I have made arrangements with (AGENT'S NAME) to show you the homes. Please meet (HIM/HER) at our office at (TIME) on (FRIDAY/SATURDAY), June (5/6). It will take approximately two hours to visit the homes.

I am looking forward to hearing your comments about the homes after the showing. If you have any questions prior to the showing, please telephone me.

Sincerely

Jessica A. Sampson

Ms. Jessica A. Sampson
Branch Manager

xx

c (NAME OF AGENT)

Document 13

Message from JESSICA SAMPSON

Key the information at the right as a table. Use SALES REPORT for the main heading and May 4 - 10 as the secondary heading. JS 5/16

Agent	Property	Price
Mark Grayson	310 Berryhill Court	$149,500
Matthew Sparks	832 Axilda Street	99,500
Mary Carlson	3725 Gulf Street	249,900
John Morgan	2690 Spring Creek	129,800
Roxanne Davis	710 Rainwood Drive	89,900
Yein Cheng	8210 Rosslyn Road	225,000
Mark Grayson	929 Whitney Street	110,200
John Morgan	2836 Yarberry Street	88,300
Matthew Sparks	218 San Felipe Street	115,600
Mark Grayson	8219 Queen Street	79,300
Roxanne Davis	5614 Monaco Road	185,400
Yein Cheng	3955 Hoyte Drive	69,500

LESSON 6 N AND G

SM: 1.5" or defaults; LS: SS

6A ◆ 8'

CONDITIONING PRACTICE

each line twice SS (slowly, then faster); DS between 2-line groups

all letters learned

home row 1 has a jak; ask a lad; a fall fad; had a jak salad;
o/t 2 to do it; as a tot; do a lot; it is hot; to dot it
e/i/r 3 is a kid; it is far; a red jar; her skis; her aide

QS

6B ◆ 20'

LEARN N AND G

each line twice SS (slowly, then faster); DS between 2-line groups; key lines 7-9 again

n *Right pointer* finger

g *Left pointer* finger

Learn n

1 j j nj nj an an and and end end ant ant land lands
2 nj nj an an en en in in on on end end and and hand
3 an en; an end; an ant; no end; on land; a fine end

DS

Learn g

4 f f gf gf go go fog fog got got fig figs jogs jogs
5 gf gf go go got got dig dig jog jog logs logs golf
6 to go; he got; to jog; to jig; the fog; is to golf

DS

Combine n and g

7 go go | no no | nag nag | ago ago | gin gin | gone gone | long
8 go on; a nag; sign in; no gain; long ago; into fog
9 a fine gig; log in soon; a good sign; lend a hand;

QS

6C ◆ 5'

IMPROVE RETURN TECHNIQUE

1. Key each line twice SS; DS between 2-line groups. Keep up your pace at the end of the line, return quickly, and begin new line promptly.
2. Rekey the drill.

1 she is gone;
2 he got an old dog;
3 she jogs in a dense fog;
4 she and he go to golf at nine;
5 he is a hand on a rig in the north;

QS

Reach out and tap Return

74B-80B ◆ (cont.)

Document 10

Message from JESSICA SAMPSON

Please send the attached letter to

Mr. Charles L. Atkins
1241 Warren Drive
Denver, CO 80221-7463

JS 5/15

Dear Mr. Atkins

It appears as though you would fit in very nicely with the "Ritter Realty Team." Your resume looks very impressive, and your references all speak very highly of you.

As you know from speaking with John Morgan about two weeks ago at the convention in Miami, we are looking for a person from outside the area who can bring in new ideas and who has been successful in the promotion and sales area. Your background shows a strength in both of these areas.

Would you be available to spend a day with us in Houston during the week of May 26-30 to discuss the position? I will call next week to determine your availability and to make arrangements for your visit.

Document 11

Message from JESSICA SAMPSON

Please key the attached PARADE OF HOMES schedule for Roxanne Davis.

JS 5/16

SCHEDULE FOR ROXANNE DAVIS)- Bold

June 5

[← Client	Phone	Time
Mr. and Mrs. Dave Johnson	555-4877	10 a.m.
Dr. and Mrs. Reed Kurth	555-8125	
Ms. Patricia Hansen	555-1143	1 p.m.
Mr. and Mrs. Scott Jones	555-1935	
Dr. Faye Snell	555-7680	4 p.m.
Mr. and Mrs. Timothy Reedsberg	555-4676	
Mr. and Mrs. Karl Hallie	555-2908	7 p.m.
Mr. and Mrs. Gregory Haas	555-1298	
Mr. Jerry Sawyer	555-1095	10 a.m.
Mr. and Mrs. Jason Walton	555-6547	
Mr. Robert Todd	555-7231	1 p.m.
Miss Sandra Kurtz	555-3452	
Ms. Gretchen Kuehn	555-9876	
Mr. and Mrs. Barry Bauer	555-2349	4 p.m.
Dr. and Mrs. Ronald Baker	555-1520	7 p.m.
Miss Tami Seymour	555-4822	

6D ◆ 17'

IMPROVE TECHNIQUE

1. Key the lines once as shown: SS with a DS between 2-line groups.
2. Key the lines again at a faster pace.

Goals

- curved, upright fingers
- quick-snap keystrokes
- down-and-in spacing
- quick return, eyes on textbook copy

reach review
```
1 a;sldkfj ed ol rf hj tf nj gf lo de jh ft nj fr a;
2 he jogs; an old ski; do a log for; she left a jar;
```
DS

n/g
```
3 an an|go go|in in|dig dig|and and|got got|end ends
4 go to; is an; log on; sign it; and golf; fine figs
```
DS

space bar
```
5 if if|an an|go go|of of|or or|he he|it it|is is|do
6 if it is|is to go|he or she|to do this|of the sign
```
DS

all keys learned
```
7 she had an old oak desk; a jell jar is at the side
8 he has left for the lake; she goes there at eight;
```
DS

all keys learned
```
9 she said he did it for her; he is to take the oars
10 sign the list on the desk; go right to the old jet
```

LESSON 7 LEFT SHIFT AND . (PERIOD)

SM: 1.5" or defaults; LS: SS

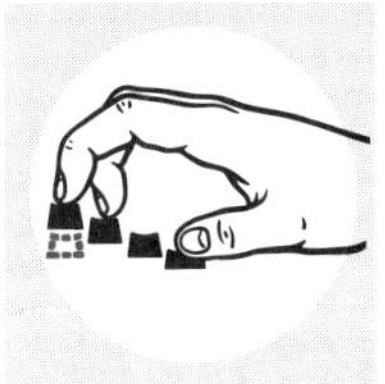
Finger-action keystrokes

Down-and-in spacing

Quick out-and-tap Return

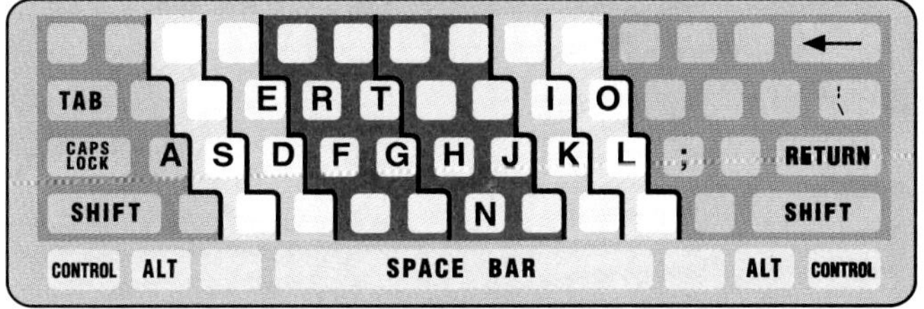

7A ◆ 8'

CONDITIONING PRACTICE

each line twice SS (slowly, then faster); DS between 2-line groups

reach review
```
1 ed ik rf ol gf hj tf nj de ki fr lo fg jh ft jn a;
```
space bar
```
2 or is to if an of el so it go id he do as in at on
```
all keys learned
```
3 he is; if an; or do; to go; a jak; an oak; of all;
```
QS

7B ◆ 5'

IMPROVE SPACE-BAR/RETURN TECHNIQUE

1. Key each line once SS; return and start each new line quickly.
2. Rekey the drill at a faster pace.

```
1 the jet is hers;
2 she has gone to ski;
3 he asked her for one disk;
4 all the girls left for the lake;
5 she is to take this list to his desk;
6 he is at the lake to ski if the fog lifts;
7 he is to see her soon if the jet lands at nine;
```
QS

74B-80B ◆ (cont.)

Document 7

Message from
JESSICA SAMPSON

Key the listing of homes that will be in this year's PARADE OF HOMES. Use Parade of Homes for the main heading and June 7-21, 19--, as the secondary heading.

JS 5/14

Location	Builder	Price
3885 Wimbledon Lane	Brock Construction	$133,000
3892 Glencliffe Lane	Murphy Homes, Inc.	95,000
114 Fernbrook Lane	J & P Construction	215,000
803 Ashmore Drive	Berry & Sons Construction	149,000
5574 Blue Hills Road	Homes by Makely	99,000
4348 Mossridge Drive	Valleyview Home Builders	105,000
3872 Glencliffe Lane	Dalton & James Realty	91,000
120 Fernbrook Lane	Your Home Builders	175,000

Document 8

Message from
JESSICA SAMPSON

Key the attached information in announcement form on a full sheet of paper. You decide on the layout; you've done a very nice job with previous announcements. The eight builders are listed with some of the other documents I've given to be keyed. Make sure to list them in alphabetical order.

JS 5/15

19-- Parade of Homes) Bold
June 7-21
Monday - Friday 5 p.m. to 9 p.m.
Saturday & Sunday 10 a.m. to 6 p.m.
Featuring homes built by
(List the eight homebuilders in alphabetical order)
Sponsored by Ritter Realty Company) - Bold

Document 9

Message from
JESSICA SAMPSON

Please send the attached letter to

Mr. and Mrs. Paul Taylor
1320 Lori Lane #3
Ogden, UT 84404-4396

JS 5/14

Dear Mr. and Mrs. Taylor

¶ Rebecca Smithson, personnel manager of Tyson Production Company, informed me that you have accepted a position with them and will be moving to Houston the first part of July. I know you will enjoy living in this area.

¶ A copy of the "Movers' Guide" published by our real estate company is enclosed. It is designed to give helpful hints on making the move as painless as possible. We hope you will find it useful as you organize for the move to Texas.

¶ If we can be of assistance to you in locating a place to rent or a home to purchase, please telephone our office.

Sincerely

7C ◆ 20'

LEARN LEFT SHIFT AND PERIOD

each line twice SS (slowly, then faster); DS between 2-line groups; rekey each line

Left Shift *Left little* finger; shift, strike, release

. Period *Right ring* finger; space twice after **.** at end of sentence

Spacing hints

Space *once* after **.** used at end of abbreviations and following letters in initials. *Do not* space after **.** *within* abbreviations. Space *twice* after **.** at the end of a sentence except at line endings. There, return without spacing.

Learn Left Shift key

1 a a Ja Ja Ka Ka La La Hal Hal Kal Kal Jae Jae Lana
2 Kal rode; Kae did it; Hans has jade; Jan ate a fig
3 I see that Jake is to aid Kae at the Oak Lake sale
DS

Learn . (period)

4 l l .l .l fl. fl. ed. ed. ft. ft. rd. rd. hr. hrs.
5 .l .l fl. fl. hr. hr. e.g. e.g. i.e. i.e. in. ins.
6 fl. ft. hr. ed. rd. rt. off. fed. ord. alt. asstd.
DS

Combine Left Shift and .

7 I do. Ian is. Ola did. Jan does. Kent is gone.
8 Hal did it. I shall do it. Kate left on a train.
9 J. L. Han skis on Oak Lake; Lt. Haig also does so.
QS

7D ◆ 17'

IMPROVE TECHNIQUE

1. Key the lines once as shown: SS with a DS between 2-line groups.
2. Key the lines again at a faster pace.

Goals

- curved, upright fingers
- finger-action keystrokes
- quiet hands and arms
- down-and-in spacing
- out-and-down shifting
- quick out-and-tap return

Technique hint: eyes on copy except when you lose your place

abbrev./initials
1 He said ft. for feet; rd. for road; fl. for floor.
2 Lt. Hahn let L. K. take the old gong to Lake Neil.
DS

3d row emphasis
3 Lars is to ask at the old store for a kite for Jo.
4 Ike said he is to take the old road to Lake Heidi.
DS

key words
5 a an or he to if do it of so is go for got old led
6 go the off aid dot end jar she fit oak and had rod
DS

key phrases
7 if so|it is|to do|if it|do so|to go|he is|to do it
8 to the|and do|is the|got it|if the|for the|ask for
DS

all letters learned
9 Ned asked her to send the log to an old ski lodge.
10 O. J. lost one of the sleds he took off the train.

74B-80B ◆ (cont.)

Document 5

Message from JESSICA SAMPSON

Here are the names of three more clients that Jeff Grayson would like invited to the private showing. A copy of the original letter is attached. Prepare a letter to each client for me to sign.

Mr. and Mrs. Chi Shen
1288 Paramount Lane
Houston, TX 77067-4310

Ms. Marjorie S. Butler
3198 Rosedale Circle
Houston, TX 77004-7120

Mr. Kevin N. King
2982 Spring Field Road
Houston, TX 77062-1312

JS
5/14

May 1, 19--

Mr. and Mrs. Jason R. Walton
1825 Victoria Drive
Houston, TX 77022-1903

Dear Mr. and Mrs. Walton

The 19-- Parade of Homes will be held **June 7-21.** This year we are planning something new. A limited number of our previous home buyers from Ritter Realty are being invited to participate in a private showing prior to the public opening of the Parade of Homes.

The private showing will give Ritter Realty agents the time needed to point out the many fine features of the quality homes being shown this year and to answer any questions you may have. With so many people taking part in the Parade of Homes, it is difficult to give our preferred customers the attention they deserve during the days the homes are shown to the public.

If you are interested in this free showing, sign and return the enclosed card. We look forward to showing you the outstanding homes built for this year's home show.

Sincerely

Jessica A. Sampson

Ms. Jessica A. Sampson
Branch Manager

xx

Enclosure

Document 6

Message from JESSICA SAMPSON

Please send the attached letter to

Mr. Nelson C. Decker
Lakeside National Bank
2310 North Main Street
Houston, TX 77009-4612

JS
5/14

---

on streamlining the mortgage process
Here is a copy of an article which may be of interest to you.
It appeared in
~~from~~ the April issue of Mortgage Banking. ~~It has~~ Several good
g
sugestions for ways of cutting the time between the application
are presented
~~date~~ and ~~the~~ closing dates. ¶ As I mentioned to you last week, we
recently *were*
have had several customers who ~~are~~ quite concerned about the
was required *the* *of*
length of time that ~~it is currently taking~~ for processing their
loans. I will be interested in your reaction to the article.

Sincerely

LESSON 8 REVIEW

SM: 1.5" or defaults; LS: SS

8A ◆ 8'

CONDITIONING PRACTICE

each line twice SS (slowly, then faster); DS between 2-line groups; practice each line again

Space once

reach review 1 ik rf ol ed nj gf hj tf .l ft. i.e. e.g. rt. O. J.

spacing 2 a an go is or to if he and got the for led kit lot

left shift 3 I got it. Hal has it. Jan led Nan. Kae is gone.

QS

8B ◆ 10'

IMPROVE RETURN TECHNIQUE

1. Key each pair of lines once as shown: SS with a DS between 2-line groups.
2. Repeat the drill at a faster pace.

Hint for Hard Return

Keep up your pace to the end of the line; return immediately; start the new line without pausing.

Eyes on copy as you return

1 Nan has gone to ski;
2 she took a train at nine.

DS

3 Janet asked for the disk;
4 she is to take it to the lake.

DS

5 Karl said he left at the lake
6 a file that has the data she needs.

DS

7 Nadia said she felt ill as the ski
8 lift left to take the girls to the hill.

QS

8C ◆ 10'

BUILD SKILL: SPACE BAR/ LEFT SHIFT

each line twice SS; DS between 2-line groups

Goals

- to reduce the pause between words
- to reduce the time taken to shift/strike key/release when making capital letters

Down-and-in spacing

Out-and-down shifting

Space Bar (Space *immediately* after each word.)

1 if is an he go is or ah to of so it do el id la ti
2 an el | go to | if he | of it | is to | do the | for it | and so
3 if she is | it is the | all of it | go to the | for an oak

DS

Left Shift key (Shift; strike key; release both quickly.)

4 Lt. Ho said he left the skiff at Ord Lake for her.
5 Jane or Hal is to go to Lake Head to see Kate Orr.
6 O. J. Halak is to ask for her at Jahn Hall at one.

QS

74B-80B ◆ (cont.)

Document 4

Message from JESSICA SAMPSON

Key the document as an unbound report. The material should answer some of the questions that first-time home buyers often ask. The two inserts are attached. Key the references on a separate page.

JS 5/13

Insert A

Rate	*Monthly Payment*
8.0%	$ 7.34
9.0	8.05
10.0	8.78
11.0	9.53
12.0	10.29
13.0	11.07

Insert B

1. *Loan origination fees*
2. *Mortgage insurance application fee*
3. *Appraisal fee*
4. *Credit report fee*
5. *Loan discount (points)*

To place a table within the body of a report, take these steps:

1. DS above and below the table; SS the body of the table.
2. Clear all tabs.
3. Determine and set a tab for each column of the table. (The table must be centered within the margins of the report.)
4. After keying the table, reset the tab for the paragraph indention before keying the remainder of the report.

HOME MORTGAGES

DS

Many types of creative financing for home loans are offered by financial institutions. However, the two most common types of mortgages are the fixed-rate mortgage and the adjustable-rate mortgage.

Fixed-Rate Mortgage The intrest rate of a fixed-rate mortgage remains the same for the duration of the loan. Even if economic conditions change, the interest rate cannot be adjusted. this can be an advantage or disadvantage, depending on whether interest rates are increased or decreasing. The table below (Wyllie, 1988, 301) illustrate the amount of a monthly mortgage payment on a 30 year loan per $1,000 borrowed. The monthly payment for a $50,000 loan for 30 years at 10 percent would be $439 ($8.78 x 50 = $439).

(Handwritten edits: ¶ before "The"; insert "e" in "intrest"; capitalize "this"; "increased" → "increasing"; "illustrate" → "illustrates"; hyphen in "30-year"; insert "For example," before "The monthly payment".)

Insert A

One percentage point canmake a sizable difference in the amount paid each month. It is to a borrowers advantage to check with several institutions to find the best interest rate available. When analyzing interest rates, how ever, a buyer should keep inmind that there are variable closing costs attached with securing a loan. These costs may include the following:

(Handwritten edits: ¶; "can make"; "borrower's"; insert "financial"; close up "however"; "in mind"; "attached" → "associated".)

Insert B

Adjustable-Rate Mortgage

Another common type of morgage offered by most financial institutions is the adjustable rate mortgage.

An adjustable-rate mortgage is a loan with an interest rate that can be adjusted up or down an agreed-upon number of times during the life of the loan. The interest rate is usually tied to changes in a monetary index, such as the interest rates on U.S. Treasury securities or the rates financial institutions must pay their depositors or investors. (Green, 1988, 441)

(Handwritten edits: "mortgage"; "adjustable-rate"; indent quotation block.)

REFERENCES

Wyllie, Eugene E., et al. Consumer Economics. 11th ed. Cincinnati: South-Western Publishing Company, 1988.

Green, D. Hayden. Consumers in the Economy. 2nd ed. Cincinnati: South-Western Publishing Co., 1988.

(Handwritten edits: "Eugene D."; "Cincinnati"; "Co."; "2d ed."; indent second line of Green entry.)

8D ◆ 22'

IMPROVE KEYING SKILL

each line twice SS (slowly, then faster); DS between 2-line groups

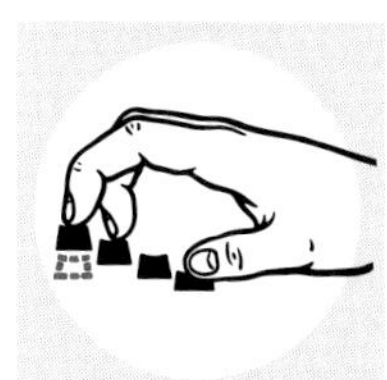

Correct finger curvature

Correct finger alignment

Key words (*Think, say,* and *key* the words.)

1 an the did oak she for off tie got and led jar all
2 go end air her dog his aid rid sit and fir ask jet
3 talk side jell gold fled sign stir fork high shall

DS

Key phrases (*Think, say,* and *key* the phrases.)

4 to do | it is | of an | if he | is to | or do | to it | if he is
5 to aid | if she | he did | of the | to all | is for | is a tie
6 is to ask | is to aid | he or she | to rig it | if she did

DS

Easy sentences (Strike keys at a brisk, steady pace.)

7 Joan is to go to the lake to get her old red skis.
8 Les asked for a list of all the old gold she sold.
9 Laska said she left the old disk list on his desk.

LESSON 9 U AND C

SM: 1.5" or defaults; LS: SS

9A ◆ 8'

CONDITIONING PRACTICE

each line twice SS (slowly, then faster); DS between 2-line groups

1 nj gf ol rf ik ed .l tf hj fr ki ft jn de lo fg l.
2 lo fir old rig lot fit gin fog left sign lend dike
3 Olga has the first slot; Jena is to skate for her.

QS

9B ◆ 5'

BUILD SKILL: SPACE BAR/ LEFT SHIFT

Key the lines once as shown: SS with a DS between 3-line groups. Keep hand movement to a minimum.

space bar

1 Ken said he is to sign the list and take the disk.
2 It is right for her to take the lei if it is hers.
3 Jae has gone to see an old oaken desk at the sale

left shift

4 He said to enter Oh. for Ohio and Kan. for Kans
5 It is said that Lt. Li has an old jet at Lake
6 L. N. is at the King Hotel; Harl is at the I

LESSONS 74-80 RITTER REALTY COMPANY (A Keyboarding Simulation)

74A-80A CONDITIONING PRACTICE

each line twice SS; then a 1' writing on line 4; find *gwam;* clear screen

alphabet 1 Judy quickly spent all her extra money on a new puzzle before leaving.
figures 2 Order No. 78966 was for 140 disks, 30 printer ribbons, and 25 manuals.
fig/sym 3 March sales ($366,680) were 24% higher than February sales ($295,700).
speed 4 The big social for their neighbor may also be held in the city chapel.

gwam 1' | 1 | 2 | 3 | 4 | 5 | 6 | 7 | 8 | 9 | 10 | 11 | 12 | 13 | 14 |

74B-80B ◆

Documents 1-3

Message from JESSICA SAMPSON

Key the attached memos.

The first memo goes to All Agents. Use PARADE OF HOMES SCHEDULE for the subject line.

The second memo goes to Mary Carlson, Sales Agent. Use REFRESHMENTS FOR PARADE OF HOMES as the subject line.

The third memo goes to John Morgan, Broker. Use ELECTRONIC MAIL as the subject line. JS 5/12

¶ The response from former home buyers who are interested in the private showing of this year's Parade of Homes has been excellent. Meeting with past customers to determine if we can be of further assistance to them with their housing requirements is a real opportunity for us. All of the individuals invited have been in their present homes for over five years and <u>may</u> be ready to consider the purchase of a new home.

¶ Michi will be coordinating schedules for the two days of the private showing. We should have your schedule ready within the next two or three days. A meeting will be held on <u>May 20</u> at <u>8:30 a.m.</u> to discuss specific details for the Parade of Homes.

¶ Mary, last month when we were discussing some of the details for the Parade of Homes private showing, you indicated that you would be willing to handle the arrangements for refreshments. I would like to take you up on that offer if it still stands.

¶ Please stop by my office sometime this week so that we can discuss a few of the specifics.

John, the information on electronic mail you brought back from the convention in Miami was intriguing. When you have a few minutes, stop by my office and let's discuss the applications that you think may be of value to our office.

9C ◆ 20'

LEARN U AND C

each line twice SS (slowly, then faster); DS between 2-line groups; repeat selected lines

U *Right pointer* finger

C *Left middle* finger

Learn u

1 j j uj uj us us us jug jug jut jut due due fur fur
2 uj uj jug jug sue sue lug lug use use lug lug dues
3 a jug; due us; the fur; use it; a fur rug; is just

DS

Learn c

4 d d cd cd cod cod cog cog tic tic cot cot can cans
5 cd cd cod cod ice ice can can code code dock docks
6 a cod; a cog; the ice; she can; the dock; the code

DS

Combine u and c

7 cud cud cut cuts cur curs cue cues duck ducks clue
8 a cud; a cur; to cut; the cue; the cure; for luck;
9 use a clue; a fur coat; take the cue; cut the cake

QS

9D ◆ 17'

IMPROVE TECHNIQUE

1. Key the lines once as shown: SS with a DS between 2-line groups.
2. Key the lines again at a faster pace.

Technique goals

- reach *up* without moving hands away from you
- reach *down* without moving hands toward your body
- use quick-snap keystrokes

3d/1st rows

1 in cut nut ran cue can cot fun hen car urn den cog
2 Nan is cute; he is curt; turn a cog; he can use it

DS

left shift and .

3 Kae had taken a lead. Jack then cut ahead of her.
4 I said to use Kan. for Kansas and Ore. for Oregon.

DS

key words

5 and cue for jut end kit led old fit just golf coed
6 an due cut such fuss rich lack turn dock turf curl

DS

key phrases

7 an urn | is due | to cut | for us | to use | cut off | such as
8 just in | code it | turn on | cure it | as such | is in luck

DS

all keys learned

9 Nida is to get the ice; Jacki is to call for cola.
10 Ira is sure that he can go there in an hour or so.

Ritter Realty Company

Learning Outcomes: As you complete this unit, you will

1. Apply your knowledge of document formats.
2. Demonstrate your ability to prepare documents from script and rough-draft copy.
3. Practice following general directions to complete a variety of keyboarding tasks.
4. Apply many of the word processing features learned.

RITTER REALTY COMPANY

A Keyboarding Simulation

Before you begin the documents on pp. 140-146, read the following copy. When planning your work, refer to the formatting guides given here to refresh your memory about the proper formatting of memos, letters, tables, and reports.

BACKGROUND

To discover if you might like a career in real estate, you are working part time for Ritter Realty. Besides assisting the realtors with showings, you also work for the Branch Manager, Ms. Jessica Sampson, in Ritter's main office.

Each year Ritter Realty sponsors a Parade of Homes. The Parade of Homes is a showing open to the general public of newly constructed homes that feature the latest innovations in the housing industry. This year the company will be inviting former clients to attend a private showing prior to the Parade of Homes. Most of the documents to be prepared will be about the Parade of Homes and the private showing. The work will include the processing of memos, tables, letters, and a report.

Directions for each document are given by Ms. Sampson. Use the date included on the instructions for all correspondence requiring a date. Ms. Sampson likes the closing lines of all her letters to read as follows:

Sincerely

Ms. Jessica A. Sampson
Branch Manager

Ms. Sampson has given you a copy of "A Quick Guide to Document Formats," which summarizes the basic features of formats used by Ritter Realty Company. Refer to this guide as needed when processing the various documents.

You will supply appropriate parts of documents when necessary. You will use your own initials for reference.

If the directions and the "Quick Guide" summary are not sufficiently detailed, use what you have learned when making formatting decisions.

You are expected to produce error-free documents, so proofread and correct your work carefully.

A QUICK GUIDE TO DOCUMENT FORMATS

Memos
Side margins: 1"
Format: Simplified
Spacing: QS below date and last paragraph. DS below other parts of memo and between paragraphs.
Date: 2" top margin
Subject: ALL CAPS

Letters
Side margins: 1"
Spacing: SS with DS between paragraphs
Format: Block with open punctuation
Date: 2" top margin

Tables
Placement: Centered
Vertical spacing: DS throughout
Horizontal spacing: 0.5" or 1" between columns
Headings: Blocked

Reports
Format: Unbound with internal citations
Side margins: 1"
First page top margin: 2"
Second page top margin: 1"
Bottom margin: 1" (or as near as possible)
Spacing: DS text; SS quotations and lists
References: On separate sheet

LESSON 10 — W AND RIGHT SHIFT

SM: 1.5" or defaults; LS: SS

10A ◆ 8'

CONDITIONING PRACTICE

each line twice SS (slowly, then faster): DS between 2-line groups

```
1 a;sldkfj a;sldkfj uj cd ik rf nj ed hj tf ol gf .l
2 is cod and cut for did end off got the all oak jug
3 Hugh has just taken a lead in a race for a record.
```

QS

10B ◆ 20'

LEARN W AND RIGHT SHIFT

each line twice SS (slowly, then faster); DS between 2-line groups; repeat each line

W *Left ring* finger

Right Shift *Right little* finger; shift, strike, release

Technique hint

Shift, strike key, and release both in a quick 1-2-3 count.

Learn w

```
1 s s ws ws sow sow wow wow low low how how cow cows
2 sw sw ws ws ow ow now now row row own own tow tows
3 to sow; is how; so low; to own; too low; is to row
```

DS

Learn Right Shift key

```
4 A; A; Al Al; Cal Cal; Ali or Flo; Di and Sol left.
5 Ali lost to Ron; Cal lost to Elsa; Di lost to Del.
6 Tina has left for Tucson; Dori can find her there.
```

DS

Combine w and Right Shift

```
7 Dodi will ask if Willa went to Town Center at two.
8 Wilf left the show for which he won a Gower Award.
9 Walt will go to Rio on a golf tour with Tom Spark.
```

QS

10C ◆ 5'

REVIEW SPACING

each line once DS

Spacing hint

Do not space after an internal period in an abbreviation.

No space — Space once

```
1 Use i.e. for that is; cs. for case; ck. for check.
2 Dr. Wong said to use wt. for weight; in. for inch.
3 R. D. Roth has used ed. for editor; Rt. for Route.
4 Wes said Ed Rowan got an Ed.D. degree last winter.
```

QS

KEYBOARDING WORKSHOP

TECHNIQUE DRILLS

1. Key each line once at a steady, easy pace.
2. Key each line again at a faster pace.
3. Key each line once more at your top speed.
4. Key a 1' writing on *each* of lines 3, 6, 9, 12, and 15; find *gwam* on each.
5. Compare *gwam* on the 5 sentences; note the 3 slowest ones.
6. Key two 1' writings on each of the 3 slowest sentences to increase speed.
7. Finally, key lines 13-15 again at your best speed, untimed.

Fingers curved, upright; quick-snap keystrokes; quiet hands and arms

alphabet review

1 show aqua vain bold left more they park suit jazz oxen code glad their
2 low key | may vex | new zoo | for cost | jet port | big quiz | that made | good mark
3 Jan analyzed her quest for perfection by examining a few vital skills.

figures/ symbols

4 AT&T 5's Model #8749 25-60% (25 to 60 percent) 130 shares at $36/share
5 My new "Eureka" XL PC is Cat. #10562; the old "Comet" XS, Cat. #37489.
6 Use Volume 13, Section 28.46, page 579, Figure 1085-A, as a reference.

double letters

7 all less hall eddy fuss been soon sorry needy apple attic lobby little
8 A tall fellow in the pool hall stuffed his jeans into his muddy boots.
9 Hollis took his little book of excellent poems to his class at school.

outside reaches

10 paw lap slow pass laws soap span walk slap slaw palm opal slash splash
11 Sasha said to swim six laps at a slow pace to warm up prior to a race.
12 Paula Quixote won all six top prizes last season for her zealous play.

fluency/ speed

13 duty pens form goal dorm land fury maps spent llama foggy slant theory
14 Their tutor may go with them when they go to the city for the bicycle.
15 Did the haughty girls pay for their own gowns for the sorority social?

gwam 1' | 1 | 2 | 3 | 4 | 5 | 6 | 7 | 8 | 9 | 10 | 11 | 12 | 13 | 14 |

TIMED WRITINGS

Take 1', 3', and 5' writings.

all letters used | A | 1.5 si | 5.7 awl | 80% hfw

	gwam 3'	5'
If you are planning to purchase a computer, you should consider the	5	3
hard disk drive feature which is available on many computers. This	9	5
feature increases the flexibility of the unit as well as the storage	14	8
space. The amount of added storage depends on the type of hard disk	18	11
purchased, but the amount can increase by the equivalent of several dozen	23	14
floppy disks. Those who use the hard disk enjoy better response time.	28	17
One concern with the hard disk is that it is quite sensitive and can	32	19
be damaged. Any information stored on the hard disk should be copied on	37	22
to a floppy disk for backup purposes. Having the second copy will assure	42	25
that important information is not lost if damage to the hard disk should	47	28
take place. Computer users often forget to make a second copy until	52	31
important information is lost from the hard disk.	55	33

gwam 3' | 1 | 2 | 3 | 4 | 5 |
5' | 1 | 2 | 3 |

10D ◆ 17'

IMPROVE TECHNIQUE

1. Key the lines once as shown: SS with a DS between 2-line groups.
2. Key the lines again at a faster pace.

Goal: finger-action reaches; quiet hands and arms

w and r. shift
1 Dr. Rowe is in Tulsa now; Dr. Cowan will see Rolf.
2 Gwinn took the gown to Golda Swit on Downs Circle.
DS

n/g
3 to go | go on | no go | an urn | dug in | and got | and a sign
4 He is to sign for the urn to go on the high chest.
DS

key words
5 if ow us or go he an it of own did oak the cut jug
6 do all and for cog odd ant fig rug low cue row end
DS

key phrases
7 we did | for a jar | she is due | cut the oak | he owns it
8 all of us | to own the | she is to go | when he has gone
DS

all keys learned
9 Jan and Chris are gone; Di and Nick get here soon.
10 Doug will work for her at the new store in Newton.

LESSON 11 B AND Y

SM: 1.5" or defaults; LS: SS

Fingers curved

Fingers upright

11A ◆ 8'

CONDITIONING PRACTICE

each line twice SS (slowly, then faster); DS between 2-line groups

reach review
1 uj ws ik rf ol cd nj ed hj tf .l gf sw ju de lo fr

c/n
2 an can and cut end cue hen cog torn dock then sick

all letters learned
3 A kid had a jag of fruit on his cart in New Delhi.
QS

11B ◆ 5'

IMPROVE TECHNIQUE

1. Key each line once SS; Return and start each new line quickly.
2. On line 4, see how many words you can key in 30 seconds (30").

1 Dot is to go at two.
2 He saw that it was a good law.
3 Rilla is to take the auto into the town.
4 Wilt has an old gold jug he can enter in the show.
QS

gwam 1' | 1 | 2 | 3 | 4 | 5 | 6 | 7 | 8 | 9 | 10 |

A standard word in keyboarding is 5 characters or any combination of 5 characters and spaces, as indicated by the number scale under line 4.

***gwam* = gross words a minute**

To find 1-minute (1') *gwam*:

1. Note on the scale the figure beneath the last word you keyed. That is your 1' *gwam* if you key the line partially or only once.
2. If you completed the line once and started over, add the figure determined in Step 1 to the figure 10. The resulting figure is your 1' *gwam*.

To find 30-second (30") *gwam*:

1. Find 1' *gwam* (total words keyed).
2. Multiply 1' *gwam* by 2. The resulting figure is your 30" *gwam*.

73B ◆ (cont.)

Table 2
CS: 1"; DS

		words
STATEHOOD		2
(Last 10 States to Join)		7
Montana	November 8, 1889	12
Washington	November 11, 1889	18
Idaho	July 3, 1890	22
Wyoming	July 10, 1890	26
Utah	January 4, 1896	30
Oklahoma	November 16, 1907	36
New Mexico	January 6, 1912	41
Arizona	February 14, 1912	46
Alaska	January 3, 1959	51
Hawaii	August 21, 1959	55

Table 3
CS: 0.5"; DS

^ insert

sp spell out

delete and close

FIGURE

WORD SKATING CHAMPIONS 6

Year	Men	Women	
1985	Aleksandr Fadev, USSR	Katerina Witt, E. Germany	22
1986	Brian Boitano USA	Debbi Thomas, USA	31
1987	Bryan Orser, Can.	Katarina Vitt, E. Germany	41
1988	Brian Boitano, USA	Katarina Witt, E. Germany	51
1989	Kurt Browning, Canada	Midori Ito, Japan	60

__________________ 82

Source: The World Almanac 1990. 92

1990 Kurt Browning, Canada Jill Trenary, USA

1991 Kurt Browning, Canada Kristi Yamaguchi, USA

11C ◆ 20'

LEARN B AND Y

each line twice SS (slowly, then faster); DS between 2-line groups; practice selected lines again

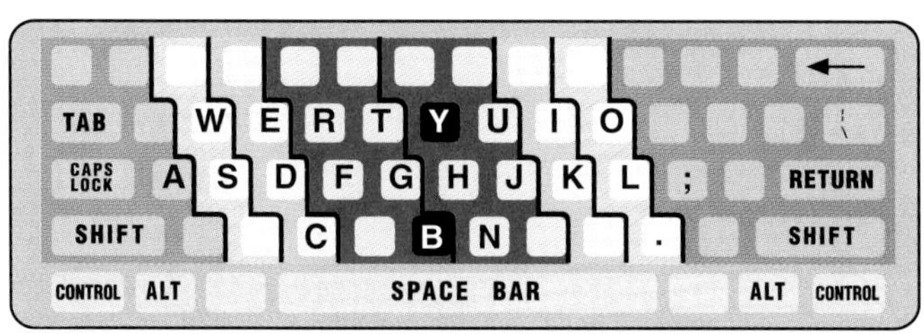

b *Left pointer* finger

y *Right pointer* finger

Learn b

1 f f bf bf fib fib rob rob but but big big fib fibs
2 bf bf rob rob lob lob orb orb bid bid bud bud ribs
3 a rib; to fib; rub it; an orb; or rob; but she bid

DS

Learn y

4 j j yj yj jay jay lay lay hay hay day day say says
5 yj yj jay jay eye eye dye dye yes yes yet yet jays
6 a jay; to say; an eye; he says; dye it; has an eye

DS

Combine b and y

7 by by buy buy boy boy bye bye byte bytc buoy buoys
8 by it; to buy; by you; a byte; the buoy; by and by
9 Jaye went by bus to the store to buy the big buoy.

QS

11D ◆ 17'

IMPROVE TECHNIQUE

1. Key the lines once as shown: SS with a DS between 2-line groups.
2. Key the lines again at a faster pace.

Goals

- reach *up* without moving hands away from you
- reach *down* without moving hands toward your body
- use quick-snap keystrokes

reach review

1 a;sldkfj bf ol ed yj ws ik rf hj cd nj tf .l gf uj
2 a kit low for jut led sow fob ask sun cud jet grow

DS

3d/1st rows

3 no in bow any tub yen cut sub coy ran bin cow deck
4 Cody wants to buy this baby cub for the young boy.

DS

key words

5 by and for the got all did but cut now say jut ask
6 work just such hand this goal boys held furl eight

DS

key phrases

7 to do | can go | to bow | for all | did jet | ask her | to buy
8 if she | to work | and such | the goal | for this | held the

DS

all letters learned

9 Kitty had auburn hair with big eyes of clear jade.
10 Juan left Bobby at the dog show near our ice rink.

gwam 1' | 1 | 2 | 3 | 4 | 5 | 6 | 7 | 8 | 9 | 10 |

72B ◆ (cont.)

Table 4

Arrange Table 2 alphabetically by state.

Table 5

Arrange Table 2 alphabetically by representatives' last names.

WordPerfect

1. Highlight text to be sorted (**Alt F4**).
2. Depress **Ctrl F9** to activate the sort definition screen. The default setting is for an Alphabetic Line Sort in Ascending Order.
3. Strike **3** (Keys) and use the right arrow key to move over to the field (the first column).
4. Key the number **2** for the field. (The left margin is the first field, although no text is keyed at the left margin.)
5. Depress **F7**, **1** (Perform action). (The column will be sorted by state.) To sort representatives' last names, repeat this procedure. In Step 4, key the number **3** (second column) for the field.

Works DOS and Works MAC

1. Copy Table 2.
2. Use the move feature to alphabetize by state.
3. Repeat these steps for Table 5.

Typewriters

1. On your document (Table 2), write a number at the left of each line to indicate alphabetical order (Example: 1 California, 2 Colorado).
2. Rekey the table.
3. Repeat these steps for Table 5.

LESSON 73 ASSESSMENT: TABLES

73A ◆ CONDITIONING PRACTICE

each line twice

alphabet 1 Their equipment manager always kept an extra five-dozen jumper cables.

figures 2 The total attendance for 1993 was 87,652, about a 40 percent increase.

fig/sym 3 The desk (#28A935) and chair (#73Z146) are usually sold for over $700.

speed 4 Sue owns the wheelchair in the shanty at the end of the big cornfield.

gwam 1' | 1 | 2 | 3 | 4 | 5 | 6 | 7 | 8 | 9 | 10 | 11 | 12 | 13 | 14 |

73B ◆ ASSESS SKILL: TABLES

File name: L73B

Table 1

CS: 1.5"; DS

		words
THE ^AL Batting^ LEADERS		5
Through July 4		8
Puckett, Twins	.345	12
Alomar, Blue Jays	.336	16
Molitor, Brewers	.322	21
E. Martinez, Mariners	.318	26
Knoblauch, Twins	.311	30
Ventura, White Sox	.309	35
Bordick, Athletics	.308	40
Baerga, Indians	.307	44
Miller, Royals	.307	48
Harper, Twins	.306	52
______________		56
Source: *Star Tribune*, July 6, 1992		64

LESSON 12 REVIEW

SM: 1.5" or defaults; LS: SS

Before you begin each practice session:

- Position your body directly in front of the keyboard (the b key should be at the center of your body). Sit erect, with feet on the floor for balance.
- Curve your fingers deeply and place them in an upright position over the home keys.
- Position the textbook or screen (if using *Alphabetic Keyboarding*) for easy reading (at about a 90° angle to the eyes).

Body properly positioned

Fingers properly curved

Fingers properly upright

12A ◆ 8'

CONDITIONING PRACTICE

each line twice SS (slowly, then faster); DS between 2-line groups; practice each line again

1 we ok as in be on by re no us if la do ah go C. J.
2 for us; in a jet; by the bid; cut his leg; to work
3 Fran knew it was her job to guide your gold truck.

QS

12B ◆ 12'

IMPROVE TECHNIQUE

1. Key the lines once as shown: SS with a DS between 2-line groups.
2. Key the lines again at a faster pace.

Down-and-in spacing

Out-and-down shifting

Space Bar (Space *immediately* after each word.)

1 an by win buy den sly won they than flay when clay
2 in a way | on a day | buy a hen | a fine day | if they win

DS

3 Jay can bid on the old clay urn he saw at the inn.
4 I know she is to be here soon to talk to the club.

DS

Shift keys (Shift; strike key; release both quickly.)

5 Lt. Su; Nan and Dodi; Karl and Sol; Dr. O. C. Goya
6 Kara and Rod are in Italy; Jane and Bo go in June.

DS

7 Sig and Bodie went to the lake with Cory and Lana.
8 Aida Rios and Jana Hardy work for us in Los Gatos.

QS

72B ◆ (cont.)

words

Table 1
CS: 1.5"; DS

OTHER OFTEN MISSPELLED WORDS		6
installation	previously	11
judgment	prior	14
monitoring	pursuant	18
opportunity	received	22
permanent	recommendation	27
personnel	reference	31
participants	similar	35
patient	successful	39
possibility	sufficient	43

Table 2
CS: 1.5"; DS

WESTERN SALES REPRESENTATIVES 6

State	Representative	14
Idaho	Chen, Jung	19
Utah	Carlton, Brenda	23
Washington	Fishback, Mary	27
Montana	O'Connor, Thomas	32
Nevada	Schofield, Robbin	37
Colorado	Hartstein, Susan	41
California	Van Noy, Adrian	46
Oregon	Moore, Brent	51
Wyoming	Buckholtz, Martin	57

Table 3
CS: 1"; DS

TOP TEN SALES REPRESENTATIVES 6

June 19-- 8

Sales Rep	Sales	Country	17
Karin Cox	$99,930	Autria	22
Sylvie Perillat	99,560	France	28
Jose Teixeira	98,288	Brazil	34
Martin McMillian	97,458	United States	41
Carlos Rosales	89,381	Nicaragua	48
Soon Choi	78,613	Hong Kong	53
Yumiko Kimura	65,980	Japan	58
Torbjorn Bengtsson	56,391	Sweden	65
Jennifer Walton	48,975	United Satse	72
Sauri, El-Shawi	46,928	Egypt	78

__________ 82

Source: July 15, 19-- Sales Report. 89

12C ◆ 15'

IMPROVE SKILL

1. Key the lines once as shown: SS with a DS between 2-line groups.
2. Key the lines again at a faster pace.

Goals

- curved, upright fingers
- quiet hands and arms
- quick spacing—no pause between words
- finger-reach action to shift keys

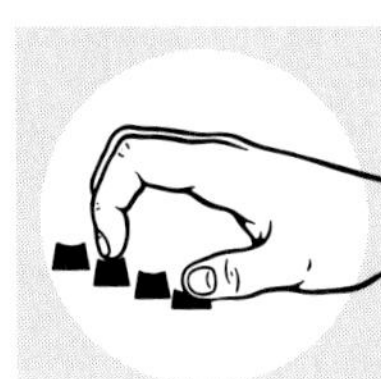

Finger-action keystrokes

Down-and-in thumb motion

Think, say, and *key* words and phrases.

```
1 by dig row off but and jet oak the cub all got rid
2 ah she own dug irk buy cog jak for yet ask led urn
                                                   DS
3 of us|if the|all of|and do|cut it|he got|to do the
4 is to be|as it is|if we do|in all the|if we own it
                                                   DS
```

Strike keys at a brisk, steady pace (all letters learned).

```
5 Judy had gone for that big ice show at Lake Tahoe.
6 Jack said that all of you will find the right job.
                                                   DS
7 Cindy has just left for work at the big ski lodge.
8 Rudy can take a good job at the lake if he wishes.
                                                   QS
```

gwam 1' | 1 | 2 | 3 | 4 | 5 | 6 | 7 | 8 | 9 | 10 |

12D ◆ 15'

CHECK SKILL

1. Key each line once DS (return twice at the end of the line).
2. Take 20" writings; find *gwam*.

Goal: At least 15 *gwam*

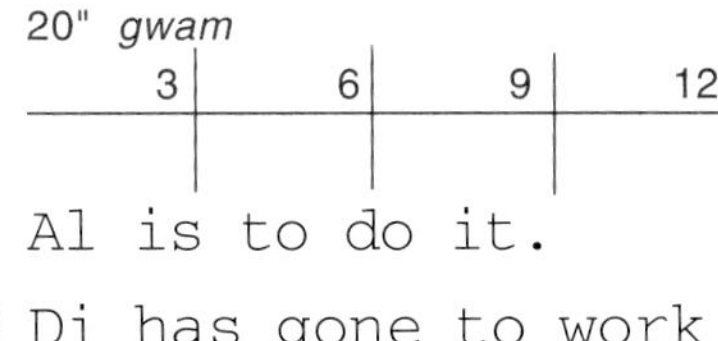

20" *gwam* 3 6 9 12 15 18 21 24 27 30

```
1 Al is to do it.
2 Di has gone to work.
3 Jan is to go to the sale.
4 Rog is to row us to your dock.
5 Harl has an old kayak and two oars.
6 She told us to set a goal and go for it.
7 It is our job to see just how high we can go.
8 Jake will go to the city to work on the big signs.
                                                    QS
```

ENRICHMENT ACTIVITY Reach Review

1. Key each line twice SS (slowly, then faster); DS between 2-line groups.
2. Rekey the drill for better control of reaches.

```
1 June had left for the club just as the news ended.
2 Bro led a task force whose goal was to lower cost.
3 Lyn knew the surf was too rough for kids to enjoy.
4 Ceil hikes each day on the side roads near school.
```

gwam 1' | 1 | 2 | 3 | 4 | 5 | 6 | 7 | 8 | 9 | 10 |

71D ◆

BUILD SKILL: TABLES

File name: L71D

Table 1

CS: 1.5"; DS

PLAYS MOST OFTEN STAGED BY HIGH SCHOOLS		words
(Times Produced by Schools Surveyed)		8
		15
You Can't Take It with You	42	21
Bye Bye Birdie	35	25
Arsenic and Old Lace	31	30
Guys and Dolls	27	33
The Music Man	24	37
____________		41
Source: International Thespian Society.		49

Table 2

CS: 1"; DS

Table 3

CS: 1"; DS

Reformat or rekey Table 2. Delete the first row of information. Include the following information:

1990 Lionel Simmons LaSalle
1991 Larry Johnson UNLV

Change source to **<u>The World Almanac</u>, 1992**.

(Total words: 73)

JOHN R. WOODEN AWARD WINNERS			
			6
(Best College Basketball Player of the Year)			15
<u>Year</u>	<u>Player</u>	<u>College</u>	22
1984	Michael Jordan	North Carolina	30
1985	Chris Mullin	St. John's	37
1986	Walter Berry	St. John's	43
1987	David Robinson	Navy	49
1988	Danny Manning	Kansas	55
1989	Sean Elliott	Arizona	61
____________			65
Source: <u>The World Almanac</u>, 1990.			75

LESSON 72 PREPARE FOR ASSESSMENT: TABLES

72A ◆

CONDITIONING PRACTICE

each line twice

alphabet 1 Max would ask very specific questions before analyzing the job issues.

figures 2 Test scores of 84, 93, 75, 62, and 100 gave Marcia an average of 82.8.

fig/sym 3 Jane wrote checks #807 & #794 for $1,650.03 and $212.50, respectively.

speed 4 He owns both the antique bottle and the enamel bottle on their mantel.

gwam 1' | 1 | 2 | 3 | 4 | 5 | 6 | 7 | 8 | 9 | 10 | 11 | 12 | 13 | 14 |

72B ◆

PREPARE FOR ASSESSMENT

To prepare for assessment in Lesson 73, format and key each of the tables on pp. 135 and 136 according to the directions given with the problems. Refer to centering procedures for your equipment on p. 127 or p. 128 as needed.

LESSON 13 M AND X

SM: 1.5" or defaults; LS: SS

13A ◆ 8'

CONDITIONING PRACTICE

each line twice SS (slowly, then faster); DS between 2-line groups

reach review 1 bf ol rf yj ed nj ws ik tf hj cd uj gf by us if ow

b/y 2 by bye boy buy yes fib dye bit yet but try bet you

all letters learned 3 Robby can win the gold if he just keys a new high.

DS

13B ◆ 20'

LEARN M AND X

each line twice SS (slowly, then faster); DS between 2-line groups; practice selected lines again

m *Right pointer* finger

x *Left ring* finger

Learn m

1 j j mj mj am am am me me ma ma jam jam ham ham yam

2 mj mj me me me may may yam yam dam dam men men jam

3 am to; if me; a man; a yam; a ham; he may; the hem

DS

Learn x

4 s s xs xs ox ox ax ax six six fix fix fox fox axis

5 xs xs sx sx ox ox six six nix nix fix fix lax flax

6 a fox; an ox; fix it; by six; is lax; to fix an ax

DS

Combine m and x

7 me ox am ax ma jam six ham mix fox men lax hem lox

8 to fix; am lax; mix it; may fix; six men; hex them

9 Mala can mix a ham salad for six; Max can fix tea.

QS

13C ◆ 5'

REVIEW SPACING WITH PUNCTUATION

each line once DS

▽ Do not space after an internal period in an abbreviation.

1 Mrs. Dixon may take her Ed.D. exam early in March.

2 Lex may send a box c.o.d. to Ms. Fox in St. Croix.

3 J. D. and Max will go by boat to St. Louis in May.

4 Owen keyed ect. for etc. and lost the match to me.

QS

70C ◆ (cont.)

Table 2

CS: 1"; DS
DS above and below the 1.5" rule before the source note.

	HEISMAN TROPHY WINNERS		words
			5
	(Best College Football Player of the Year)		13
Year	Player	College	21
1984	Doug Flutie	Boston College	27
1985	Bo Jackson	Auburn	32
1986	Vinny Testaverde	Miami (Fla.)	39
1987	Tim Brown	Notre Dame	44
1988	Barry Sanders	Oklahoma State	51
1989	Andre Ware	Univ. of Houston	57
______________			61
Source: The World Almanac, 1990.			71

Table 3

CS: 1"; DS
Using the information at the right, update or rekey Table 2.
(Total words: 80)

1990	Ty Detmer	BYU
1991	Desmond Howard	Michigan

____

Source: The World Almanac, 1992.

LESSON 71 TABLES

71A ◆ CONDITIONING PRACTICE

each line twice

alphabet 1 Marquis Becks enjoyed expanding his vast knowledge of Arizona history.

figures 2 Games of 36, 28, 24, and 21 gave Brian a 1990 season average of 27.25.

fig/sym 3 Stone Realty sold the houses on Lots #3 & #6 for $87,950 and $104,200.

speed 4 The proficient man was kept busy with the problem with the city docks.

gwam 1' | 1 | 2 | 3 | 4 | 5 | 6 | 7 | 8 | 9 | 10 | 11 | 12 | 13 | 14 |

71B ◆ BUILD SKILL: TABLES

File name: L71B

Using Table 2 above, see how quickly you can format and key the copy.

1. Review vertical/horizontal centering on p. 127 or p. 128 if necessary.
2. Check work for proper placement. Are the LM and RM about the same width? Are the top and bottom margins about equal?

71C ◆ FILE MANAGEMENT

Refer to 56D, p. 107 if necessary before deleting files.

Delete the following files:
L60B L62B
L61B L63B
L61D L64B

13D ◆ 17'

IMPROVE KEYING TECHNIQUE

1. Key the lines once as shown: SS with a DS between 2-line groups.
2. Key the lines again at a faster pace.

Technique goals

- reach *up* without moving hands away from you
- reach *down* without moving hands toward your body
- quiet hands and arms

3d/1st rows
1 by am end fix men box hem but six now cut gem ribs
2 me ox buy den cub ran own form went oxen fine club
DS

space bar
3 an of me do am if us or is by go ma so ah ox it ow
4 by man buy fan jam can any tan may rob ham fun guy
DS

key words
5 if us me do an sow the cut big jam rub oak lax boy
6 curl work form born name flex just done many right
DS

key phrases
7 or jam|if she|for me|is big|an end|or buy|is to be
8 to fix|and cut|for work|and such|big firm|the call
DS

all keys learned
9 Jacki is now at the gym; Lex is due there by four.
10 Joni saw that she could fix my old bike for Gilda.

LESSON 14 P AND V

SM: 1.5" or defaults; LS: SS

14A ◆ 8'

CONDITIONING PRACTICE

each line twice SS (slowly, then faster); DS between 2-line groups; if time permits, practice each line again

all letters learned

one-hand words
1 in we no ax my be on ad on re hi at ho cad him bet

phrases
2 is just|of work|to sign|of lace|to flex|got a form

all letters learned
3 Jo Buck won a gold medal for her sixth show entry.
QS

14B ◆ 6'

IMPROVE SHIFT-KEY/RETURN TECHNIQUE

Key each 2-line sentence once as "Return" is called. SS; DS between sentences.

Goal: Reach end of each line just as "Return" is called.

Eyes on copy as you shift and as you return

		gwam 30"	20"
1	Marj is to choose a high goal	12	18
2	and to do her best to make it.	12	18
	DS		
3	Gig said he had to key from a book	14	21
4	for a test he took for his new job.	14	21
	DS		
5	Alex knows it is good to hold your goal	16	24
6	in mind as you key each line of a drill.	16	24
	DS		
7	Nan can do well many of the tasks she tries;	18	27
8	she sets new goals and makes them one by one.	18	27
	QS		

69D ◆

CREATE AT KEYBOARD

File name: L69D

1. Select three of the questions and compose a response. Number your responses and DS between paragraphs.
2. Edit your copy, making corrections and changes to improve sentence structure and organization.
3. Prepare the final copy.

Questions

What would you like to be doing five years from now?

Do your grades accurately reflect your ability? Explain why or why not.

Are you considering further education? Explain why or why not.

What are your major accomplishments in life?

If you could travel anywhere in the world, where would you go? Explain why.

LESSON 70 TABLES

70A ◆

CONDITIONING PRACTICE

each line twice

alphabet 1 Making a yearly budget was a very unique experience for Jonathan Zorn.

figures 2 There were 386 blue, 274 green, and 159 yellow lights on the 10 trees.

fig/sym 3 Computer Model #364-A8 sells for $1,250; Model #365-A7 sells for $995.

speed 4 I may work with the city on their problems with the city turn signals.

gwam 1' | 1 | 2 | 3 | 4 | 5 | 6 | 7 | 8 | 9 | 10 | 11 | 12 | 13 | 14 |

70B ◆

BUILD SKILL IN FORMATTING TABLES

CS: 1"; DS all lines
File name: L70B

Using Table 2 on p. 131, see how quickly you can format and key the copy.

1. Review vertical/horizontal centering steps on p. 127 (typewriters) or 128 (computers) if necessary.
2. Check work for proper placement. Are the LM and RM about the same width? Are the top and bottom margins about equal? Is there 1.5" between columns?

70C ◆

FORMAT THREE-COLUMN TABLES

File name: L70C
Block column headings as shown.

Table 1

CS: 1"; DS

Keying Total Lines

1. Underline the last figures in the columns so that the underlines extend over the *Total* figures.
2. DS below the underlined figures.
3. Indent the word "Total" 5 spaces (0.5"); key the totals; align figures at decimals.

			words
UNITED WAY CONTRIBUTIONS			5
(In Thousands)			8
Department	Goal	Final	16
Accounting	$ 2.5	$ 3.0	22
Credit	2.0	2.3	25
Human Resources	3.8	3.9	30
Management Information	1.3	1.4	36
Manufacturing/Shipping	5.6	7.1	42
Marketing/Sales	9.4	10.2	47
Purchasing	2.0	2.7	51
Word Processing	2.0	2.8	58
Total	$28.6	$33.4	63

14C ◆ 20'

LEARN P AND V

each line twice SS (slowly, then faster); DS between 2-line groups; practice selected lines again

p *Right little* finger

v *Left pointer* finger

Learn p

```
1 ; ; p; p; pa pa up up apt apt pen pen lap lap kept
2 p; p; pa pa pa pan pan nap nap paw paw gap gap rap
3 a pen; a cap; apt to pay; pick it up; plan to keep
```
DS

Learn v

```
4 f f vf vf via via vie vie have have five five live
5 vf vf vie vie vie van van view view dive dive jive
6 go via; vie for; has vim; a view; to live; or have
```
DS

Combine p and v

```
7 up cup vie pen van cap vim rap have keep live plan
8 to vie; give up; pave it; very apt; vie for a cup;
9 Vic has a plan to have the van pick us up at five.
```
QS

14D ◆ 16'

IMPROVE TECHNIQUE

1. Key the lines once as shown: SS with a DS between 2-line groups.
2. Key the lines again at a faster pace.

Technique goals

- reach up without moving hands away from you
- reach down without moving hands toward your body
- use quick-snap keystrokes
- keep action in fingers

reach review

```
1 vf p; xs mj ed yj ws nj rf ik tf ol cd hj gf uj bf
2 if lap jag own may she for but van cub sod six oak
```
DS

3d/1st rows

```
3 by vie pen vim cup six but now man nor ton may pan
4 by six but now may cut sent me fine gems five reps
```
DS

key words

```
5 with kept turn corn duty curl just have worn plans
6 name burn form when jury glad vote exit came eight
```
DS

key phrases

```
7 if they|he kept|with us|of land|burn it|to name it
8 to plan|so sure|is glad|an exit|so much|to view it
```
DS

all letters learned

```
9 Kevin does a top job on your flax farm with Craig.
10 Dixon flew blue jets eight times over a city park.
```

LESSON 69 TABLES

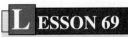

69A ◆ CONDITIONING PRACTICE

each line twice

alphabet 1 They are moving to a new development just back of the Vasquez complex.
figures 2 Between 1987 and 1993 there were 203,564 recorded births in our state.
fig/sym 3 The balance due on Account #2849 after the 10% down payment is $3,756.
speed 4 The proficient auditor was in dismay due to the problem with an audit.

gwam 1' | 1 | 2 | 3 | 4 | 5 | 6 | 7 | 8 | 9 | 10 | 11 | 12 | 13 | 14 |

69B ◆ ALIGN FIGURES

File name: L69B

Drill 1
Center horizontally the drill at the right; SS; CS 1".

Drill 2
Center horizontally the drill at the right; DS; CS: 1.5".

Computer users:
Set a *right* tab at the end of each column to align the figures.

Typewriter users:
Set a tab for the number in each column that requires the least forward and backward spacing to align the figures at the right. To align the figures, space forward or backward from the tab as necessary.

492	1640	2288
63	930	826
110	4610	1049
374	475	638
85	928	1177
211	2017	405

69C ◆ TABLES WITH SECONDARY HEADINGS

File name: L69C

Table 1
Center table vertically and horizontally; CS: 1"; DS all headings and column entries.

BASIC UNITS OF METRIC MEASURE		words
Units and Names		6
		9
Unit of length	meter (m)	14
Unit of mass (weight)	kilogram (kg)	21
Unit of temperature	kelvin (K)	28
Unit of time	second (s)	32
Unit of electrical current	ampere (A)	40
Unit of luminous intensity	candela (cd)	48
Unit of substance	mole (mol)	54

Table 2
Center table vertically and horizontally; CS: 1.5"; DS all headings and column entries.

SUMMER SCHOOL COURSE OFFERINGS		6
Summer 19--		9
Computer Basics	June 22	13
Integrated Software	June 29	19
Desktop Publishing	July 6	24
Spreadsheet Basics	July 13	30
Graphics	July 20	33
Database Fundamentals	August 8	39
Word Processing	August 10	44

LESSON 15 Q AND , (COMMA)

SM: 1.5" or defaults; LS: SS

15A ◆ 8'

CONDITIONING PRACTICE

each line twice SS (slowly, then faster); DS between 2-line groups; if time permits, practice selected lines again

all letters learned 1 do fix all cut via own buy for the jam cop ask dig

p/v 2 a map; a van; apt to; vie for; her plan; have five

all letters learned 3 Beth will pack sixty pints of guava jam for David.

QS

15B ◆ 20'

LEARN Q AND , (COMMA)

each line twice SS (slowly, then faster); DS between 2-line groups; practice each line again

q *Left little* finger

, *Right middle* finger; space once after , used as punctuation

Learn q

1 a qa qa aq aq quo quo qt. qt. quad quad quit quits

2 qa quo quo qt. qt. quay quay aqua aqua quite quite

3 a qt.; pro quo; a quad; to quit; the quay; a squad

DS

Learn , (comma)

4 k k ,k ,k kit, kit; Rick, Ike, or I will go, also.

5 a ski, a ski; a kit, a kit; a kite, a kite; a bike

6 Ike, I see, is here; Pam, I am told, will be late.

DS

Combine q and ,

7 Enter the words quo, quote, quit, quite, and aqua.

8 I have quit the squad, Quen; Raquel has quit, too.

9 Marquis, Quent, and Quig were quite quick to quit.

QS

15C ◆ 5'

REVIEW SPACING WITH PUNCTUATION

each line once DS

▽ Space once after comma used as punctuation.

1 Aqua means water, Quen; also, it is a unique blue.

2 Quince, enter qt. for quart; also, sq. for square.

3 Ship the desk c.o.d. to Dr. Quig at La Quinta Inn.

4 Q. J. took squid and squash; Monique, roast quail.

QS

LESSON 68 TABLES

68A ♦ CONDITIONING PRACTICE

each line twice

alphabet	1	Mozambique was the place Karen most enjoyed visiting in exotic Africa.
figures	2	South High School had 350 graduates in 1986 and 284 graduates in 1987.
fig/sym	3	Order #3845-6079 was damaged during shipment by J&B Express on May 21.
speed	4	The lame lapdog may wish to dognap on the burlap by the antique chair.

gwam 1' | 1 | 2 | 3 | 4 | 5 | 6 | 7 | 8 | 9 | 10 | 11 | 12 | 13 | 14 |

68B ♦ REVIEW CENTERING

File name: L68B

1. Review vertical and horizontal centering steps on p. 127 (typewriters) or p. 128 (computers) for your equipment.
2. Using the model table on p. 129, see how quickly you can format and key the copy.
3. Proofread and correct errors before removing the table from typewriter or screen.
4. Check work for proper format. Are the top and bottom margins about equal? Are the left and right margins about the same width? If not, review the centering procedures on p. 127 or p. 128 once more.

68C ♦ TABLES WITH MAIN HEADINGS

File name: L68C

Table 1

Format and key the information at the right as a table. Center vertically and horizontally; leave 1" between columns (CS: 1").

PERSONNEL RECORD		words
		3
Employee Name	Jorge L. Ortega	9
Street Address	1624 Melody Drive	16
City	Midwest City	20
State	OK	21
ZIP Code	73110-2856	25
Telephone	733-1958	29

Table 2

Format and key the information at the right as a table. Center vertically and horizontally; leave 1.5" between columns (CS: 1.5").

Table 3

Reformat or rekey Table 2. Leave 2" between columns. Change the title to **WORDS COMMONLY MISSPELLED**.

COMMONLY MISSPELLED WORDS		
		5
accommodate	corporate	10
adequate	customer	13
appropriate	electrical	18
categories	eligible	22
committee	employees	26
compliance	immediately	30
compliment	implemented	35
correspondence	international	41

15D ◆ 17'

IMPROVE TECHNIQUE

1. Key the lines once as shown: SS with a DS between 2-line groups.
2. Key the lines again at a faster pace.

Technique goals

- reach *up* without moving hands away from you
- reach *down* without moving hands toward your body
- use quick-snap keystrokes

reach review	1	qa .l ws ,k ed nj rf mj tf p; xs ol cd ik vf hj bf
	2	yj gf hj quo vie pay cut now buy got mix vow forms
		DS
3d/1st rows	3	six may sun coy cue mud jar win via pick turn bike
	4	to go|to win|for me|a peck|a quay|by then|the vote
		DS
key words	5	pa rub sit man for own fix jam via cod oak the got
	6	by quo sub lay apt mix irk pay when rope give just
		DS
key phrases	7	an ox|of all|is to go|if he is|it is due|to pay us
	8	if we pay|is of age|up to you|so we own|she saw me
		DS
all letters learned	9	Jevon will fix my pool deck if the big rain quits.
	10	Verna did fly quick jets to map the six big towns.

LESSON 16 REVIEW

SM: 1.5" or defaults; LS: SS

Fingers properly curved

Fingers properly aligned

16A ◆ 8'

CONDITIONING PRACTICE

each line twice SS (slowly, then faster); DS between 2-line groups; practice each line again

review	1	Virgil plans to find that mosque by six with Jack.
shift keys	2	Pam, Van, and McQuin should be in New Gate by two.
easy sentence	3	Vi is to aid the girl with the sign work at eight.
		QS

gwam 1' | 1 | 2 | 3 | 4 | 5 | 6 | 7 | 8 | 9 | 10 |

16B ◆ 10'

KEY BLOCK PARAGRAPHS

each paragraph (¶) once SS; DS between ¶s; then key the ¶s again at a faster pace

Typewriter users: Key each ¶ line for line as shown.

Computer users: Do not return at end of each line. The computer will return automatically with what is called a "soft return." You must, however, strike Return/Enter twice at the end of ¶1 to leave a DS between ¶s ("hard return").

	gwam 1'
Paragraph 1	
When you strike the return or enter key at the end	10
of a line to space down and start a new line, this	20
process is called a hard return.	26
DS	
Paragraph 2	
If a machine returns at line ends for you, what is	10
known as a soft return or wordwrap is in use. You	20
must use a hard return, though, between paragraphs.	30
QS	

gwam 1' | 1 | 2 | 3 | 4 | 5 | 6 | 7 | 8 | 9 | 10 |

LESSON 67 TABLES

67A ◆ CONDITIONING PRACTICE

each line twice SS; DS between 2-line groups; then three 1' writings on line 4; find *gwam;* clear screen

alphabet 1 Jacob was quite puzzled when Mr. Grifey told us to take the exam over.

figures 2 There are 1,503 engineering majors; 879 are males and 624 are females.

fig/sym 3 My 1992 property tax increased by 6.75% ($241); I paid $3,580 in 1991.

speed 4 Helen owns the six foals and the lame cow in the neighbor's hay field.

gwam 1' | 1 | 2 | 3 | 4 | 5 | 6 | 7 | 8 | 9 | 10 | 11 | 12 | 13 | 14 |

67B ◆ REVIEW HORIZONTAL CENTERING

Horizontally center each of the lines at the right. If necessary, review horizontal centering procedure before you begin:
Computers—22C, p. 42
Typewriters—27C, p. 52

CENTERING CONCEPTS

Horizontal: side to side

Vertical: top to bottom

Horizontal center: half left; half right

Vertical center: half top; half bottom

67C ◆ FORMAT A TWO-COLUMN TABLE

File name: L67C

Table 1

1. Study the procedures for vertical and horizontal centering given for your equipment on page 127 (typewriters) or 128 (computers) .
2. Format and key the model copy at the right. Leave 1" between columns (CS: 1").

Table 2

The yearbook staff has added an **Assistant Business Manager (Mitchell Chang)**. Prepare another table reflecting the new staff member.

YEARBOOK STAFF

Editor-in-Chief	Susan Druhan
Assistant Editor	Elizabeth Poole
Business Manager	Robert Banks
Photography/Layout	Denise Richardson
Advertising/Sales	Diane Blust
Advisor	Anthony Diaz

16C ◆ 12'

BUILD SKILL: SPACE BAR/SHIFT KEYS

each line twice SS; DS between 4-line groups

Goals

- to reduce the pause between words
- to reduce the time taken to shift/strike key/release when making capital letters

Down-and-in spacing

Out-and-down shifting

Space Bar (Space immediately after each word.)

1 so an if us am by or ox he own jay pen yam own may
2 she is in | am to pay | if he may | by the man | in a firm
DS

3 I am to keep the pens in a cup by a tan mail tray.
4 Fran may try to fix an old toy for the little boy.
DS

Shift keys (Shift; strike key; release both quickly.)

5 J. V., Dr. or Mrs., Ph.D. or Ed.D., Fourth of July
6 Mrs. Maria Fuente; Dr. Mark V. Quin; Mr. T. C. Ott
DS

7 B. J. Marx will go to St. Croix in March with Lex.
8 Mae has a Ph.D. from Miami; Dex will get his Ed.D.
QS

16D ◆ 10'

IMPROVE SKILL

each line twice SS (slowly, then faster); DS between 4-line groups

Technique goals

- quick-snap keystrokes
- quick joining of letters to form words
- quick joining of words to form phrases

Think, say, and *key* words and phrases.

1 ox jam for oak for pay got own the lap via sob cut
2 make than with them such they when both then their
DS

3 to sit | an elf | by six | an oak | did go | for air | the jam
4 to vie | he owns | pay them | cut both | the quay | for they
DS

Strike keys at a brisk, steady pace.

all letters learned
5 I may have six quick jobs to get done for low pay.
6 Vicky packed the box with quail and jam for Signe.
DS

all letters learned
7 Max can plan to bike for just five days with Quig.
8 Jim was quick to get the next top value for Debby.
QS

16E ◆ 10'

CHECK SKILL

Take a 30" writing on each line; find *gwam*.

Goal: At least 18 *gwam*

30" *gwam*

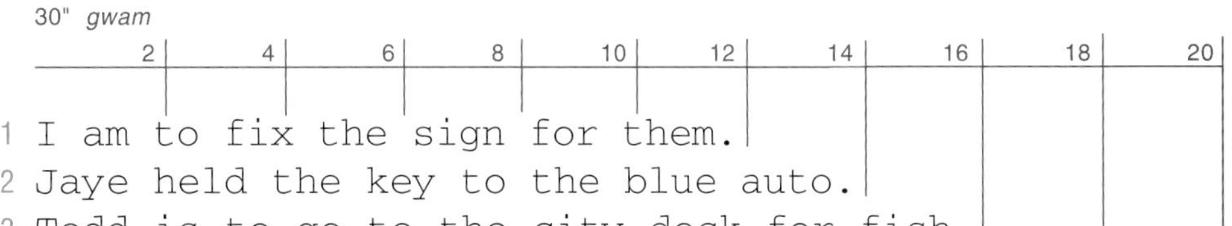

2 | 4 | 6 | 8 | 10 | 12 | 14 | 16 | 18 | 20

1 I am to fix the sign for them.
2 Jaye held the key to the blue auto.
3 Todd is to go to the city dock for fish.
4 Vi paid the girl to make a big bowl of salad.
5 Kal may keep the urn he just won at the quay show.

2 | 4 | 6 | 8 | 10 | 12 | 14 | 16 | 18 | 20

If you finish a line before time is called and start over, your *gwam* is the figure at the end of the line PLUS the figure above or below the point at which you stopped.

HORIZONTAL CENTERING

WORDPERFECT

1. Turn the centering feature on (**Shift F6**).
2. Key the longest entry from the first column.
3. Space over the amount of space to be left between the first and second column.
4. Key the longest entry from the second column. (If more than two columns, repeat Steps 3 and 4 for each additional column.)
5. Write down the Position **(Pos)** number where tab stops will be set for each column. (For relative tabs, subtract 1" for left margin.)
6. Delete the centered line.
7. Clear existing tabs (review p. 124).
8. Set tabs at the beginning of each left aligned column, at the decimal point for each decimal aligned column, and at the right for each right aligned column.
9. Set for DS (**Shift F8**, **L**, **S**, **2**, **F7**, **F7**).
10. Turn on vertical centering feature as outlined below.
11. Key the table.

WORKS DOS

1. Key the longest entry from the first column.
2. Space over the amount of space to be left between the first and second column.
3. Key the longest entry from the second column. (If more than two columns, repeat Steps 2 and 3 for each additional column.)
4. Center the keyed line (**Ctrl C**).
5. Clear existing tabs (**Alt**, **T**; **T**; **Alt A**).
6. Set tabs. Set tabs at the beginning of each left aligned column, at the decimal point of each decimal aligned column, and at the right of each right aligned column.
7. Change spacing to DS (**Ctrl 2**).
8. Delete the centered line.
9. Key the main and secondary headings and strike Return.
10. Change justification to left (**Ctrl L**).
11. Key the table.
12. Center table vertically as outlined below.

WORKS MAC

1. Key the longest entry from the first column.
2. Space over the amount of space to be left between the first and second column.
3. Key the longest entry from the second column. (If more than two columns, repeat steps 3 and 4 for each additional column.)
4. Center the line (**Format, Justification, Center**).
5. Set tabs. Set tabs at the beginning of each left aligned column, at the decimal point of each decimal aligned column, and at the right of each right aligned column.
6. Delete the centered line.
7. Set spacing to DS.
8. Key the main and secondary headings and strike Return.
9. Change justification to left.
10. Key the table.
11. Center table vertically as outlined below. (Set spacing to SS before inserting the hard returns.)

VERTICAL CENTERING

WORDPERFECT

The feature used for vertical centering is called the center page feature or the top/bottom feature:

1. Place the cursor at upper left on the page (Pos 1, Line 1).
2. Use **Shift F8**.
3. Strike **P**(age).
4. Strike **C**(enter).
5. Choose **Y**(es); **F7**.

WORKS DOS

1. Count the number of lines to be used to key the table (include blank lines).
2. Subtract lines needed from 54 total lines available. (There are 66 lines on a sheet of paper. When the default top and bottom margins of 1" are deducted, 54 lines remain.)
3. Divide the remainder by 2 to determine page beginning (PB). If the number that results ends in a fraction, drop the fraction. If an odd number results, use the next lower even number.

   Example for table on p. 129:

Lines available =	54
Total lines to be used for table =	13
	41
41 ÷ 2 =	$20^1/_2$
PB =	line 20

4. If SS, insert 19 hard returns, starting at top of screen (line 1); if DS, insert 9 hard returns, starting at top of screen (line 2).

WORKS MAC

The number of lines on a page varies by the font and point size used:

1. Key the table, beginning on the first line of the screen.
2. Determine the number of lines left on the page below the table by inserting/counting hard returns until a soft page break appears.
3. Divide the number of returns by 2.
4. Place the cursor at the beginning of the document and insert the number of returns determined in Step 3.

Alternative method: The default setting (Geneva, 12 point, 1" top and bottom margins) leaves 40 lines for copy.

1. Count the number of lines to be used to key the table (include blank lines).
2. Subtract this number from 40.
3. Divide the remainder by 2. (If the number that results ends in a fraction, drop the fraction.)
4. Insert this number of hard returns.

   Example for table on p. 129:

Lines available =	40
Total lines to be used for table =	13
	27
27 ÷ 2 =	$13^1/_2$
Lines in top margin =	13
PB =	14

LESSON 17 Z AND : (COLON)

SM: 1.5" or defaults; LS: SS

17A ◆ 8'

CONDITIONING PRACTICE

each line twice SS; then a 1' writing on line 3; find *gwam*: total words keyed

all letters learned 1 Jim won the globe for six quick sky dives in Napa.

spacing 2 to own | is busy | if they | to town | by them | to the city

easy sentence 3 She is to go to the city with us to sign the form.

gwam 1' | 1 | 2 | 3 | 4 | 5 | 6 | 7 | 8 | 9 | 10 |

17B ◆ 20'

Z AND : (COLON)

each line twice SS (slowly, then faster); DS between 2-line groups; practice selected lines again

Z *Left little* finger

: Left Shift and strike **:** key

Language skills notes

- Space twice after **:** used as punctuation.
- Capitalize the first word of a complete sentence following a colon.

Learn z

1 a a za za zap zap zap zoo zoo zip zip zag zag zany

2 za za zap zap zed zed oz. oz. zoo zoo zip zip maze

3 zap it, zip it, an adz, to zap, the zoo, eight oz.

Learn : (colon)

4 ; ; :; :; Date: Time: Name: Room: From: File:

5 :; :; To: File: Reply to: Dear Al: Shift for :

6 Two spaces follow a colon, thus: Try these steps:

Combine z and :

7 Zelda has an old micro with : where ; ought to be.

8 Zoe, use as headings: To: Zone: Date: Subject:

9 Liza, please key these words: zap, maze, and zoo.

10 Zane read: Shift to enter : and then space twice.

17C ◆ 5'

SPACING CHECKUP

Key each line once SS. In place of the blank line at the end of each sentence, key the word "once" or "twice" to indicate the proper spacing.

1 After a . at the end of a sentence, space _____.

2 After a ; used as punctuation, space _____.

3 After a . following an initial, space _____.

4 After a : used as punctuation, space _____.

5 After a , within a sentence, space _____.

6 After a . following an abbreviation, space _____.

Master Simple Table Format

Learning Outcomes: After completing this unit, you will be able to

1. Format and key 2- and 3-column tables.
2. Align numbers of varying lengths.

PARTS OF A SIMPLE TABLE

A table is a systematic arrangement of data, usually in rows and columns. Tables range in complexity from those with only two columns and a main heading to those with several columns and special features. The tables in this unit are limited to those with the following parts:

1. Main Heading (title) in ALL CAPS
2. Secondary Heading in capital and lowercase letters
3. Column Headings (blocked)
4. Body (column entries)
5. Source Note
6. Total line

HORIZONTAL/VERTICAL PLACEMENT OF TABLES

Tables are placed on the page so that the left and right margins (LM, RM) are approximately equal and the column spacing (CS), or number of spaces between columns, is exactly equal. This means about half the characters and spaces in each line are at the left of horizontal center; about half are at the right.

Tables prepared on separate sheets are placed so that the top and bottom margins are approximately equal. This means about half the lines are above vertical center; about half are below. Tables that are placed slightly above vertical center ("reading position") are considered to look more appealing than those that are placed at or below exact vertical center.

Short, simple tables are usually double-spaced (DS) throughout, but single-spaced (SS) column entries for longer tables are acceptable.

ALIGNING DATA IN COLUMNS

Words in columns are aligned at the left. Figures, however, are usually aligned at the right or at the decimal point. On typewriters, alignment is done by spacing forward or backward from the tab stops. With computer software, aligning is done automatically by setting a decimal or a right alignment tab.

VERTICAL CENTERING—TYPEWRITER

1. Count the lines to be used to key the table (include blank lines).
2. Subtract lines needed from total lines available on page (66 lines).
3. Divide the remainder by 2 to determine top margin. If the number that results ends in a fraction, drop the fraction.

   Example for table on p. 129:

Lines available =	66
Total lines to be used for table =	13
	53
53 ÷ 2 =	$26\frac{1}{2}$
Lines in top margin =	26
PB =	line 27

4. Insert 27 hard returns.

HORIZONTAL CENTERING—TYPEWRITER

1. Move margin stops to ends of scale.
2. Clear all tabulator stops.
3. Move printing point to horizontal center of paper, which is 42 for 10-pitch type and 51 for 12-pitch type.
4. Set left margin stop.
   a. From horizontal center point, backspace once for each 2 characters and spaces in longest line of each column and once for each 2 spaces to be left between columns. If longest line in one column has an odd number of strokes, combine extra stroke with first stroke in next column of text. If you have 1 stroke left over after backspacing for all columnar items, disregard the extra stroke.
   b. Set LM at point where all backspacing ends.
5. Set tabs.
   a. From LM, space forward once for each character and space in longest line of first column and once for each space to be left between first and second columns.
   b. Set tab stop at this point for second column.
   c. When there is a third column, continue spacing forward in the same way to set a tab stop for it.

HORIZONTAL CENTERING—COMPUTER

The center feature used for centering lines of text between the left and right margins also may be used for centering columns. The operator must key the longest line in the table (longest entry in each column, plus space between columns). The center feature places half of this line to the left of center point and half to the right. The tab positions are determined by text in this line.

VERTICAL CENTERING—COMPUTER

Vertical centering involves subtracting the number of lines of text from the number of lines available and dividing the remaining number of unused lines equally between the top and bottom margins. WordPerfect software has a feature that performs this procedure automatically. On Works software, the operator must figure the number of lines in the top margin and insert hard returns above the first line of text.

17D ◆ 17'

IMPROVE TECHNIQUE

1. Key the lines once as shown: SS with a DS between 2-line groups.
2. Key the lines again at a faster pace.

Technique goals

- curved, upright fingers
- quiet hands and arms
- steady keystroking pace

q/z
1 zoo qt. zap quo zeal quay zone quit maze quad hazy
2 Zeno amazed us all on the quiz but quit the squad.

p/x
3 apt six rip fix pens flex open flax drop next harp
4 Lex is apt to fix apple pie for the next six days.

v/m
5 vim mam van dim have move vamp more dive time five
6 Riva drove them to the mall in my vivid lemon van.

easy sentences
7 Glen is to aid me with the work at the dog kennel.
8 Dodi is to go with the men to audit the six firms.

alphabet
9 Nigel saw a quick red fox jump over the lazy cubs.
10 Jacky can now give six big tips from the old quiz.

LESSON 18 CAPS LOCK AND ? (QUESTION MARK)

SM: 1.5" or defaults; LS: SS

18A ◆ 8'

CONDITIONING PRACTICE

each line twice SS; then a 1' writing on line 3; find *gwam*: total words keyed

alphabet 1 Lovak won the squad prize cup for sixty big jumps.
z/: 2 To: Ms. Mazie Pelzer; From: Dr. Eliza J. Piazzo.
easy sentence 3 He is to go with me to the dock to do work for us.

gwam 1' | 1 | 2 | 3 | 4 | 5 | 6 | 7 | 8 | 9 | 10 |

18B ◆ 7'

KEY BLOCK PARAGRAPHS

Key each paragraph (¶) once; DS between ¶s; then key the ¶s again at a faster pace. Take a 1' writing on each ¶; find *gwam*.

To find 1-minute (1') *gwam*:

1. Note the figure at the end of your last complete line.
2. Note from the scale under the ¶s the figure below where you stopped in a partial line.
3. Add the two figures; the resulting number is your *gwam*.

Paragraph 1 — *gwam* 1'

The space bar is a vital tool, for every fifth or 10
sixth stroke is a space when you key. If you use 20
it with good form, it will aid you to build speed. 30

Paragraph 2

Just keep the thumb low over the space bar. Move 10
the thumb down and in quickly toward your palm to 20
get the prized stroke you need to build top skill. 30

gwam 1' | 1 | 2 | 3 | 4 | 5 | 6 | 7 | 8 | 9 | 10 |

KEYBOARDING WORKSHOP

SKILL DRILLS

1. Key each line once at a steady, easy pace.
2. Key each line again at a faster pace.
3. Key each line once more at your top speed.
4. Key a 1' writing on *each* of lines 3, 6, 9, 12, and 15; find *gwam* on each.
5. Compare *gwam* on the 5 sentences; note the 3 slowest ones.
6. Key two 1' writings on each of the 3 slowest sentences to increase speed.
7. Finally, key lines 13-15 again at your best speed, untimed.

Fingers curved, upright; quick-snap keystrokes; quiet hands and arms

alphabet review

1 axis quiz cost have main buys what rode pack flag jell game open excel
2 to quit | can wait | your firm | just plan | gold fork | jazz band | have the exam
3 The judge observed as the expert workers quickly froze the boned meat.

figures/symbols

4 $47/sq. yd. six percent (6%) son-in-law p's and q's Use <u>were</u>, not <u>was</u>.
5 We will print 850 cards, 731 calendars, 96 leaflets, and 42 circulars.
6 Use Customer's I.D. #472903 on our Invoice #16582 (dated November 16).

adjacent keys

7 are port mask spot news went coin there point threw smart trial stores
8 Every owner was there to report the trade union's prior point of view.
9 Open bidding on truck tires will suit the clerk's priority quite well.

long-direct reaches

10 any cent must curb numb many myth bring doubt plume curve nylon center
11 The rainy day became sunny after we ate lunch under a bright umbrella.
12 Since the sun was bright, the umpire did not notice the runner swerve.

fluency/speed

13 for wish land make risk also they their angle sight spend fight visual
14 When he signs the form, title to all the lake land may go to the city.
15 They may all go to the auto firms to fix the panel signs if they wish.

gwam 1' | 1 | 2 | 3 | 4 | 5 | 6 | 7 | 8 | 9 | 10 | 11 | 12 | 13 | 14 |

TIMED WRITINGS

Key 1', 3', and 5' writings.

all letters used | A | 1.5 si | 5.7 awl | 80% hfw

gwam 3' | 5'

A firm interested in improving both the quality and quantity of the 5 3
documents produced by the office staff may want to consider the latest 9 6
word processing equipment now on the market. Word processing equipment 14 8
which was too expensive in the past is now affordable for even the small- 19 11
est office. This is due in large part to the vast strides that have been 24 14
made in the field of computer technology. 27 16

The advanced packages of word processing software turn a computer 31 19
into a word processor which has most of the features of the more advanced 36 22
word processing equipment. It is now a simple job to review and edit 41 24
letters, reports, and tables on a computer. Insert, move copy, replace, 45 27
and delete are common features of most packages. This has made the job 50 30
of an office worker in many organizations much easier than it used to be. 55 33

gwam 3' | 1 | 2 | 3 | 4 | 5 |
5' | 1 | 2 | 3 |

18C ◆ 15'

LEARN CAPS LOCK AND ?

each line twice SS (slowly, then faster); DS between 2-line groups; practice each line again

Depress Caps Lock to key a series of capital letters.

To release the Lock for lowercase letters, strike Left or Right Shift key on most typewriters; strike the Lock again on most computers. Learn now how this is done on the equipment you are using.

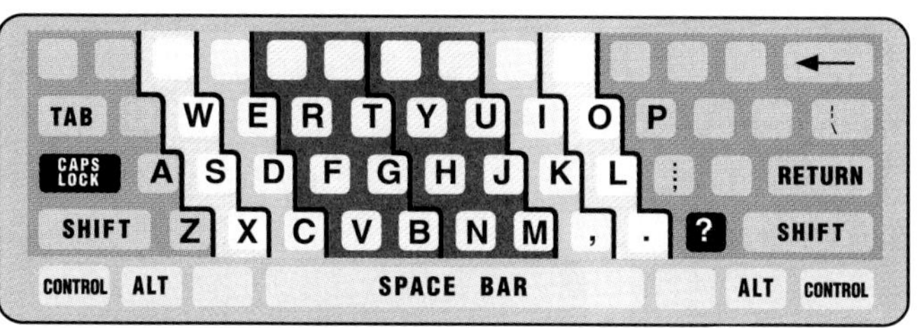

Caps Lock *Left little* finger

? Left shift; then *right little* finger

Learn Caps Lock

1 Hal read PENTAGON and ADVISE AND CONSENT by Drury.
2 Oki joined FBLA when her sister joined PBL at OSU.
3 Zoe now belongs to AMS and DPE as well as to NBEA.

Learn ? (question mark) — Space twice

4 ; ; ?; ?; Who? What? When? Where? Why? Is it?
5 Who is it? Is it she? Did he go? Was she there?
6 Is it up to me? When is it? Did he key the line?

18D ◆ 20'

IMPROVE TECHNIQUE

1. Key the lines once as shown: SS with a DS between 2-line groups.
2. Key the lines again at a faster pace.
3. Take a 1' writing on line 11 and then on line 12; find *gwam*.

Technique goals

- keep hands and arms quiet
- use finger-action keystrokes
- use Caps Lock to make ALL CAPS

caps lock/?
1 Did she join OEA? Did she also join PSI and DECA?
2 Do you know the ARMA rules? Are they used by TVA?

z/v
3 Zahn, key these words: vim, zip, via, zoom, vote.
4 Veloz gave a zany party for Van and Roz in La Paz.

q/p
5 Paul put a quick quiz on top of the quaint podium.
6 Jacqi may pick a pink pique suit of a unique silk.

key words
7 they quiz pick code next just more bone wove flags
8 name jack flax plug quit zinc wore busy vine third

key phrases
9 to fix it is to pay to aid us or to cut apt to own
10 is on the if we did to be fit to my pay due at six

alphabet 11 Lock may join the squad if we have six big prizes.
easy sentence 12 I am apt to go to the lake dock to sign the forms.

gwam 1' | 1 | 2 | 3 | 4 | 5 | 6 | 7 | 8 | 9 | 10 |

To find 1' *gwam*: Add 10 for each line you completed to the scale figure beneath the point at which you stopped in a partial line. The total is your 1' *gwam*.

LESSON 66 UNBOUND REPORTS

66A ◆ CONDITIONING PRACTICE

each line twice

alphabet 1 Everyone except Zelda Jenkins will be required to go to the math fair.
figures 2 Jo's Nursery sold 370 trees and 458 shrubs between May 29 and June 16.
fig/sym 3 The checks written on 8/4 ($81.52) and 9/3 ($68.70) were not recorded.
speed 4 The box with the emblem of the bugle is on the mantle by the fishbowl.

gwam 1' | 1 | 2 | 3 | 4 | 5 | 6 | 7 | 8 | 9 | 10 | 11 | 12 | 13 | 14 |

66B ◆ ASSESS SKILL: UNBOUND REPORTS

File name: L66B

1. Format and key the report in unbound style.
2. Format the reference list on a separate sheet.

REFERENCES

Hamel, Ruth. "Making Summer Earnings Work for You." <u>USA Weekend</u>, 2-4, June 1989, 10-11.

Kushner, John. <u>How to Find and Apply for a Job</u>. Cincinnati: South-Western Publishing Co., 1989.

3. Prepare a title page using your name and school name and the current date.

words

THE IMPORTANCE OF WORK EXPERIENCE 7

A part-time or summer job pays more than money. Although the money 20
earned is important, the work experience gained has a greater long-term 35
value when one applies for a full-time job after graduation from school. Job 50
application forms (the application blank and the personal data sheet) ask you 66
to list jobs you have held and to list as references the names of individuals 82
who supervised your work. As one young person was heard to remark, "You 96
can't get a job without experience and you can't get experience without a 111
job." That dilemma can be overcome, however, by starting to work early in 126
life and by accepting simpler jobs that have no minimum age limit and do not 141
require experience. 146

<u>Jobs Teens Can Do</u> 153

Start early at jobs that may not pay especially well but help to establish a 168
working track record: baby-sitting, delivering newspapers, mowing lawns, 183
assisting with gardening, and the like. Use these work experiences as spring- 198
boards for such later jobs as sales clerk, gas station attendant, fast food 213
worker, lifeguard, playground supervisor assistant, and office staff assistant 229
(after you have developed basic office skills). As you progress through these 245
work exploration experiences, try increasingly to get jobs that have some re- 260
lationship to your career plans. If, for example, you want a career involving 276
frequent contact with people--as in sales--seek part-time and summer work 291
that gives you experience in dealing with people (Hamel, 1989, 10). 305

<u>How to Handle Yourself on the Job</u> 318

Whatever the job you are able to get, the following pointers will help you 333
succeed in getting a good recommendation for the next job you seek. 347

1. Be punctual. Get to work on time and return from lunch and other 361
breaks promptly. 364

2. Get along well with others. Do your job well and offer to assist others 380
who may need help. Take direction with a smile instead of a frown. 394

3. Speak proper English. Teenage jargon is often lost on the adults who 408
are likely to be your supervisors. 416

4. Dress the part. Observe the unwritten dress code; dress as others on 430
the job do. Always be neat and clean. 438

references 487

LESSON 19 TABULATOR

SM: 1.5" or defaults; LS: SS

19A ◆ 8'

CONDITIONING PRACTICE

each line twice SS; then a 1' writing on line 3; find *gwam*: total words keyed

On most typewriters: Comma and period as well as colon and question mark can be keyed when the caps lock is on.

On most computers: Caps Lock affects only the letter keys; shifted punctuation marks require the use of one of the Shift keys.

alphabet 1 Zosha was quick to dive into my big pool for Jinx.

caps lock 2 Vi found ZIP Codes for OR, MD, RI, NV, AL, and PA.

easy sentence 3 Ian kept a pen and work forms handy for all of us.

gwam 1' | 1 | 2 | 3 | 4 | 5 | 6 | 7 | 8 | 9 | 10 |

19B ◆ 12'

LEARN TABULATOR

Typewriters

To clear electronic tabs:

1. Strike Tab key to move print element to the tab stop you want to clear.
2. Depress the Tab Clear key to remove the stop.
3. To remove all stops, depress Tab Clear key, then Repeat key.

To clear electric tabs:

1. Move print element to extreme right using Space Bar or Tab key.
2. Hold Clear key down as you return print element to extreme left to remove all tab stops.

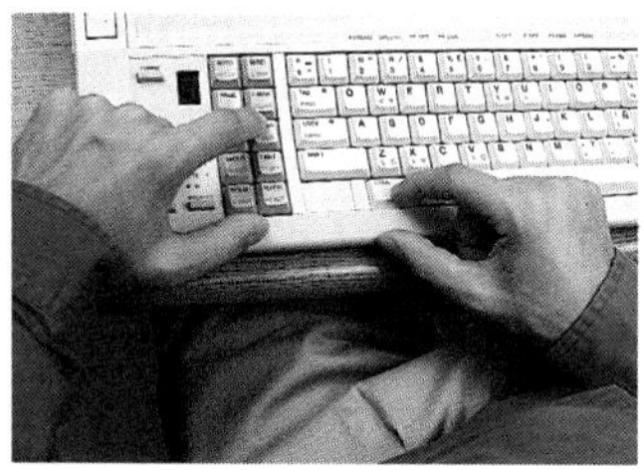

To set tab stops (all typewriters):

1. Move print element to desired tab position by striking Space Bar or Backspace key.
2. Depress Tab Set key. Repeat procedure for each stop needed.

Computers

Most computer programs have preset (default) tabs as shown by vertical lines in the following ruler line (*Alphabetic Keyboarding*):

```
       LM    Tab   Tab   Tab
=======*=====|=====|=====|
```

This illustration shows tabs preset every 5 spaces, beginning at Position 5 (5 spaces from the default left margin). For now you will use the default tabs; later you will learn how to clear these tabs and set tabs at other positions.

Tabulating procedure: Strike the Tab key with the closest little finger; release it quickly and return the finger to home-key position.

Computer users begin at Step 3 below.

1. Clear all tab stops, as directed above.
2. Set a tab stop 5 spaces to the right of left margin.
3. Key the paragraphs (¶s) once SS, indenting the first line of each ¶.

Note: A hard return is required at end of each ¶.

Tab→ The tab key is used to indent blocks of copy such as these.

Tab→ It should also be used for tables to arrange data quickly and neatly into columns.

Tab→ Learn now to use the tab key by touch; doing so will add to your keying skill.

65C ◆

WORD PROCESSING FEATURES

File name: L65C

1. Study the information at the right about the tab feature.
2. Complete the drill below.

Tab. A tab is a feature that causes the cursor to skip across the screen to a point set by the operator or to the default tabs preset every five spaces (0.5"). Three types of tabs (left, right, and decimal) align copy for easy reading. A left tab places text to the right of the tab. A right tab places text to the left of the tab. A decimal tab aligns numbers at the decimal point.

WORDPERFECT

1. Depress **Shift F8**
2. Strike **L**(ine)
3. Strike **T**(ab Set)
4. Depress Home, Home, ←
5. Depress **Ctrl End** (clears tabs)
6. Key number for new tab and strike Return for each tab to be set. If a Decimal or Right tab is desired, key the first letter of the desired type (D or R) after keying number and striking Return key.
7. Depress **F7** twice

Notes: Tabs can be set for relative or absolute by adjusting **T**(ype) in the tab command list. The default is set for relative: Tabs are measured from the left margin and will change automatically when the left margin is changed.

A single tab can be deleted by moving the cursor to the tab and striking the Delete or Backspace key.

WORKS DOS

1. **Alt**, **T**
2. Strike **T**(abs)
3. **Alt A** (clears existing tabs)
4. Key number for new tab setting
5. Strike Return
6. If you wish to change the alignment (left, right, decimal), use arrow keys to make new selection. Once you have all selections made, strike Return.
7. After you finish keying tab settings, depress **Alt D** to return to input screen.

Note: Preset tabs to the left of a newly set tab are automatically removed when the new tab is set.

WORKS MAC

1. Move the pointer to the position just beneath the ruler where you want a tab set.
2. To set a left tab [~]; to set a right tab [~,~]; and to set a decimal tab [~,~,~].

Notes: A tab can be removed by dragging the tab set down into the text and releasing the mouse button.

Preset tabs to the left of a newly set tab are automatically removed when the new tab is inserted.

Drill 1

1. Clear the screen.
2. Following procedure outlined above for your equipment, set a left tab at 1", 3", and 5".
3. Key the information at the right.
4. Insert a page break.

1st tab (left)	2d tab (left)	3d tab (left)
Mary Smith	June 20	1956
Jose Martinez	September 8	1961
Roberto Sanchez	February 7	1966
Leo Vang	April 15	1965
Marsha Cey	July 2	1959

Drill 2

1. Clear all existing tabs using procedure outlined above for your equipment.
2. Set a left tab at 1", a decimal tab at 4", and a right tab at 6".
3. Key the information at the right.
4. Save file.

1st tab (left)	2d tab (decimal)	3d tab (right)
Jay Chang	125.00	Senior
Tim Ellickson	95.25	Junior
Mike Lofton	63.75	Sophomore
Mary Skidmore	180.50	Junior
Maria Valdez	92.75	Sophomore
Vladamar Getz	88.90	Freshman

19C ◆ 10'

IMPROVE TECHNIQUE

each pair of lines twice SS; DS between 4-line groups

tabulator
1 Tab→ Indent five spaces the first line of a series
2 of lines written as a paragraph.

shift-key sentences
3 The best dancers are: Ana and Jose; Mag and Boyd.
4 Did Ms. Paxon send us the letter from Dr. LaRonde?

caps lock
5 Masami saw the game on ESPN; Krista saw it on NBC.
6 The AMS meeting is on Tuesday; the DPE, on Friday.

19D ◆ 14'

BUILD SPEED

1. Key each pair of lines once; SS with a DS between pairs.
2. Take a 1' writing on each of lines 5-8; find *gwam* on each writing.
3. Take another 1' writing on line 7 and line 8 to improve speed.

Goal: At least 21 *gwam*

Think, *say*, and *key* words and phrases.

1 ad my we in be on at up as no are him was you gets
2 girl quay turn rush duty down maps rich laid spend

3 an ad|to fix|an oak|to get|the zoo|via jet|in turn
4 if they|to risk|by them|the duty|and paid|she kept

Key the words at a brisk, steady pace.

5 He is to aid the girls with the work if they wish.
6 Jan may go to the city for the bid forms for them.

7 He may go to the lake by dusk to do the dock work.
8 I did all the work for the firm for the usual pay.

gwam 1' | 1 | 2 | 3 | 4 | 5 | 6 | 7 | 8 | 9 | 10 |

19E ◆ 6'

CHECK SKILL

1. **Typewriter:** Clear tab stops and set a new stop 5 spaces to the right of the left margin.
   Computer: Use default tabs.
2. Key each ¶ once SS; DS between ¶s.
3. Take a 1' writing on each ¶; find *gwam* on each writing. (1' *gwam* = figure above the last word keyed.)

. 2 . 4 . 6 . 8 .
¶1 Good form means to move with speed and quiet
10 . 12 . 14 . 16 . 18 .
control. My next step will be to size up the job
20 . 22 . 24 . 26 . 28
and to do the work in the right way each day.

. 2 . 4 . 6 . 8 .
¶2 To reach my goal of top speed, I have to try
10 . 12 . 14 . 16 . 18 .
to build good form. I will try for the right key
20 . 22 . 24 . 26 . 28
each time, but I must do so in the right way.

65B ◆

FORMAT TOPIC OUTLINES

File name: L65B
SM: 1"; TM: 2"

Outline 1

1. Review procedures for setting tabs. Typewriter users, see p 35. Computer users, complete 65C before completing this activity.
2. Review the information at the right.
3. Format and key the outline.

Typewriter

Set tabs at 5, 9, and 13 spaces from the left margin.

WordPerfect and Works DOS

Tabs are relative to the left margin. For example, a relative tab set at 0.5 is one-half inch from wherever the left margin is set. Set tabs at 0.5, 0.9, and 1.3.

Works MAC

Each mark on the ruler is 1/8". Set tabs at 3/8", 5/8", and 7/8".

Outline 2

Format and key the outline shown at the right.

- For typewriter, WordPerfect, and Works DOS users, 2 spaces follow the period at each subheading.
- For Works MAC users, 2 or 3 spaces follow the period at each subheading.

```
                    SPACING TOPIC OUTLINES
                                          QS
 I.  VERTICAL SPACING
                                DS
     A.  Title of Outline
         1.  Two-inch top margin
         2.  Followed by 3 blank line spaces (QS)
     B.  Major Headings
         1.  First major heading preceded by a QS; all
             others preceded by 1 blank line space (DS)
         2.  All followed by a DS
         3.  All subheadings single-spaced (SS)
                                                DS
II.  HORIZONTAL SPACING
                      DS
     A.  Title of Outline Centered over the Line of Writing
     B.  Major Headings and Subheadings
         1.  Identifying Roman numerals at left margin (periods
             aligned) followed by 2 spaces
         2.  Identifying letters and numbers for each subsequent
             level of subheading aligned below the first word of
             the preceding heading, followed by 2 spaces
```

Annotations: 1st tab; Space forward once from margin; 1st tab; 2nd tab; 3rd tab; Hard return and then *tab 3 times*

```
                    EMPLOYMENT COMMUNICATIONS
                                        QS
  I.  PERSONAL DATA SHEET

      A.  Personal Information      lc
          1.  Name, address, and Telephone number       if needed
          2.  Social Security number (work permit number)
          3.  Personal interests:  hobbies/recreational interests
      B.  Educational Information
          1.  Schools attended and dates of attendance
          2.  Special areas of study; activities; awards received
      C.  Work Experience
          1.  Jobs held; what you experienced; commendations
          2.  Volunteer work
  DS
      D.  References (Teachers, Work Supervisors)
 II.  LETTER OF APPLICATION

      A.  Source of Information about Job Opening
      B.  Expression of Interest in Being Interviewed for the Job
      C.  Brief Summary of Work Skills and How They Fit the Job
          1.  Special courses that are applicable to the job
          2.  Work experiences that make you qualified for the job
      D.  Request for Interview

III.  THANK-YOU LETTER FOLLOWING INTERVIEW
  DS
      A.  Appreciation for Courtesies Shown During Company Visit
      B.  Positive Impressions of Company and Employees
      C.  Expression of Continued Interest in the Job
```

LESSON 20 REVIEW/CHECK

SM: 1.5" or defaults; LS: SS

20A ◆ 8'

CONDITIONING PRACTICE

each line twice SS; then a 1' writing on line 3; find *gwam*

alphabet 1 Quig just fixed prize vases he won at my key club.
spacing 2 Marcia works for HMS, Inc.; Juanita, for XYZ Corp.
easy sentence 3 Su did vow to rid the town of the giant male duck.

gwam 1' | 1 | 2 | 3 | 4 | 5 | 6 | 7 | 8 | 9 | 10 |

20B ◆ 20'

IMPROVE TECHNIQUE

each line once SS; key each line again at a faster pace

Ask your teacher to check your keyboarding technique as you key the following lines.

Fingers curved

Fingers upright

Finger-action key-stroking

Down-and-in spacing

Reach review (Keep on home row the fingers not used for reaching.)

1 old led kit six jay oft zap cod big laws five ribs
2 pro quo|is just|my firm|was then|may grow|must try
3 Olga sews aqua and red silk to make six big kites.

Space Bar emphasis (*Think*, *say*, and *key* the words.)

4 en am an by ham fan buy jam pay may form span corn
5 I am|a man|an elm|by any|buy ham|can plan|try them
6 I am to form a plan to buy a firm in the old town.

Shift-key emphasis (Reach *up* and reach *down* without moving the hands.)

7 Jan and I are to see Ms. Han. May Lana come, too?
8 Bob Epps lives in Rome; Vic Copa is in Rome, also.
9 Oates and Co. has a branch office in Boise, Idaho.

Easy sentences (*Think*, *say*, and *key* the words at a steady pace.)

10 Eight of the girls may go to the social with them.
11 Corla is to work with us to fix the big dock sign.
12 Keith is to pay the six men for the work they did.

gwam 1' | 1 | 2 | 3 | 4 | 5 | 6 | 7 | 8 | 9 | 10 |

20C ◆ 6'

THINK AS YOU KEY

Key each line once SS. In place of the blank line at the end of each sentence, key the word that correctly completes the adage.

1 All that glitters is not ________.
2 Do not cry over spilt ________.
3 A friend in need is a friend ________.
4 A new broom always sweeps ________.
5 A penny saved is a penny ________.

64B ◆ UNBOUND REPORT

Process report with references on page 2; prepare title page; correct errors. File name: L64B

words

READING FOR KEYBOARDING AND FORMATTING 8

When learning to key, format, and process 16
documents, a major portion of one's time is 25
spent reading. Two different reading processes 35
are used in learning: reading for meaning and 44
reading for "copy getting." 50

Reading for Meaning 58

When one reads an explanation and descrip- 66
tion of a document format or directions for com- 75
pleting a keying task, the purpose of reading is 85
to process information and to acquire meaning 94
or understanding (de Fossard, 1990, 1). Such 103
reading requires focusing on the content: its 113
organization, sequence, ideas, terms, and facts. 123
The objective is to assimilate them, store them, 133
and recall them in proper order for later use. 142
Reading for meaning is very important when 151
learning terms, concepts, and procedures. Such 160
reading is preferably done with speed followed 170
by review. 172

Reading for Copy Getting 182

When one reads a drill or document for the 191
purpose of copying it by means of a keyboard, 200
one reads to "get the copy" to feed through the 210
brain at the speed the fingers are able to re- 219
cord it by striking the keys (West, 1983, 227
130). The purpose is not to understand the 236
message or to get meaning from it; rather, the 245
purpose is to reproduce the message character 254
for character. In initial learning, this process 264
is done on a letter-by-letter basis. As skill 274
grows, however, the process begins to include 283
"chains" of letters and short words that are 292
perceived and responded to as units. Rarely, 301
though, can a keyboard operator feed the fin- 310
gers more than one or two words at a time un- 319
less the words are short. 324

Reading for copy getting requires that the 333
speed of reading be synchronized with the fin- 342
gers' ability to make the keystrokes required to 352
reproduce the words. In this process, the mind 361
is concerned with the form and sequence of the 371
letters and words, not with the meaning of the 380
message the letters and words convey. This 389
kind of reading must be done at a slower pace 398
that is deliberate but harmonious. 405

REFERENCES 407

de Fossard, Esta. Reading in Focus. 3d ed. 420
Cincinnati: South-Western Publishing Co., 428
1990. 430

West, L. J. Acquisition of Typewriting Skills. 446
2d ed. Indianapolis: Bobbs-Merrill Educa- 455
tional Publishing, 1983. 459

64C ◆ COMPUTER ACTIVITY

File name: L64C

Retrieve file L62B and edit the first paragraph to match the copy at the right.

```
     For over a decade, office automation experts have specu-
lated about the demise of the typewriter. In their view the
computer will assume the word processing role held by the type-
writer for more than a century. Ironically, a recent report
(Fernberg, 1989, 49-50) indicates that electronic typewriter
sales over the last three years averaged about a billion dol-
lars each year.
```

LESSON 65 UNBOUND REPORTS

65A ◆ CONDITIONING PRACTICE

each line twice

alphabet 1 For the next two weeks you could save the big quilts for major prizes.

figures 2 Kane received 1,845 votes; Kennedy, 973 votes; and Mertins, 602 votes.

fig/sym 3 Their bill came to $68.19 ($47.63 for paper and $20.56 for envelopes).

speed 4 Their neighbor on the cozy island is the chair of the sorority social.

gwam 1' | 1 | 2 | 3 | 4 | 5 | 6 | 7 | 8 | 9 | 10 | 11 | 12 | 13 | 14 |

20D ◆ 7'

IMPROVE SPEED

Take a 30" writing on each line; find *gwam*. Try to increase your speed.

Goal: At least 22 *gwam*

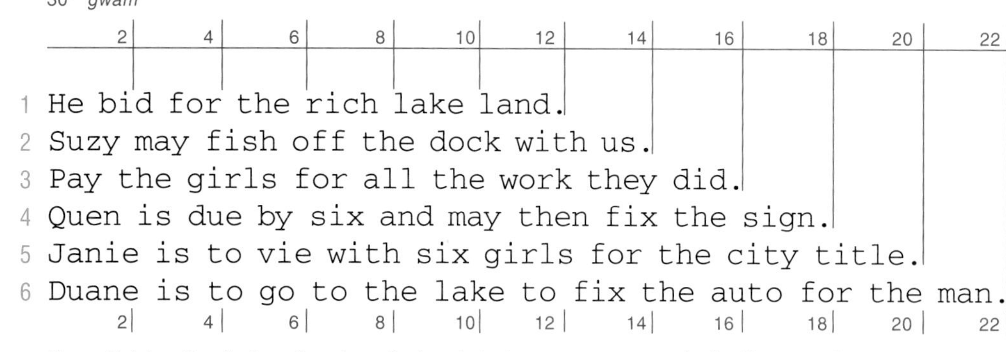

30" *gwam*

2 | 4 | 6 | 8 | 10 | 12 | 14 | 16 | 18 | 20 | 22

1 He bid for the rich lake land.
2 Suzy may fish off the dock with us.
3 Pay the girls for all the work they did.
4 Quen is due by six and may then fix the sign.
5 Janie is to vie with six girls for the city title.
6 Duane is to go to the lake to fix the auto for the man.

2 | 4 | 6 | 8 | 10 | 12 | 14 | 16 | 18 | 20 | 22

If you finish a line before time is called and start over, your *gwam* is the figure at the end of the line PLUS the figure above or below the point at which you stopped.

20E ◆ 9'

IMPROVE SPEED

1. Take a 1' writing on each paragraph (¶) SS; find *gwam* on each writing.
2. Using your better *gwam* as a base rate, select a practice goal and follow the practice procedure shown at the bottom of the page.

all letters used | E | 1.2 si | 5.1 awl | 90% hfw

Tab→ How you key is just as vital as the copy you work from or produce. What you put on paper is a direct result of the way in which you do the job.

Tab→ If you expect to grow quickly in speed, take charge of your mind. It will then tell your eyes and hands how to work through the maze of letters.

GUIDED WRITING PROCEDURE

Select a practice goal

1. Take a 1' writing on ¶1 of a set of ¶s that contain superior figures for guided writings, as in 20E above.
2. Using the *gwam* as a base, add 4 *gwam* to determine your goal rate.
3. Choose from Column 1 of the table at the right the speed nearest your goal rate. At the right of that speed, note the 1/4' points in the copy you must reach to maintain your goal rate.

Quarter-minute checkpoints

gwam	1/4'	1/2'	3/4'	Time
16	4	8	12	16
20	5	10	15	20
24	6	12	18	24
28	7	14	21	28
32	8	16	24	32
36	9	18	27	36
40	10	20	30	40

4. Note from the word-count dots and figures above the lines in ¶1 the checkpoint for each quarter minute. (Example: Checkpoints for 24 *gwam* are 6, 12, 18, and 24.)

Practice procedure

1. Take two 1' writings on ¶1 at your goal rate guided by the quarter-minute calls (1/4, 1/2, 3/4, time).
   Goal: To reach each of your checkpoints just as the guide is called.
2. Take two 1' writings on ¶ 2 of a set of ¶s in the same way.
3. Take a 2' writing on the set of ¶s combined, without the guides.

Speed level of practice

When the purpose of practice is to reach out into new speed areas, use the *speed* level. Take the brakes off your fingers and experiment with new stroking patterns and new speeds. Do this by:

1. Reading 2 or 3 letters ahead of your keying to foresee stroking patterns.
2. Getting the fingers ready for the combinations of letters to be keyed.
3. Keeping your eyes on the copy in the book.

63B ◆ (cont.)

words

A Place to Study 171

Choose the best place to study and use the same one every day. Doing so 185
will help to put you in a study mood when you enter that place. According to 201
Usova (1989, 37), "The library is not always a desirable place to study." Choose 217
a place that has the fewest distractions such as people traffic, conversation, 233
telephone, TV, and outside noises. Study is usually best done alone and in the 249
absence of sights and sounds that distract the eye and ear. In your chosen 264
quiet place, force the mind to concentrate on the task at hand. 277

A Plan for Study 284

Research on the effects of specific study skills on student performance 298
(Dansereau, 1985, 39) suggests that the following study tactics help to im- 313
prove academic performance. 319

Enumerated Items
1. Block a series of numbered items 5 spaces (0.5") from the LM.
2. SS each item, but DS between items and above and below the series.
3. Use the procedures outlined in 62B on p. 119 for indenting.

1. Skim a unit or a chapter, noting headings, topic sentences, key words, 334
and definitions. This overview will clue you to what you are about to 348
study. 350

2. As you read a unit or chapter, convert the headings into questions; then 365
seek answers to those questions as you read. 374

3. If you own the book, use color marking pens to highlight important 389
ideas: headings, topic sentences, special terms, definitions, and support- 403
ing facts. If you don't own the book, make notes of these important ideas 418
and facts. 421

4. After you have completed a unit or chapter, review the highlighted 435
items (or your notes which contain them). 444

5. Using the headings stated as questions, see if you can answer those 458
questions based on your reading. 465

6. Test yourself to see if you can recall definitions of important terms and 480
lists of supporting facts or ideas. 488

A high correlation exists between good study habits and good grades for 502
the courses taken in school. 508

Document 2
Title Page
Format and key a title page for the report using your name, your school name, and the current date.

REFERENCES 510

Dansereau, D.F. "Learning Strategy Research." Thinking and Learning 529
Skills. Vol. 1. Hillsdale, NJ: Lawrence Erlbaum , 1985, 21-40. 543
Usova, George M. Efficient Study Strategies. Pacific Grove, CA: Brooks/ 563
Cole Publishing Company, 1989. 569

LESSON 64 UNBOUND REPORTS

64A ◆ CONDITIONING PRACTICE

each line twice

alphabet 1 The vast Cox farm was just sold by the bank at quite an amazing price.
figures 2 Their firm constructed 340 of the 560 new homes between 1987 and 1992.
fig/sym 3 Martin paid Invoice #382 ($56.79 with a 5% discount) with check #1084.
speed 4 The girls and the maid may go downtown to pay for the six giant signs.

gwam 1' | 1 | 2 | 3 | 4 | 5 | 6 | 7 | 8 | 9 | 10 | 11 | 12 | 13 | 14 |

KEYBOARDING WORKSHOP

KEYBOARD MASTERY

Each line has at least 6 uses of the letter it is intended to emphasize. The lines may be used for a comprehensive keyboard review or for intensive keyboard mastery practice on selected letters.

Comprehensive review

1. In each of several class periods, select a set of lines beginning with lines 1-5.
2. Key each line twice: first, slowly to gain control; then, at a faster pace to extend the skill.

Intensive letter mastery

1. In each of several class periods, select 5 lines that emphasize letters you may not have mastered; for example, x-z-q-v-p.
2. Key each line 3 times: first, slowly to gain control; next, faster to force quick motions; then, at an in-between rate.

A 1 Aida said her aunt gave her a pass to the theater.
B 2 Bobby did bobble the ball but made the big basket.
C 3 Cyd can make a quick copy of the check for a cent.
D 4 Donda did the drill at top speed for a good grade.
E 5 Ellen sent a check to each of the men on the crew.

F 6 Fran left half the forms in the file for the chef.
G 7 Gig used grit to gain his goal and get top grades.
H 8 Harv has high hopes that he can go to that school.
I 9 Inga is to sign the will this week and to file it.
J 10 Jean has a major job she enjoys with a just judge.

K 11 Kirk took a kid for a risky ride in the oak kayak.
L 12 Lena lost this list at the old mall when she fell.
M 13 Maxim made his mark on your swim team this summer.
N 14 Nina can lend a pen to the woman to sign the note.
O 15 Owen knows he is too old to be on our soccer team.

P 16 Pam put pepper on the pork chops and the new peas.
Q 17 Quen was quite quick to quiz my squad about squid.
R 18 Ruby worked on a report to be read by four jurors.
S 19 Sid said his sister has six silver charms to sell.
T 20 Tim got a taxi to the city square for the concert.

U 21 Uri is sure you will sue our county for a big sum.
V 22 Viv can have five vans of vivid color take voters.
W 23 Wes saw a bowl in the window and wished to own it.
X 24 Xerxes indexed by week the sixty excise tax forms.
Y 25 You say you are not yet ready to dye the old yarn.
Z 26 Zoe saw a zebra nuzzle a lazy zebu at the new zoo.

gwam 1' | 1 | 2 | 3 | 4 | 5 | 6 | 7 | 8 | 9 | 10 |

CHECK/IMPROVE SPEED

Take 1' guided writings as directed by your teacher.

Quarter-minute checkpoints

gwam	1/4'	1/2'	3/4'	Time
16	4	8	12	16
20	5	10	15	20
24	6	12	18	24
28	7	14	21	28
32	8	16	24	32
36	9	18	27	36
40	10	20	30	40

all letters used | E | 1.2 si | 5.1 awl | 90% hfw |

gwam 2'

If you do not make your goal the first time, 5
do not give up or quit. Size up the task and try 10
it again in a new way. Try to focus on what will 15
help you make your rate the next time. 18

It may be that you need just to slow down in 23
order to speed up. That is to say, do not try so 28
hard to force your speed. Relax, read with care, 33
and just let the words flow from your fingers. 37

gwam 2' | 1 | 2 | 3 | 4 | 5 |

words

62B ◆ (cont.)

Document 2
Reference Page

Format and key a reference page from the information at the right.

Document 3
Title Page

Format and key a title page for the report. Use your name, your school name, and the current date.

Document 4
(computer users only)

Use the move feature to move the final side heading (*Typewriter Sophistication*) and the last ¶ of text. Place this text below the first ¶ of the report.

<u>Typewriter Sophistication</u> 492

Electronic typewriters range from low-end machines with 503
limited features and without editing windows to high-end 514
machaines with full page displys, diskete storage, and com- 526
plete text-editing capabilities. The price range varies with 539
the amount of advanced features included. Some machines are 551
upgradable so that the aprorpriate level of sophistocation 563
can be obtained without replacing machines. 572

REFERENCES 574

Audion, Mark. "Using Electronic Typewriters:The Basics, 584
Plus. . . ." <u>Today's Office</u>, July 1986, 55-64. 597

Fernberg, Patricia M. "Electrie Typewriters:Understanding 610
the Product." <u>Modern Office Technology</u>, March 1989, 625
48-50. 627

Paze, Patricia. "Typewriters: Technology with an Easy 638
Touch." <u>Today's Office</u>, September 1985, 55-72. 650

LESSON 63 UNBOUND REPORTS

63A ◆
CONDITIONING PRACTICE

each line twice

alphabet 1 **Jackson believed he might maximize profits with a quality sales force.**
figures 2 **Jo's social security number, 504-18-2397, was recorded as 504-18-2396.**
fig/sym 3 **Invoice #689 (dated 10/24) for $3,575 was paid on Tuesday, November 1.**
speed 4 **Their neighbor may dismantle the ancient ricksha in the big cornfield.**

gwam 1' | 1 | 2 | 3 | 4 | 5 | 6 | 7 | 8 | 9 | 10 | 11 | 12 | 13 | 14 |

words

63B ◆
FORMAT ENUMERATED ITEMS

File name: L63B

Document 1
Report

Format and key the copy at the right and on the next page as an unbound report. Place the reference list below the last line of copy on page 2 of the report. Correct errors as you key.

BASIC STRATEGIES FOR EFFECTIVE STUDY 7

Effective learning depends upon good study habits. Efficient study skills 22
do not simply occur; they must first be learned and then applied consis- 37
tently. Good study strategies include a preset time for study, a desirable 52
place to study, and a well-designed study plan. 62

<u>A Time for Study</u> 68
All of us think we have more things to do than we have time to do, and 82
studying gets shortchanged. It is important to prepare a schedule of daily ac- 98
tivities that includes time slots for doing the studying we have to do. Within 114
each study slot, write in the specific study activity; for example, "Read Unit 6 130
of accounting; do Problems 1-5." Keep the schedule flexible so that it can be 146
modified after you assess your success in meeting your study goals within 161
each time slot. 164

(continued, p. 121)

Master Word Processing Features

Learning Outcomes: After completing this unit, you will be able to

1. Use cursor move, insert, and typeover features.
2. Use bold, underline, and center features.
3. Use status/ruler line and set line spacing.

LESSON 21 LEARN CURSOR MOVE, INSERT, AND TYPEOVER

SM: defaults; LS: SS

21A ◆ 8' CONDITIONING PRACTICE

each line twice SS; then three 1' timed writings on line 3; find *gwam*

alphabet 1 Marjax made five quick plays to win the big prize.
caps lock 2 Did you say to send the cartons by UPS or by USPS?
easy 3 I am to pay the six men if they do the work right.

gwam 1' | 1 | 2 | 3 | 4 | 5 | 6 | 7 | 8 | 9 | 10 |

21B ◆ 20' LEARN WORD PROCESSING FEATURES

Cursor move

Being able to move the cursor quickly from one location to another in a document allows you to edit and revise copy/text in an efficient manner. You have already used the up and down arrow keys to move the cursor from line to line and the right and left arrow keys to move the cursor to the right or left one character at a time. Larger cursor movements can be made by using specific keys or key combinations or by using the mouse.

WordPerfect and Works DOS: The cursor can be moved to the beginning or end of the line and to the top or bottom of the screen by depressing a specific key or key combinations. (See Cursor Move Summary at the right.)

Works MAC: The cursor can be moved to any location of entered text by moving the I-beam pointer to the desired location and clicking and releasing the mouse. (The words *Click* and *Click on* are represented throughout this textbook by this symbol: ~.)

Cursor Move Summary

To move cursor to:	Word Perfect	Works/ DOS
Beginning of Line	Home, ←	Home
End of Line	Home, →	End
Top of Screen	Home, ↑	CTRL PgUp
Bottom of Screen	Home, ↓	CTRL PgDn
Right One Word	Ctrl →	Ctrl →
Left One Word	Ctrl ←	Ctrl ←

When a comma (,) separates the keys used, strike first key and then strike second key. When no comma separates commands, depress and hold first key while depressing second key.

Insert mode

New text can be inserted into existing text by using the insert mode, which is automatically on when you enter the software program. Move the cursor to the location where the new text is to be inserted and key the new text. When the insert mode is on, existing text will move to the right.

Typeover mode

The typeover mode allows you to replace current text with newly keyed text.

WordPerfect and Works DOS 3.0 (no typeover mode for Works 2.0): Depress the Ins key to change from the insert mode to the typeover mode. Move cursor to beginning of text to be replaced and key replacement text.

Works MAC: Move the I-beam to the beginning of the text to be replaced. Click (~) and hold as you drag (→) the I-beam over the text you want replaced. Release and key the replacement text.

62B ◆

REPORT WITH LONG QUOTATION

File name: L62B

Document 1
Report

Format and key the report shown at the right and on the next page as a 2-page unbound report, DS. Correct errors as you key.

Long Quotations

When keying quotations of more than 3 typed lines, SS and indent them 5 spaces (0.5") from the LM. Leave a DS above and below them.

To indent a block of text 5 spaces from the left margin do the following:

Typewriter

Reset left margin over 5 spaces for the quote.

WordPerfect

Depress F4 at beginning of the paragraph.

Works DOS

1. Depress Alt, T.
2. Strike A (spacing).
3. Change the left indent to 0.5".
4. Strike return. After keying the long quotation, return to start the next line.
5. Reset the left indent to 0.

Works MAC

1. Drag the left margin (and paragraph indent) 0.5" to the right.
2. Key the long quotation; return to start the next line.
3. Drag the left margin back (to the left) 0.5".

words

TYPEWRITERS: AN ENDANGERED SPECIES? 7

For well over a decade, experts in office automation 18
have predicted the demise of the typewriter. In their view 30
the computer is destined to take over the word processing 42
role enjoyed by the typewriter for over a century. Yet, a 53
recent report (Fernberg, 1989, 49-50) indicates that elec- 65
tronic typewriter shipments over the last three years aver- 76
aged about a billion dollars a year. Further, the Computer 88
and Business Equipment Manufacturers' Association projects 100
that the annual growth rate will remain constant at 1.5 per- 112
cent over the next five years. With sales holding steady at 124
over a million units a year, the electronic typewriter does 136
not appear endangered. It is likely here to stay--and for 148
good reasons. 151

<u>Typewriter Familiarity</u> 160

Virtually anyone who has learned to key can sit down at 171
the electronic typewriter and within a few minutes operate it 184
with amazing ease and speed. According to Paez (1985, 55): 196

> A familiar keyboard, which requires fewer keystrokes and 207
> has a simpler, less code-intensive user interface, makes 219
> the transition to a high-end typewriter much easier than 230
> the transition to a personal computer with the same func- 241
> tions. 243

<u>Typewriter Flexibility</u> 252

An electronic typewriter can preform some function com- 263
puters cannot, but a personal computer (PC) cannot be used as 275
a mere typewriter (nor should it be). Perhaps that is why 287
one large survey found that 85 percent of secretaries who use 299
PCs also use typewriters. Using microchip technology, sophis- 312
ticated electronic typewriters can perform many of the auto- 324
matic functions and editing functions of which computers are 336
capable. 338

<u>Automatic Functions</u>. Among the features of electric 353
typewriters are autamatic centering, returning, right margin 365
justifing and hang-indenting. These features are aviable on 378
computers as well, but some users of both kinds of equipment 390
say that the typewriter is more "user fredndly." 400

<u>Editing Functions</u>. Many electronic typewriters permit 415
operators to backspace/delete, insert copy, move copy from 426
one plce to another, and search and replace specific words or 439
terms in an document. Some are equiped with templates that 451
make form fill-in easy; others permits the merging of in- 462
formation from diferent sources. All these functions are 474
performed without needing to rekey documents. 482

(continued, p. 120)

21B ◆ (cont.)

1. Study word processing (wp) features on previous page.
2. Key sentence 1; edit as instructed.
3. Repeat activity trying to edit more efficiently.

1. Key the following.

Mark will be in California on Monday.

2. Make the following changes, using the Cursor move keys and insert mode.

```
Mark will be in California on Monday.
```

[handwritten insertions: Mark ^Meyers will be in ^San Diego, California^, on Monday^, *Memorial Day*.]

3. Make these additional changes. Use typeover mode to change day and holiday.

```
Mark Meyers will be in San Diego, California, on Monday,
Memorial Day.
```

[handwritten edits: ^*Mr.* Mark Meyers^, *the new mayor,* will be in San Diego, California, on ~~Monday~~ *Friday*, ~~Memorial~~ *Columbus* Day.]

21C ◆ 12'

CHECK/IMPROVE SPEED

Take 1' writings on each ¶ and 2' writings on ¶1 and 2 combined; find *gwam* on each writing.

all letters used | E | 1.2 si | 5.1 awl | 90% hfw |

```
Line      .     2     .     4     .     6     .     8     .   gwam 2'
1      You must realize by now that learning to key             5
  10    .    12     .     14     .     16     .     18     .
2 requires work.  However, you will soon be able to            10
  20    .    22     .     24     .     26     .     28     .
3 key at a higher speed than you can write just now.           15
        .     2     .     4     .     6     .     8     .
4      You will also learn to do neater work on the            19
  10    .    12     .     14     .     16     .     18     .
5 machine than you can do by hand.  Quality work at            24
  20    .    22     .     24     .     26     .     28     .
6 higher speeds is a good goal for you to have next.           29
gwam 2' |   1   |   2   |   3   |   4   |   5   |
```

21D ◆ 10'

REVIEW WORD PROCESSING FEATURES

1. Rekey the two paragraphs of 21C.
2. Make the changes outlined at the right.

Line 1 Insert **how** between *learning* and *to*.
2 Insert **time and hard** between *requires* and *work*.
3 Insert **much** between *a* and *higher*.

Line 4 Insert **how** between *learn* and *to*.
5 Insert **ever** between *can* and *do*.
6 Typeover *have next* with **work towards**.

LESSON 22 LEARN BOLD, UNDERLINE, AND CENTER

SM: defaults; LS: SS

22A ◆ 8'

CONDITIONING PRACTICE

each line twice SS; then three 1' timed writings on line 3; find *gwam*

```
alphabet 1 Jack viewed unique forms by the puzzled tax agent.
       ? 2 Where is Elena?  Did she call?  Is she to go, too?
    easy 3 Title to all of the lake land is held by the city.
 gwam 1' | 1 | 2 | 3 | 4 | 5 | 6 | 7 | 8 | 9 | 10 |
```

1" TM

total words

Page number — 2 DS

data, retrieve and change it, or select certain data (such as an 276
address) to be used in documents. Software users can manipulate 289
and print data in report form for decision-making purposes. DS 302

Side heading — <u>Spreadsheet Software</u> DS 310

"A spreadsheet is an electronic worksheet made up of columns 322
Internal citation — and rows of data" (Oliverio and Pasewark, 1989, 489). Spread- 334
sheet software may direct a program to apply mathematical opera- 347
tions to the data and to print reports that are useful in summa- 360
rizing and analyzing business operations and in planning for the 373
1" LM future. DS 1" RM 375

Employment personnel look favorably upon job applicants who 387
are familiar with these kinds of software and how they are used. 400
QS (space down 2 DS)

REFERENCES QS, then change to SS 402

List of references — Clark, James F., et al. <u>Computers and Information Processing</u>. 415
2d ed. Cincinnati: South-Western Publishing Co., 1990. DS 426

Oliverio, Mary Ellen, and William R. Pasewark. <u>The Office</u>. 438
Cincinnati: South-Western Publishing Co., 1989. 448

Unbound Report, Page 2

61E ◆ COMPUTER ACTIVITIES

Retrieve file L61B and bold the headings in the report. If you need to, refer to 46D, p. 82.

Delete the following files from your disk (refer to 56D, p. 107 if necessary):

BLANCO	BURK
L58B	L59C
L59B	

LESSON 62 UNBOUND REPORTS

62A ◆ CONDITIONING PRACTICE

each line twice

alphabet 1 Morgan Sanchez was frequently invited to exhibit her artwork in Japan.
figures 2 We purchased 3,148 of her 7,260 shares on Thursday, December 15, 1992.
fig/sym 3 Frederick & Gilbertson paid me $635,000 for the 460 acres on 12/17/89.
speed 4 She may make us visit the big chapel in the dismal city on the island.

gwam 1' | 1 | 2 | 3 | 4 | 5 | 6 | 7 | 8 | 9 | 10 | 11 | 12 | 13 | 14 |

22B ◆ 8'

REVIEW WORD PROCESSING FEATURES

Using the insert and typeover modes, make the changes to the conditioning practice sentences you just finished keying as outlined at the right.

```
        Smith      the       style of      baffled         , Jake Nix
Jack^ viewed^ unique ~~forms by~~ the ~~puzzled~~ tax agent^.
           Helen                        today         with us  ?
Where is ~~Elena~~?  Did she call^?  Is she to go^, too.
                                          kept            manager
Title to all of the lake land is ~~held~~ by the city^.
```

22C ◆ 20'

LEARN WORD PROCESSING FEATURES

Review the word processing features; study the command summary for the software you are using. Though letter-key commands appear as capitals, such as **Ctrl B** or **⌘ U**, you will key lowercase letters.

Bold
A feature that prints the designated text darker than the rest of the copy to add emphasis.

Underline
A feature that underlines text as it is keyed.

Center
A feature that centers text horizontally as it is keyed.

Command Summary

Software	Bold	Underline	Center
WordPerfect On	F6	F8	Shift F6
WordPerfect Off	F6	F8	Return
Works DOS On	Ctrl B	Ctrl U	Ctrl C
Works DOS Off	Ctrl Space Bar	Ctrl Space Bar	Ctrl L
Works MAC On	⌘B	⌘U	Format Justification Center
Works MAC Off	⌘B	⌘U	Format Justification Left

Use the new word processing features to key the text at the right; use the center feature to center lines 7-10. Repeat activity to increase your skill at using the new features.

1 Fred uses **Microsoft Works**; Jayne uses **WordPerfect**.

2 **Troy Day** will not be here; **Joan Mays** will be here.

3 **Christmas** will be on **Sunday** this year, not **Monday**.

4 I was in **Atlanta** on Monday and **Chicago** on Tuesday.

5 Return to Excellence was written by **Jeffrey Chang**.

6 Both Cheryl Marx and Robert Oyen are **FBLA** members.

7 **Yellowstone**, Wyoming

8 **Mount McKinley**, Alaska

9 **Yosemite**, California

10 **Mount Rainier**, Washington

total words

Title ELECTRONIC KEYBOARD APPLICATIONS 2" Top Margin 1
QS (space down 2 DS)

Report body Learning to key is of little value unless one applies it in 19
preparing something useful--a record or document of some kind. 31
Three basic kinds of software have been developed to assist those 45
with keyboarding skill in applying their skill electronically. DS 57

Side heading <u>Word Processing Software</u> DS 67
Word processing software is "software specially designed to 79
assist in the document preparation needs of an individual or 91
Internal citation business" (Clark et al., 1990, 193). Word processing software 104
permits the user to enter text, format it, manipulate or revise 117
it, and print a copy. The software can be used to process a wide 130
variety of documents such as letters, memos, reports, and tables. DS 143
This software has special features such as automatic center- 155
1" LM ing and word wrap that reduce time and effort. In addition, it 1" RM 168
permits error corrections, format and sequence changes, and 180
insertion of variables "on screen" before a copy is printed. 193
These features increase efficiency by eliminating document 204
rekeying. DS 207

Side heading <u>Database Software</u> DS 214
A database is "any collection of related items stored in 225
Internal citation computer memory" (Oliverio and Pasewark, 1989, 573). The data in 238
a database may be about club members, employee payroll, company 251
sales, and so on. Database software allows the user to enter 263

At least 1"

Shown in 10-pitch type, photo-reduced

22D ◆ 14'

IMPROVE SPEED

Take 1' and 2' writings as your teacher directs you.

all letters used | E | 1.2 si | 5.1 awl | 90% hfw

```
                                                   gwam 2'
      .    2    .    4    .    6    .    8    .
     Many boys and girls have major goals in life     4
 10    .   12    .   14    .   16    .   18    .
that they hope to reach.  To hope is easy, but to     9
 20    .   22    .   24    .   26    .   28    .
get will take much effort.  Many of us have a lot    14
 30    .   32    .   34    .   36    .   38    .
of hope but lack the drive to do the needed work.    19
      .    2    .    4    .    6    .    8    .
     To reach a goal, we must first set up a plan    24
 10    .   12    .   14    .   16    .   18    .
of action.  Next, we must put that plan in motion    29
 20    .   22    .   24    .   26    .   28    .
step by step.  If we quit before we take the last    34
 30    .   32    .   34    .   36    .   38    .
step, we will not take the prize we wanted to win.   39
gwam 2' |    1    |    2    |    3    |    4    |    5    |
```

LESSON 23 LEARN STATUS/RULER LINE AND LINE SPACING

SM: defaults; LS: SS

23A ◆ 8'

CONDITIONING PRACTICE

each line twice SS; then three 1' writings on line 3; find *gwam*

```
alphabet 1 Kevin can fix the unique jade owl as my big prize.
capitalization 2 Rule:  When : precedes a sentence, cap first word.
easy 3 Dodi is to make a visit to the eight island towns.
gwam 1' | 1 | 2 | 3 | 4 | 5 | 6 | 7 | 8 | 9 | 10 |
```

23B ◆ 22'

LEARN WORD PROCESSING FEATURES

Status/Ruler Line. In word processing software, a status or ruler line serves as a compass. Among other information, the status/ruler line shows the position of the cursor in relation to the edges of a printed page.

WORDPERFECT STATUS LINE

Information displayed in the lower right corner of screen telling you the location of the cursor. Indicates the Document (**Doc 1**) you are keying (either Doc 1 or Doc 2), the page (**Pg**) of the document you are keying, the line (**Ln**) on the page you are keying, and the position (**Pos**) of the cursor. Pos or Pos number changes as the bold, underline, and ALL CAPS features are activated.

WORKS DOS STATUS LINE

Information displayed in the bar at the bottom of the screen telling you the total number of pages of the current document and the page where the cursor is presently located. Also shows when bold (**B**), underline (**U**), and italics (**I**) are turned on.

WORKS DOS AND MAC RULER LINE

Shows location of left and right margins. The cursor location can be seen in relation to the ruler line.

LESSON 61 UNBOUND REPORTS

61A ♦ CONDITIONING PRACTICE

each line twice SS; then three 1' writings on line 3; find *gwam*; clear screen

alphabet 1 Pamela Jaworski inquired about the exact size of the very large house.

figures 2 Flight 687 from Boston will arrive at 10:45 a.m. on May 29 at Gate 13.

fig/sym 3 The 5% sales tax on Order #394 is $16.80; for Order #202 it is $17.50.

speed 4 The haughty man may signal with a giant emblem or with the usual sign.

gwam 1' | 1 | 2 | 3 | 4 | 5 | 6 | 7 | 8 | 9 | 10 | 11 | 12 | 13 | 14 |

61B ♦ FORMAT A REPORT AND REFERENCE LIST

File name: L61B

1. Study the report formatting information on p. 115.
2. Format and key the model report and references shown on pp. 117-118. Correct your errors as you key.

Note: Depending on the equipment you are using, line endings may be different from those of the model.

61C ♦ CENTER LINES HORIZONTALLY

Center each of the lines at the right horizontally. Start the first line 2" from the top of the page. DS between lines.

Typewriter: Move the *printing point* to center of paper. Backspace once for each 2 characters and spaces in the line to be centered. If necessary, refer to 27E, p. 52.

WordPerfect: Shift F6

Works DOS: Control C

Works MAC: Format, Justification, Center

HORIZONTAL CENTERING

Equal Left and Right Margins

Half of Copy to Left of Center

Half of Copy to Right of Center

Variance of One or Two Spaces Acceptable

61D ♦ FORMAT A TITLE PAGE

File name: L61D

A cover or title page is prepared for many reports. Using the following guides, format a title page for the report you prepared in 61B.

1. Center the title in ALL CAPS 2" from the top.
2. Center your name in capital and lower-case letters 5" from the top.
3. Center the school name a DS below your name.
4. Center the current date 9" from the top.

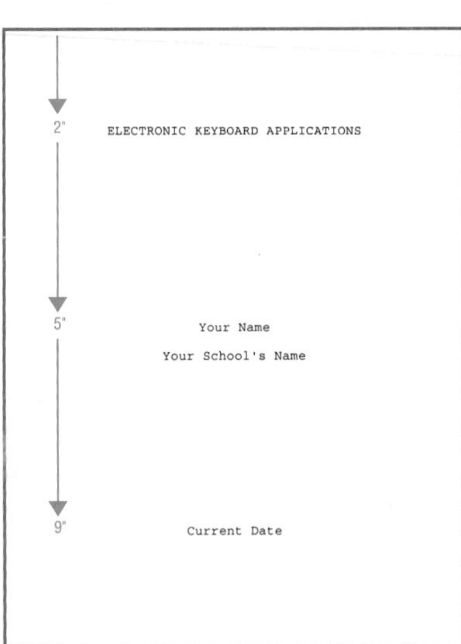

2"
ELECTRONIC KEYBOARD APPLICATIONS
5"
Your Name
Your School's Name
9"
Current Date

Line Spacing. You can set the number of blank lines left between lines of text with the spacing feature. Single spacing (SS) means there are no blank lines between text, while double spacing (DS) means there is one blank line left between lines of text.

WORDPERFECT

1. **Shift F8**; **L**(ine); **S**(pacing)
2. Key **1**, Return for single (**Key 2**, Return for double)
3. Depress **F7**

WORKS DOS

Ctrl 1 for Single Spacing
Ctrl 2 for Double Spacing

WORKS MAC

1. Format; Spacing
2. Single (or Double)

Margins. Specification of the number of spaces (or inches) at the left and right of printed lines.

1. Review the wp features; study the specific commands on this page for the software you are using.
2. Change the left and right margin settings to 2".
3. Key the first paragraph in 23C below; return twice after keying the paragraph.
4. Change the spacing to double spacing (DS); change the margins to 1".
5. Key the second paragraph (23C); return twice after keying the paragraph.
6. Change the spacing to single spacing (SS); change the margins to 1.5" inches.
7. Key the two paragraphs again; return twice after keying the last paragraph.
8. Change the spacing to double spacing (DS); change the margins to the default settings.

WORDPERFECT

The default margin setting is 1". To change the margins to 2":

1. **Shift F8**; **L**(ine); **M**(argins)
2. Strike **2** (2" left margin), Return
3. Strike **2** (2" right margin), Return
4. Depress **F7**

WORKS DOS

The default margin setting is 1.3" for the left margin and 1.2" for the right margin. To change the margins to 2":

1. **Alt, P**
2. **M**(argins)
3. **Alt E**, strike **2** (2" left margin)
4. **Alt R**, strike **2** (2" right margin)
5. Return

WORKS MAC

Underneath the ruler line are two triangles (▷ ◁). You can change the left (▷) and right (◁) margins by clicking and dragging the triangles to the desired location. The default margins are 1". To change the left margin to 2", click and drag (~←) the ▷ to 1 on the ruler. To change the right margin to 2", click and drag (~→) the ◁ from 6.5 to to 5.5 on the ruler.

The indent feature (■) is embedded inside the left margin. If you want the margin changed with no indent, you will need to drag both the ■ and the ▷ to the same location. If you want a 5 space paragraph indention, drag the ■ five spaces past the ▷.

23C ◆ 10'

IMPROVE SPEED

Take 1' writings on each ¶ and 2' writings on both ¶s; find *gwam*.

all letters used | E | 1.2 si | 5.1 awl | 90% hfw |

gwam 2'

```
     .    2    .    4    .    6    .    8    .
     In the months and years ahead, you will have    4
10   .   12    .   14    .   16    .   18    .
many times to be proud of your new skill.  If you    9
20   .   22    .   24    .   26    .   28    .
go on to college and then get a job, you may have   14
30   .   32    .   34    .   36    .   38    .
to key quite often.  So build more skill to prize.  19
     .    2    .    4    .    6    .    8    .
     In a short while you will be able to key the   24
10   .   12    .   14    .   16    .   18    .
copy with just a little thought.  By then you can   29
20   .   22    .   24    .   26    .   28    .
learn to format papers in proper style for actual   34
30   .   32    .   34    .   36    .   38    .
use.  Make your next goal a higher level of skill.  39
```

gwam 2' | 1 | 2 | 3 | 4 | 5 |

23D ◆ 10'

REVIEW FEATURES

1. Rekey ¶1 and underline <u>many</u>, <u>quite</u>, and <u>more</u>; bold **proud**, **key**, and **prize**.
2. Rekey ¶2 and underline <u>short</u>, <u>use</u>, and <u>higher</u>.
3. Center and bold the last sentence in ¶1.
4. Center the last 5 words in ¶2 in ALL CAPS (omit the period).

Master Report Format

Learning Outcomes: After completing this unit, you will be able to

1. Format and key unbound reports.
2. Format and key reference lists.
3. Format and key title pages.
4. Format and key topic outlines.

UNBOUND REPORT FORMAT

Many short reports are prepared without covers or binders. Such reports are called unbound reports. If they consist of more than one page, the pages are fastened together in the upper left corner by a staple or paper clip.

Standard Margins

Unbound reports are formatted with standard 1-inch (1") side margins (SM). A top margin of 2" is customarily used on the first page of unbound reports. Typewriter users will place the title on line 13. Computer users should remember the 1" default top margin .

A 1" bottom margin is recommended. Because the internal spacing of report parts varies, a bottom margin of exactly 1" is often not possible. For that reason, a bottom margin of at least 1" is acceptable. For typewriter users an exact 1" bottom margin would place the last line of copy on line 60 from the top edge of the paper.

Page Numbering

The first page of an unbound report is usually not numbered. On the second and subsequent pages, there is a 1" top margin. Typewriter users will place the page number on line 7 at the right margin (RM). Computer users who have a default top margin of 1" will place the page number on the first line of the input screen. A DS is left below the page number.

Internal Spacing of Reports

A QS is left between the report title and the first line of the body. Multiple-line titles are DS. A DS is left above and below side headings and between paragraphs, which are usually DS but may be SS when specified.

Internal Citations

References used to give credit for quoted or paraphrased material are cited in parentheses in the report body. This internal citation method of documentation is rapidly replacing the footnote method because it is easier and quicker. Internal citations should include the name(s) of the author(s), the year of publication, and the page number(s) of the material cited.

Quotation marks are used for direct quotes but not for paraphrased material.

An ellipsis (. . .) is used to indicate any material omitted from a quotation:

> "Many changes are occurring today in office organization . . . and technology" (VanHuss and Daggett, 1990, 1).

Reference Lists

All references cited in a report are listed alphabetically by author surnames at the end of a report (usually on a separate page) under the heading REFERENCES. A QS appears between the heading and the first reference. The reference page uses the same top margin and side margins as the first page of the report, but a page number is included at the RM, 1" from the top of page.

Each reference is SS with a DS between references. The first line of each reference begins at the LM; other lines are indented 5 spaces (0.5"). If the reference list appears on the last page of the report body, a QS is left between the last line of copy and the heading REFERENCES.

Master Keying and Word Processing Skills

Learning Outcomes: After completing this unit, you will be able to

1. Demonstrate better keying technique and use of service keys.
2. Demonstrate greater control of letter reaches and improved speed.
3. Computer users: Demonstrate mastery of basic word processing functions.

LESSON 24 KEYBOARDING/WORD PROCESSING

SM: 1.5" or defaults; LS: SS

24A ◆ 6' CONDITIONING PRACTICE

each line twice SS; then a 1' writing on line 3; find *gwam*

alphabet 1 Nat will vex the judge if she bucks my quiz group.
punctuation 2 Al, did you use these words: vie, zeal, and aqua?
easy sentence 3 She owns the big dock, but they own the lake land.

gwam 1' | 1 | 2 | 3 | 4 | 5 | 6 | 7 | 8 | 9 | 10 |

COMPUTER on-screen changes

Line 1 Change *Nat* to **Nan**.
2 Change *aqua* to **lazy**.

Line 3 Change *She owns* to **They own** and, later in the line, *they own* to **she owns**.

24B ◆ 22' RESPONSE PATTERNS

1. Key each pair of lines twice SS; DS between 4-line groups.
2. Take 1' writings on selected lines to increase speed; find *gwam*.
3. Take another 1' writing on the slower line to increase your speed.

Practice hints

Balanced-hand lines: *Think*, *say*, and *key* the words by word response at a fast pace.

One-hand lines: *Think*, *say*, and *key* the words by letter response at a steady but unhurried pace.

Letter response

Many one-hand words (as in lines 3-4) are not easy to key. Such words may be keyed letter-by-letter and with continuity (steadily, without pauses).

Word Response

Short, balanced-hand words (as in lines 1-2) are so easy to key that they can be keyed as words, not letter-by-letter. Think and key them at your top speed.

balanced-hand words
1 ah do so go he us if is of or to it an am me by ox
2 ha for did own the for and due pay but men may box

one-hand words
3 as up we in at on be oh ax no ex my ad was you are
4 ad ink get ilk far him few pop set pin far imp car

balanced-hand phrases
5 of it | he is | to us | or do | am to | an ox | or by | is to do
6 do the | and for | she did | all six | the map | for the pay

one-hand phrases
7 as on | be in | at no | as my | be up | as in | at him | saw you
8 you are | oil tax | pop art | you get | red ink | we saw him

balanced-hand sentences
9 The man is to go to the city and do the auto work.
10 The girl is to go by bus to the lake for the fish.

one-hand sentences
11 Jimmy saw you feed a deer on a hill up at my mill.
12 Molly sat on a junk in oily waters at a bare reef.

gwam 1' | 1 | 2 | 3 | 4 | 5 | 6 | 7 | 8 | 9 | 10 |

KEYBOARDING WORKSHOP

SKILL DRILLS

1. Key each line once at a steady, easy pace.
2. Key each line again at a faster pace.
3. Key each line once more at your top speed.
4. Key a 1' writing on *each* of lines 3, 6, 9, 12, and 15; find *gwam* on each.
5. Compare *gwam* on the 5 sentences; note the 3 slowest ones.
6. Key two 1' writings on each of the 3 slowest sentences to increase speed.
7. Finally, key lines 13-15 again at your best speed, untimed.

Fingers curved, upright; quick-snap keystrokes; quiet hands and arms

alphabet review

1 axle zone corn vent both play make jogs quit flow drop name paid major
2 for us | got by | a zone | did quit | can make | just them | open vent | if we excel
3 Gomez jokes expertly with a friend but can be very shy and very quiet.

figures/ symbols

4 10-15% forty dollars ($40) S&K Kim & Perez $483.74 Flight #2956 is in.
5 Her phone number is 836-9572; her address is 3014 Jefferson Boulevard.
6 The Grade "A" carpet cost $31.90 per square yard ($56.78 less $24.80).

space bar

7 ham buy pan jay tam any plan glum duty slam twin gory swim given ivory
8 buy the pan | can pay him | any of them | try her plan | may be ivory | am handy
9 Pam may try to work with ten men and women on a new plan for the city.

shift keys/ LOCK

10 Karen and Coy Sparks are skiing in the Alps with Maye and Nancy Apple.
11 Janie saw Patsy, Lauren, Ellen, and Claudia while she was in Columbus.
12 T. J. Wurtz expects Sun & Co. to merge with ROBO, a subsidiary of TMW.

fluency/ speed

13 both rich girl name when make lend right small ivory handy shall eight
14 The girls cut and curl their hair when they visit their rich neighbor.
15 He is apt to make the men go to the island for the coalfish and clams.

gwam 1' | 1 | 2 | 3 | 4 | 5 | 6 | 7 | 8 | 9 | 10 | 11 | 12 | 13 | 14 |

TIMED WRITINGS

Key 1', 3', and 5' writings, following your teacher's directions.

all letters used | A | 1.5 si | 5.7 awl | 80% hfw

gwam 3' | 5'

People in business are concerned about what is communicated by the 4 3
written word. As they write memos, letters, and reports, they may plan 9 6
for the content but may not plan for the image of the message. Experts, 14 8
however, realize that neglecting the way a document looks can be costly. 19 11

Many times a written piece of correspondence is the only basis on 23 14
which a person can form an impression of the writer. Judgments based on 28 17
a first impression that may be formed by the reader about the writer 33 20
should always be considered before mailing a document. 36 22

The way a document looks can communicate as much as what it says. 41 25
Margins, spacing, and placement are all important features to consider 46 27
when you key a document. A quality document is one that will bring the 50 30
interest of the reader to the message rather than to the way it appears. 55 33

gwam 3' | 1 | 2 | 3 | 4 | 5 |
5' | 1 | 2 | 3 |

24C ◆ 22'

CHECK/IMPROVE KEYING SPEED

LS: DS

Take 1' guided writings and 2' unguided writings; find *gwam* for each writing.

1' *gwam* goals
- ▽ 17 = acceptable
- ⊡ 21 = average
- ⊙ 25 = good
- ◊ 29 = excellent

all letters used | E | 1.2 si | 5.1 awl | 90% hfw

	gwam 2'
Keep in home position all of the fingers not	5
being used to strike a key. Do not let them move	10
out of position for the next letters in your copy.	15
Prize the control you have over the fingers.	19
See how quickly speed goes up when you learn that	24
you can make them do just what you expect of them.	29

gwam 2' | 1 | 2 | 3 | 4 | 5 |

COMPUTER on-screen changes

Reset side margins to 1.5" and line spacing to DS; then rekey ¶s from book with these changes as you key:

Line 1 Change *Keep* to **Hold**.
3 Change *copy* to **text**.
5 Insert **just** after *See*.

Line 2 Boldface **Do not**.
3 Underline Prize.

LESSON 25 KEYBOARDING/WORD PROCESSING

SM: 1.5" or defaults; LS: SS

25A ◆ 6'

CONDITIONING PRACTICE

each line twice SS; then a 1' writing on line 3; find *gwam*

alphabet 1 Wusov amazed them by jumping quickly from the box.
spacing 2 am to | is an | by it | of us | an oak | is to pay | it is due
easy 3 It is right for the man to aid them with the sign

gwam 1' | 1 | 2 | 3 | 4 | 5 | 6 | 7 | 8 | 9 | 10 |

COMPUTER on-screen changes

Line 1 Change *jumping quickly* to **quickly jumping**.

Line 3 Change *It is* to ***Is it***, *man* to ***men***, and **.** to **?**.

25B ◆ 12'

OUTSIDE REACHES

1. Key the lines once as shown: SS with a DS between 2-line groups.
2. Key the lines again to improve keying ease and speed.

Technique goals
- fingers deeply curved and upright
- eyes on copy
- finger-action keystrokes
- hands and arms quiet, almost motionless

Outside reaches with 3d and 4th fingers

o/p/l
1 ol po opt old owl apt pow lap pod pal low ape soap
2 Lola is apt to opt for a job in the park all fall.

w/s/x
3 ws xs ox ow six own sow lax paw fox laws oxen swap
4 Lex will swap two onyx owls he owns for six swans.

a/z/q
5 za aq zap qt. adz quo zip aqua zone quit jazz quip
6 Liza quit the zany jazz band for a quiet quay job.

alphabet
7 Olive Penz packed my bag with six quarts of juice.
8 Jud aims next to play a quick game with Bev Fritz.
9 Greta may just pack the box with five dozen quail.
10 Jacques Veloz keeps the new form by the tax guide.

gwam 1' | 1 | 2 | 3 | 4 | 5 | 6 | 7 | 8 | 9 | 10 |

60B ◆ (cont.)

words

Document 2
Personal-Business Letter

2274 Cogswell Road | El Monte, CA 91732-3846 | December 3, 19-- | Mrs. Alice 14
M. Wiggins | 11300 Lower Azusa Road | El Monte, CA 91732-4725 | Dear Mrs. 28
Wiggins 30

Thanks to you and other PTA members who brought guests, our November 18 44
meeting was a tremendous success. Dr. Gibson was overwhelmed by the 58
high level of interest in computer literacy shown by parents of our students. 74

You will be pleased to know that two of the guests you brought have now reg- 89
istered to become regular PTA members. The total new-member registra- 103
tion was nine. 106

The other officers of the El Monte PTA join me in appreciation of the active 121
role you are taking this year. 128

Cordially yours | Ms. Laura J. Marsh 134

Document 3
Business Letter

December 4, 19-- | Mr. Duane R. Burk, Office Manager | Huesman & Schmidt, 14
Inc. | 662 Woodward Avenue | Detroit, MI 48226-1947 | Dear Mr. Burk 27

Miss Chun and I certainly enjoyed our discussions with you last week. We 41
are highly pleased that you have given us an opportunity to work with you to 57
maximize your office space. 63

Based upon your plan to regroup certain personnel, Miss Chun is reworking 77
her design to accommodate the changes. That work should be completed 91
next week. At that time we shall also have a firm bid to show you. 105

Would next Friday at ten o'clock be a convenient time for us to show you the 121
new plans? If not, please suggest another date and time. 132

Sincerely yours | Virgil P. Thompson | Assistant Sales Manager | xx (105) 145

Document 4
Simplified Memo

Date: **December 4, 19--**
Addressee: **Vincente W. Lugo**
Subject: **NEW SERVICE CONTRACT FOR OFFICE EQUIPMENT**
Writer: **Danielle E. Bogarde**
Reference: **your initials**

opening lines 15

¶ We have just signed a new service contract with the 25
Lee & Perin Company. Henceforth, they will clean, service, 37
and repair all our keyboarding and word processing 48
equipment. 50
¶ L&P has asked me to notify all supervisors that only 61
L&P personnel should do internal cleaning or make repairs 72
on any typewriter, computer, or word processor. When service 85
is required, please call 555-8590 to make your request. 96
¶ Make sure everyone under your supervision knows 106
about this change. 110

closing lines 114

Document 5

Computer users: Make a copy of Document 2 and then make these changes.

Address the letter to:

Mr. Jon Galen
Silverbay Avenue
El Monte, CA 91732-6782

Change the date to **February 1**

Make these changes in ¶1:
November 18 to **January 25**
Dr. Gibson to **Dr. Linton**
computer literacy to **teenage drug abuse.**

25C ◆ 18'

RESPONSE PATTERNS

1. Key each set of lines twice SS (slowly, then faster); DS between 6-line groups.
2. Take 1' writings on selected lines; find *gwam* and compare rates.
3. Rekey the slowest line.

Combination response

Normal copy (as in lines 7-9) includes both word- and letter-response sequences.

Use *top* speed for easy words, *lower* speed for words that are harder to key.

letter response
1 be in as no we kin far you few pin age him get oil
2 see him|was nil|vex you|red ink|wet mop|as you saw
3 Milo saved a dazed polo pony as we sat on a knoll.

word response
4 ox if am to is may end big did own but and yam wit
5 do it|to cut|he got|for me|jam it|an owl|go by air
6 He is to go to the city and to do the work for me.

combination response
7 am at of my if on so as to be or we go up of no by
8 am in|so as|if no|is my|is up|to be|is at|is up to
9 Di was busy at the loom as you slept in the chair.

letter 10 Jon gazed at a phony scarab we gave him in a case.
combination 11 Pam was born in a small hill town at the big lake.
word 12 Keith is off to the lake to fish off the big dock.

gwam 1' | 1 | 2 | 3 | 4 | 5 | 6 | 7 | 8 | 9 | 10 |

25D ◆ 14'

CHECK/IMPROVE KEYING SPEED

LS: DS

Take 1' guided writings and 2' unguided writings; find *gwam* on the 2' writings.

1' *gwam* goals

- ▽ 19 = acceptable
- ⊡ 23 = average
- ⊙ 27 = good
- ◊ 31 = excellent

all letters used	E	1.2 si	5.1 awl	90% hfw

gwam 2'

The level of your skill is a major item when 5
you try to get a job. Just as vital, though, may 10
be how well you can express ideas in written form. 15

It might amaze you to learn what it is worth 19
to a company to find those who can write a letter 24
of quality as they key. Learn to do so in school. 29

gwam 2' | 1 | 2 | 3 | 4 | 5 |

COMPUTER on-screen changes

Line 1 Change *is* to **will be**.
2 Change *though* to **however**.
5 Change *letter* to **report**.
6 Change *do so* to **compose as you key**.

On the line above the first ¶, center in **bold** the heading **COMPOSING AND KEYING**; then return. (You insert two hard returns each time you strike the return key when using DS.)

Key ¶s again from book, making these changes as you key:
(1) Underline major in line 1;
(2) **Bold** the last sentence in ¶2.

59C ◆ CREATING TEXT

File name: L59C

1. Compose at the keyboard 1 or 2 paragraphs on one of the questions at the right. DS paragraph(s).
2. Edit your copy, marking corrections and changes to improve sentence structure and organization.
3. Prepare the final copy.

Questions

If you received a check for $100,000 in the mail today, what would you do with it?

What qualities do you think an employer would look for in a prospective employee?

Would you buy a stereo on credit? Explain.

59D ◆ IMPROVE SKILL: SCRIPT COPY

File name: L59D

all letters used | LA | 1.4 si | 5.4 awl | 85% hfw

gwam 2'

Whether you key documents for personal or for business 5
use, much of the copy will be in handwritten or rough-draft 11
form. So adjust your speed in order to do work of quality. 18
Seize the next opportunity to prove that you can handle both 24
kinds of copy without too great a loss in speed and control. 30
With practice, you can process such copy with speed and ease. 36

LESSON 60 BUSINESS LETTERS

60A ◆ CONDITIONING PRACTICE

each line twice

alphabet	1	Jack answered many questions about the exact value of each topaz ring.
figures	2	On Monday, November 14, 1988 I bought pattern numbers 32A57 and 60B94.
fig/sym	3	The 1992 cost ($414) was 15 percent greater than the 1987 cost ($360).
speed	4	The neighbor's dog was with the girl by the big sign in the cornfield .

gwam 1' | 1 | 2 | 3 | 4 | 5 | 6 | 7 | 8 | 9 | 10 | 11 | 12 | 13 | 14 |

60B ◆ ASSESS FORMATTING

File name: L60B

1. Format and key Documents 1-3 (at right and on p. 113).
2. Proofread and correct errors before removing documents.

Document 1
Simplified Memo

Date: **November 13, 19--**
Addressee: **DeRon Jackson**
Subject: **APPOINTMENT FOR GENESIS INSTALLATION**
Writer's name: **Kermit L. Dahms**
Reference: **your initials**

words

opening lines 16

Miss Blanco of Dolphin Vocational High School called to con- 28
firm the appointment for you to install the six Genesis GS 39
computers and two printers in her word processing lab. 52
The appointment is at 3 p.m. on Friday, November 18. 64

Be sure to take the three <u>User's Manuals</u> for the basic 78
software programs we are providing. Miss Blanco wants 90
three of her teachers to have a brief hands-on demonstration 101
of the basic operating procedures. 108

closing lines 111

K EYBOARDING WORKSHOP

RESPONSE PATTERNS

1. Key each line of a group 3 times:
   a. To improve technique
   b. To improve speed
   c. To improve control of finger motions.
2. Take 1' writings on the lines your teacher selects.
3. Record your speed scores; watch your skill grow.

Balanced-hand words (Use word response.)

words

1 of is it he to by or us an so if do am go me the six and but
2 a box may did pay end man air own due big for they with when
3 make them also then such than form work both city down their
4 end they when wish hand paid name held down sign field world

phrases

5 to me | of us | and may | pay for | big box | the six | but due | own them
6 am to work | is to make | a big city | by the name | to do such work

sentences

7 He may wish to go to the city to hand the work form to them.
8 The city is to pay for the field work both men did for them.

gwam 1' | 1 | 2 | 3 | 4 | 5 | 6 | 7 | 8 | 9 | 10 | 11 | 12 |

One-hand words (Use letter response.)

words

9 a in be on we up as my at no was you are him get few see set
10 far act war tax only were best date case fact area rate free
11 you act few ever only fact card upon after state great water

phrases

12 at no | as my | on you | we are | at best | get set | you were | only date
13 get you in | act on my case | you set a date | get a rate on water

sentences

14 Get him my extra tax card only after you set up a case date.
15 As you see, you are free only after you get a case date set.

gwam 1' | 1 | 2 | 3 | 4 | 5 | 6 | 7 | 8 | 9 | 10 | 11 | 12 |

Double-letter words (Speed up double letters.)

words

16 all see too off will been well good miss feel look less call
17 too free soon week room fill keep book bill tell still small
18 off call been less free look need week soon will offer needs

phrases

19 a room | all week | too soon | see less | call off | need all | will see
20 see a need | fill a book | miss a bill | all will see | a good offer

sentences

21 It is too soon to tell if we will need that small book room.
22 They still feel a need to offer a good book to all who call.

gwam 1' | 1 | 2 | 3 | 4 | 5 | 6 | 7 | 8 | 9 | 10 | 11 | 12 |

Balanced-hand, one-hand, and double-letter words

words

23 of we to in or on is be it as by no if at us up an my he was
24 and all war six see you men too are may get off pay him well
25 such will work best then keep were good been only city needs
26 make soon ever wish tell area name bill upon paid tell great

phrases

27 is too great | they will be | box was small | their offer was good
28 if at all | may get all | off the case | to tell him | to keep after

sentences

29 If you wish to get to the rate you set, keep the hand still.
30 All of us do the work well, for only good form will pay off.

gwam 1' | 1 | 2 | 3 | 4 | 5 | 6 | 7 | 8 | 9 | 10 | 11 | 12 |

LESSON 59 BUSINESS LETTERS

59A ◆ CONDITIONING PRACTICE

each line twice

alphabet	1	Jacques has asked to be given one week to reply to this tax quiz form.
figures	2	Raul must study Section 2, pages 75-190, and Section 4, pages 246-380.
fig/sym	3	The new rate on Glenn & Taylor's $2,856 note (due 4/13/97) is 10 1/2%.
speed	4	Jo may sign the usual form by proxy if they make an audit of the firm.

gwam 1' | 1 | 2 | 3 | 4 | 5 | 6 | 7 | 8 | 9 | 10 | 11 | 12 | 13 | 14 |

59B ◆ IMPROVE LETTER FORMATTING SKILL

1. Format and key the letters below in block style with open punctuation.
2. Proofread (and spell check); correct errors before removing documents.

File name: L59B

Letter 1 words

899 Farmers Loop Road 4
Fairbanks, AK 99712-3647 9
November 18, 19-- 12

Attention Customer Service 18
Outergear, Inc. 21
1354 Market Street 25
San Francisco, CA 94103-2746 31

Ladies and Gentlemen 35

On October 30, I ordered from your winter cata- 44
log a Heavyweight Fleece Tee Shirt (#M628). 53
Although the packing slip and the printed plastic 63
bag label clearly state that the shirt is a large, 73
the shirt label shows that the size is medium. 83
Large was the size I ordered. 89

Because I have had a similar experience twice 98
in the past, my confidence in your ability to fill 108
my orders accurately is reduced. To avoid the 118
nuisance and expense of packaging and return- 126
ing the shirt, I will keep it to use as a gift. 136

Will you please caution your packers or the 145
appropriate manufacturers to check sizes and 154
colors more carefully before placing garments 163
in prelabeled bags. I'm certain that the extra 173
care will make your other customers happier, 182
too. 183

Sincerely yours 186

Roland C. Marshall 190

Letter 2 words

November 18, 19-- 4

Mr. Leslie D. Banks 8
George Washington High School 14
2165 E. 2700 South Street 19
Salt Lake City, UT 84109-3720 25

Dear Mr. Banks 28

Your question about the effect of word process- 37
ing equipment on the need for keying accuracy 46
is a good one. 50

Accuracy of documents processed is just as 58
vital now as ever before. The ease with which 68
keying errors can now be corrected, however, 77
has shifted the emphasis from number of input 86
errors made to skill in finding and correcting 95
these errors. 98

A major weakness of those who take employ- 106
ment tests is their inability to detect and correct 117
the errors they make. Therefore, we suggest 126
that employee training should emphasize proof- 135
reading and error correction rather than error- 144
free initial input. 148

A grading system rewarding efficient proofread- 158
ing and correction skills instead of penalizing 167
errors of initial input is worthy of your serious 177
consideration. (words in body: 152) 180

Sincerely yours 184

Ms. Audrey M. Lindsay 188
Employment Office Manager 193

xx 194/**214**

MODULE 2

Master Alphanumeric Keyboarding Technique

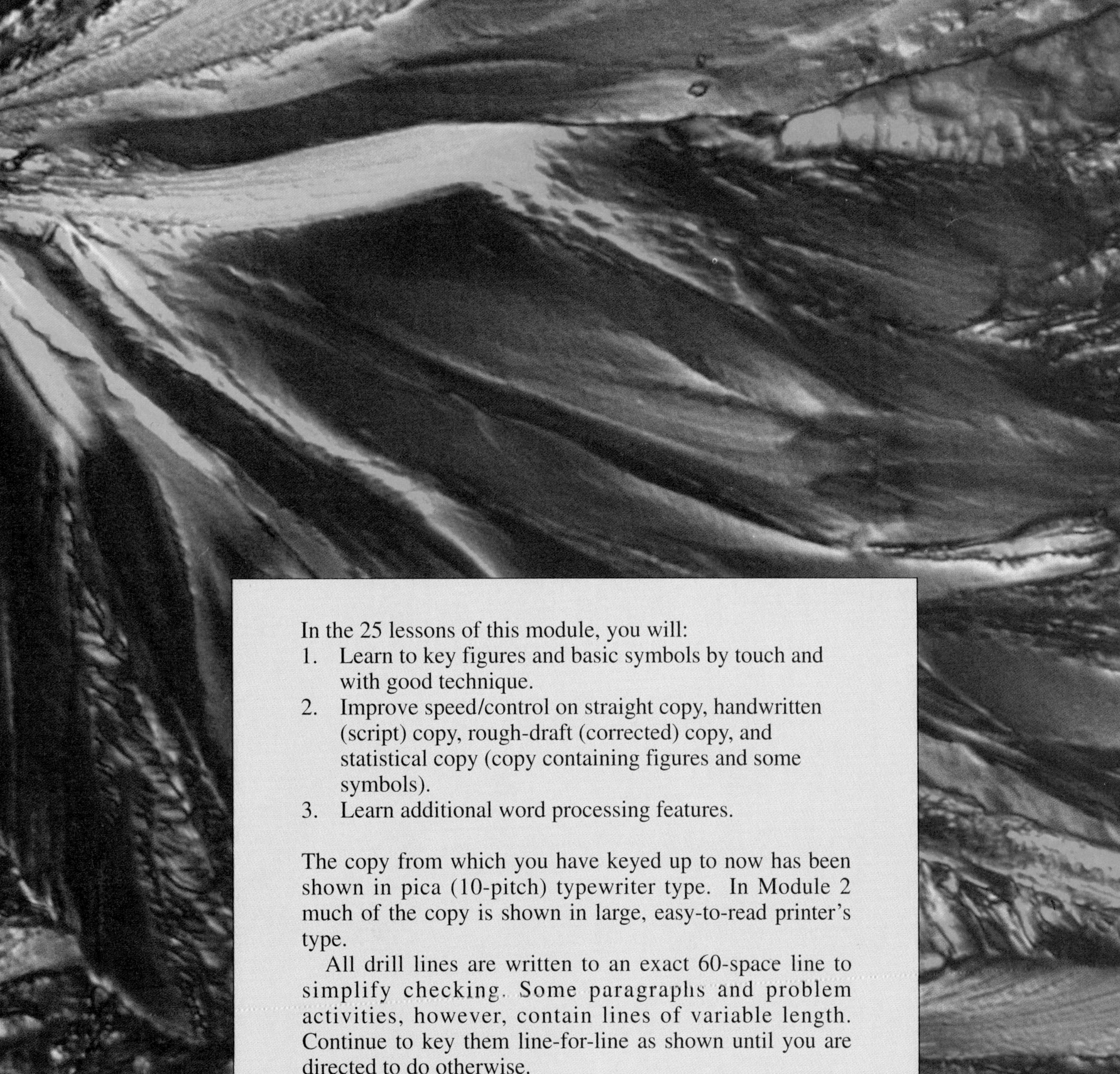

In the 25 lessons of this module, you will:

1. Learn to key figures and basic symbols by touch and with good technique.
2. Improve speed/control on straight copy, handwritten (script) copy, rough-draft (corrected) copy, and statistical copy (copy containing figures and some symbols).
3. Learn additional word processing features.

The copy from which you have keyed up to now has been shown in pica (10-pitch) typewriter type. In Module 2 much of the copy is shown in large, easy-to-read printer's type.

All drill lines are written to an exact 60-space line to simplify checking. Some paragraphs and problem activities, however, contain lines of variable length. Continue to key them line-for-line as shown until you are directed to do otherwise.

58B ◆

BUSINESS LETTERS

File name: L58B

Proofread and correct errors before removing documents.

Letter 1

Format and key the letter at the right. Review Drill 2, p. 105 for placement of attention and subject lines if necessary.

words

November 14, 19-- | Attention Sales Manager | Business Management 12
Systems | 748 S. Market Street | Tacoma, WA 98402-1365 | Ladies and 25
Gentlemen | IMPROVE SALES BY 10 PERCENT 33

If you could close 10 percent more sales a year, would you spend a day of 48
your time to learn how? If so, we want to welcome you to 59

SUCCESS BY VISUAL PERSUASION 65

This special seminar is designed for high-level managers like you who want 80
quick, easy ways to prepare visual presentations that are a cut above the 95
chalkboard and flipchart. Using a lecture/electronic technique, a seminar 110
leader will show you how to use built-in outlining, drawing, and charting tools. 127
You will even learn how to get full-color effects in overheads and slides. 142

To improve your sales by 10 percent a year, read the enclosed brochure 156
about the seminar; then complete and return the registration card. You will 171
be glad you did. (143) 175

Sincerely yours | Robert L. Marsh, Director | xx | Enclosure 186

Letter 2

1. Format and key the letter at the right.
2. Use the U.S. Postal Service address style as shown. (See 56E, p. 107.)

Letter 3

Make the following changes to Letter 2:

Date: **November 17, 19--**

Address (in the style shown):
Mr. Edwin C. Phipps
Elmwood Vocational School
1262 Asylum Avenue
Hartford, CT 06105-2828

Salutation: supply one

Subject: **WORLD CHAMPIONS**

Copy notation: **c Ms. Eloise M. Rozic**

words

November 16, 19-- 4

MISS JANELLE A QUIN 8
CENTRAL HIGH SCHOOL 12
1000 LINCOLN AVENUE 16
EVANSVILLE IN 47714-2330 21

Dear Miss Quinn 24

Thanks for conveying the intrest of your students inthe 36
keying speeds acheived by those who have won international 48
typewriting contests. 52

Margaret Hama won hte last inter national contest, held 64
in 1941. She keyed for an hour on an electric typewriter 75
at a speed of 149 net words a minute (errors penalized). 87
The next highest speed was attained by Albert Tangore, who 99
won the 1923 contest on a manual typewrite atthe rate of 110
147 words a minute 115

Even though later claims have been made to the title World 126
Champion Typist," the international contests were discon- 137
tinued during World War II and to our knowledge have not 149
been started again. 152

Good luck to you and you students as you seek champion- 163
ship speed. (141) 166

Sincerely Yours 169

Mrs. Allison K. Boyles 173
Educational Director 178

xx (Use your initials.) 178/195

Master Figure-Key Operation

Learning Outcomes: After completing this unit, you will be able to

1. Operate the figure keys (top row) with correct technique by touch.
2. Key copy containing figures as well as words at acceptable speed.
3. Center lines of copy horizontally.

LESSON 26 — 8 AND 1

SM: 1" (or defaults); LS: SS

26A ◆ 6' CONDITIONING PRACTICE

each line twice SS; then a 1' writing on line 3; find *gwam*

alphabet 1 Max was quick to fly a big jet plane over the frozen desert.
spacing 2 Any of them can aim for a top goal and reach it if they try.
easy 3 Nan is to go to the city hall to sign the land forms for us.

gwam 1' | 1 | 2 | 3 | 4 | 5 | 6 | 7 | 8 | 9 | 10 | 11 | 12 |

26B ◆ 18' LEARN 8 AND 1

each line twice SS (slowly, then faster); DS between 4-line groups; practice each line again

8 *Right pointer* finger

1 *Left little* finger

Learn 8

1 k k 8k 8k kk 88 k8k k8k 88k 88k Reach up for 8, 88, and 888.
2 Key the figures 8, 88, and 888. Please open Room 88 or 888.

Learn Figure 1

3 a a 1a 1a aa 11 a1a a1a 11a 11a Reach up for 1, 11, and 111.
4 Add the figures 1, 11, and 111. Has just 1 of 111 finished?

Combine 8 and 1

5 Key 11, 18, 81, and 88. Just 11 of the 18 skiers have left.
6 Reach with the fingers to key 18 and 188 as well as 1 and 8.
7 The stock person counted 11 coats, 18 slacks, and 88 shirts.

57B ◆ (cont.)

Letter 3

File name: SABIN

Typewriter users: Rekey Letter 1 making the changes outlined at the right.

Computer users: Retrieve Letter 1 and use the word processing features you have learned to make the changes outlined at the right.

Send the letter to: Mrs. Ellen Sabin, Chair
Business Education Department
Riverside High School
968 Blakely Drive
Cleveland, OH 44143-1342

Mrs. Sabin ordered eight Genesis GS computers and three printers. The equipment will be delivered on November 25 at four o'clock.

57C ◆
RENAME A FILE

Letter 1 should have been saved under the name of the addressee (Blanco), rather than under the name of the sender (Dahms). Using the rename feature outlined below, save the Dahms letter under BLANCO. The same is true for Letter 2. Save the Thompson letter under BURK.

Rename File. At times, you may want to change the name of an existing file. To rename a file, follow the instructions outlined for your particular software.

WORDPERFECT

1. Depress **F5** (select disk drive if necessary)
2. Strike Return
3. Use arrow keys to highlight file to be renamed
4. Strike **M**(ove/Rename)
5. Key in new file name; strike Return
6. Depress **F7**

WORKS DOS

1. Use **Alt**, **F**
2. Strike **F**(ile Management)
3. Strike **R**(ename); strike Return
4. Use arrow keys to highlight file to be renamed
5. Strike Return
6. Key in new file name (include extension)
7. Strike Return; strike Esc

WORKS MAC

With the file open, select the Save As command in the File Menu. Key new file name and strike Return key. (Document is saved under the new name, leaving the old file intact. If you do not want the document saved under both names, delete the old file.)

LESSON 58 BUSINESS LETTERS

58A ◆
CONDITIONING PRACTICE

each line twice

alphabet 1 Brave jockeys and large quarter horses whiz past farmers in box seats.
figures 2 Your Order No. 648 calls for 103 chairs, 29 typewriters, and 75 desks.
fig/sym 3 She wired them $365 on May 29 for the items ordered on Invoice #40187.
speed 4 Cy may be the right man to blame for the big fight in the penalty box.

gwam 1' | 1 | 2 | 3 | 4 | 5 | 6 | 7 | 8 | 9 | 10 | 11 | 12 | 13 | 14 |

26C ◆ 14'

MASTER TECHNIQUE

1. Each pair of lines (1-6) twice SS (slowly, then faster); DS between 4-line groups.
2. A 1' writing on line 7 and on line 8; find *gwam* on each writing.

Technique goals

- reach *up* without moving the hand forward
- reach *down* without twisting the wrists or moving the elbows in and out

Row emphasis

home/3d
1 she quit | with just | that play | fair goal | will help | they did go
2 Dru said you should try for the goal of top speed this week.

home/1st
3 hand axe | lava gas | can mask | jazz band | lack cash | a small flask
4 Ms. Hamm can call a cab, and Max can flag a small black van.

figures
5 The quiz on the 18th will be on pages 11 to 18 and 81 to 88.
6 Just 11 of the 118 boys got 81 of the 88 quiz answers right.

easy
7 Ty is to pay for the eight pens she laid by the audit forms.
8 Keith is to row with us to the lake to fix six of the signs.

gwam 1' | 1 | 2 | 3 | 4 | 5 | 6 | 7 | 8 | 9 | 10 | 11 | 12 |

26D ◆ 12'

GUIDED WRITING

On each ¶, take a 1' writing to find base rate; then, 1' guided writings.

Quarter-minute checkpoints

gwam	1/4'	1/2'	3/4'	Time
16	4	8	12	16
20	5	10	15	20
24	6	12	18	24
28	7	14	21	28
32	8	16	24	32
36	9	18	27	36
40	10	20	30	40

all letters used | E | 1.2 si | 5.1 awl | 90% hfw |

gwam 2'

How much time does it take you to return at the end of 6
the line? Do you return with a lazy or a quick reach? Try 12
not to stop at the end of the line; instead, return quickly 18
and move down to the next line of copy. 21

How much time does it take you to strike the shift key 27
and the letter to make a capital? Just a bit more practice 33
will help you cut by half the time you are now using. When 39
you cut the time, you increase your speed. 43

gwam 2' | 1 | 2 | 3 | 4 | 5 | 6 |

LESSON 27 9 AND 4

SM: 1" (or defaults); LS: SS

27A ◆ 6'

CONDITIONING PRACTICE

each line twice

alphabet 1 Joby quickly fixed a glass vase and amazed the proud owners.
spacing 2 She told us to add the figures 11, 88, 18, 81, 118, and 881.
easy 3 Ciel may make a bid on the ivory forks they got in the city.

gwam 1' | 1 | 2 | 3 | 4 | 5 | 6 | 7 | 8 | 9 | 10 | 11 | 12 |

27B ◆ 12'

IMPROVE SPEED: GUIDED WRITING

Practice again the 2 ¶s above, using the directions in 26D.

Goal: To improve your speed by 2-4 *gwam.*

LESSON 57 BUSINESS LETTERS

57A ◆ CONDITIONING PRACTICE

each line twice

alphabet	1	Monkeys in the quaint park watched a fat lizard devour six juicy bugs.
figures	2	The telephone number for your 120 N. Lotus Drive location is 378-4569.
fig/sym	3	The rates varied from 15 1/2% to 17 1/4% on loans from $98 to $36,500.
speed	4	Kay may make an authentic map of the ancient city for the title firms.

gwam 1' | 1 | 2 | 3 | 4 | 5 | 6 | 7 | 8 | 9 | 10 | 11 | 12 | 13 | 14 |

57B ◆ BUSINESS LETTERS

1. Format and key the letters below in block style with open punctuation (shown).
2. Proofread (and spell check); correct errors before removing the documents.

Letter 1
File name: DAHMS

words

November 12, 19-- 4

Miss Carmen J. Blanco, Chair 9
Business Education Department 15
Dolphin Vocational High School 22
104 N. Andrews Avenue 26
Fort Lauderdale, FL 33301-2859 32

Dear Miss Blanco 36

Your order for six Genesis GS computers and two printers is being processed. We are pleased to include you in the growing number of users of this quality equipment. 45 54 64 69

We plan to deliver and install these machines at three o'clock on November 18 to avoid disrupting classroom activities. Please let me know if this date and time are convenient for you. 79 88 98 107

Only a few minutes are required to install the equipment, but we want to test two or three programs to be certain that everything is working properly. 116 125 134 137

Please telephone me at the number shown above to confirm or change the appointment. 147 154
(words in body: 121)

Sincerely yours 158

Kermit L. Dahms, Sales Manager 164

xx 164

c DeRon S. Jackson 168

Letter 2
File name: THOMPSON

words

November 12, 19-- 4

Mr. Duane R. Burk, Office Manager 10
Huesman & Schmidt, Inc. 15
662 Woodward Avenue 19
Detroit, MI 48226-1947 24

Dear Mr. Burk 27

Thank you for letting our representative, Miss Tina Chun, discuss with you and your staff our new line of landscaped office modules. 36 46 54

Using in-scale templates, Miss Chun has redesigned the general work area of your word processing center. Her mock-up offers you important features: ideal use of space in individual workstations, stationary panels to create private work areas without a feeling of cloister, and traffic patterns that are least disruptive to others. 63 71 80 89 99 109 118 121

May we show you this portable display and discuss the low cost of improving the productivity and harmony of your office staff. A color photograph of the mock-up is enclosed. Please call me to set a convenient date and time for us to spend about an hour with you. 130 140 149 159 168 174
(words in body: 149)

Sincerely yours 178

Virgil P. Thompson 181
Assistant Sales Manager 186

xx 187

Enclosure 189

27C ◆ 18'

LEARN 9 AND 4

each line twice SS (slowly, then faster); DS between 4-line groups; practice each line again

9 *Right ring* finger

4 *Left pointer* finger

Learn 9

use the letter "l"

1 l l 91 91 ll 99 191 191 991 991 Reach up for 9, 99, and 999.
2 Key the figures 9, 99, and 999. Have only 9 of 99 finished?

Learn 4

3 f f 4f 4f ff 44 f4f f4f 44f 44f Reach up for 4, 44, and 444.
4 Add the figures 4, 44, and 444. Please study pages 4 to 44.

Combine 9 and 4

5 Key 44, 49, 94, and 99. Only 49 of the 94 joggers are here.
6 Reach with the fingers to key 49 and 499 as well as 4 and 9.
7 My goal is to sell 44 pizzas, 99 tacos, and 9 cases of cola.

27D ◆ 5'

MASTER KEYBOARDING TECHNIQUE: FIGURES

1. Key each line twice SS (slowly, then faster); DS between 2-line groups.
2. Key each line again to improve speed.

Figure sentences

use the figure "1"

1 Keep the fingers low as you key 11, 18, 19, 48, 94, and 849.
2 On March 8, 1991, 44 people took the 4 tests for the 8 jobs.
3 He based his May 1 report on pages 449 to 488 of Chapter 19.

27E ◆ 9'

CENTER LINES HORIZONTALLY

Get typewriter ready to center

1. Set LM and paper guide at 0; set RM at 85 (10-pitch) or 102 (12-pitch).
2. Clear all tab stops.
3. Set a tab stop at center point: 42 (10-pitch) or 51 (12-pitch).
4. Study *How to center manually* at the far right.
5. Follow the *Drill procedure.*

Drill procedure*

1. Beginning on line 10, center each line of Drill 1 horizontally (side to side), SS.
2. Space down 4 times and center each line of Drill 2 horizontally, SS.
3. Center Drill 3 in the same manner.

*Even if your equipment allows automatic centering, use the manual procedure to complete Steps 1-3. Then repeat the drills as follows: On a computer, use the center feature (see page 42, 22C). On a typewriter with automatic centering, use that feature.

How to center manually

1. On a typewriter, tabulate to center point; on a computer, space (strike the Space Bar) to center point.
2. From center, backspace *once* for each 2 letters, spaces, figures, or punctuation marks in the line.
3. Do not backspace for an odd or leftover stroke at the end of the line.
4. Begin keying where backspacing ends.

Example:

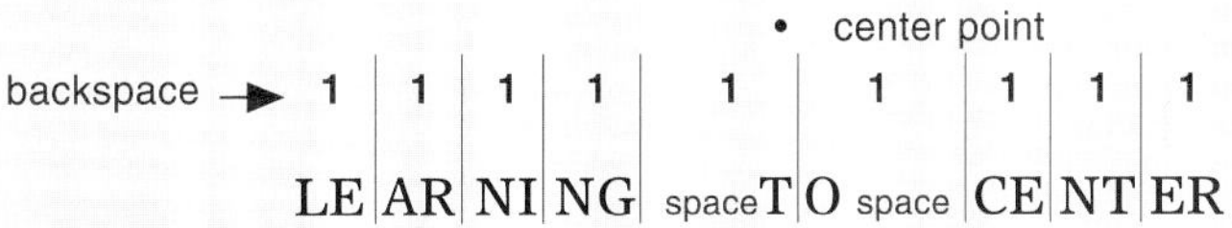

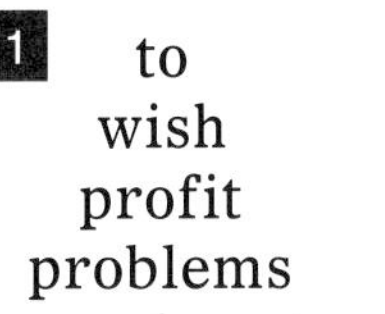

1
to
wish
profit
problems
amendments

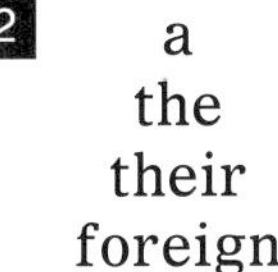

2
a
the
their
foreign
committee

3
I
work
handle
quantity
patient

56D ◆
DELETE A FILE

Delete the following files from your disk:

WIGGINS	GALEN
RYAN	L52C
TUTOR	L53B

Deleting a File. When a file is no longer needed, it should be deleted (removed) from the disk. Doing so frees up disk space and makes it easier to manage the remaining files.

WORDPERFECT

1. Depress **F5**
2. Strike Return (see note below)
3. Use arrow keys to highlight file to be deleted
4. Strike **D**(elete)
5. Strike **Y**(es)
6. Depress **F7** to return to input screen

Note: If the file to be deleted is not on the default drive, you will have to change disk drives after you depress F5.

WORKS DOS

1. Depress **Alt**, **F**
2. Strike **F**(ile Management)
3. Strike **D**(elete File)
4. Strike Return
5. Use arrow keys to highlight file to be deleted
6. Strike Return twice
7. Strike the Esc key

WORKS MAC

1. Select File
2. Select Delete
3. ~ file to be deleted
4. ~ delete
5. ~ OK

56E ◆
LEARN TO ADDRESS ENVELOPES

1. Study the guides at right and the illustrations below.
2. Format a small (No. 6 3/4) and a large (No. 10) envelope for each of the addresses. Use your own return address on the small envelopes.

MISS AMEKI IGAWA
C/O THE DESERT MANOR
102 FREMONT STREET
LAS VEGAS NV 89101-2277

MR HUANG KUO FU MANAGER
DELGADO & HUANG INC
758 N FIGUEROA STREET
LOS ANGELES CA 90012-3650

Envelope address

Set a tab 2.5" from the left edge of a small envelope and 4" from the left edge of a large envelope.

Space down about 2" from top edge of the envelope. Begin the address at the tab position.

Style

Use block style, SS. Use ALL CAPS; omit punctuation. Place city name, 2-letter state abbreviation, and ZIP Code + 4 on last address line. One space precedes the ZIP Code + 4.

Return address

Use block style, SS, and caps and lowercase or ALL CAPS. Begin on line 2 from top of envelope, 3 spaces from left edge.

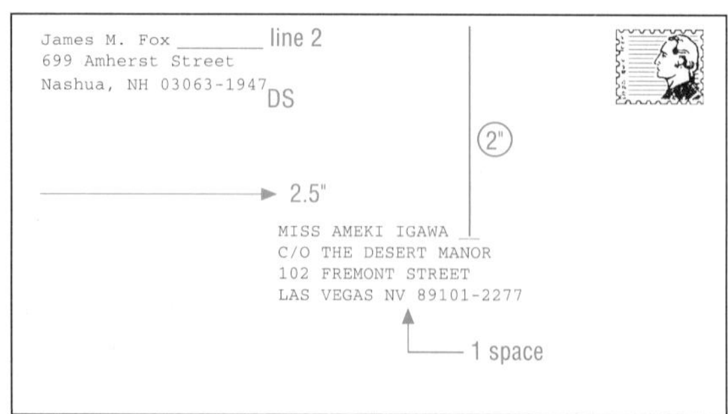

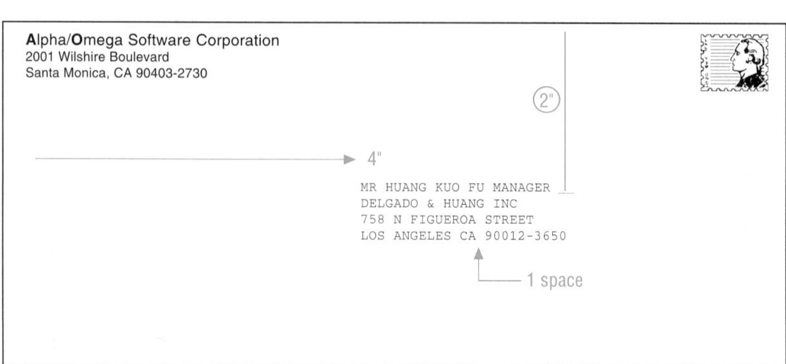

LESSON 28 — 0 AND 5

SM: 1" (or defaults); LS: SS

28A ◆ 6' CONDITIONING PRACTICE

each line twice

alphabet 1 Roz may put a vivid sign next to the low aqua boat for Jack.
figures 2 Please review Figure 8 on page 94 and Figure 14 on page 189.
easy 3 Tien may fix the bus panel for the city if the pay is right.

gwam 1' | 1 | 2 | 3 | 4 | 5 | 6 | 7 | 8 | 9 | 10 | 11 | 12 |

28B ◆ 18' LEARN 0 AND 5

each line twice SS (slowly, then faster); DS between 4-line groups; practice each line again

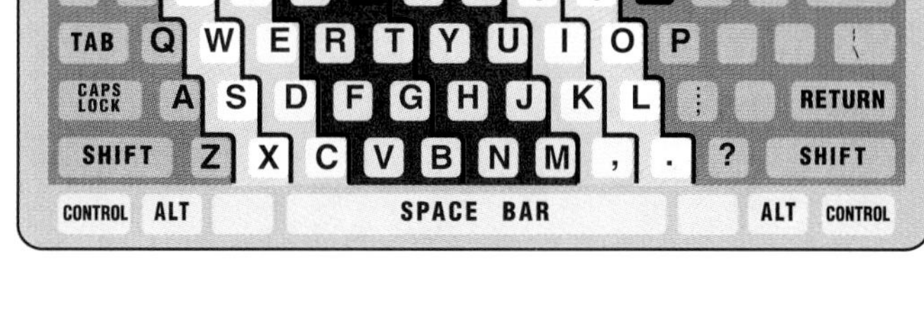

0 *Right little* finger

5 *Left pointer* finger

Learn 0 (zero)

1 ; ; 0; 0; ;; 00 ;0; ;0; 00; 00; Reach up for 0, 00, and 000.
2 Snap the finger off the 0. I used 0, 00, and 000 sandpaper.

Learn 5

3 f f 5f 5f ff 55 f5f f5f 55f 55f Reach up for 5, 55, and 555.
4 Reach up to 5 and back to f. Did he say to order 55 or 555?

Combine 0 and 5

5 Reach with the fingers to key 50 and 500 as well as 5 and 0.
6 We asked for prices on these models: 50, 55, 500, and 5500.
7 On May 5, I got 5 boxes each of 0 and 00 steel wool for her.

28C ◆ 12' TECHNIQUE: FIGURES

each line twice SS; DS between 2-line groups

Spacing note:
No space is left before or after : when used with figures to express time.

Capitalization note:
Most nouns before numbers are capitalized; exceptions include *page* and *line*.

No space

1 Flight 1049 is on time; it should be at Gate 48 at 5:50 p.m.
2 The club meeting on April 5 will be in Room 549 at 8:10 a.m.
3 Of our 185 workers in 1990, 14 had gone to new jobs by 1991.
4 I used Chapter 19, pages 449 to 458, for my March 10 report.
5 Can you meet us at 1954 Maple Avenue at 8:05 a.m. August 10?
6 Of the 59 studcnts, 18 kcycd at least 40 w.a.m. by April 18.

MERKEL-EVANS, Inc.

1321 Commerce Street • Dallas, TX 75202-1648 • Tel. (214) 871-4400

		words in parts	total words
Date	November 10, 19-- QS 2" TM (Line 13)	4	4
Letter address	Mrs. Evelyn M. McNeil	8	8
	4582 Campus Drive	12	12
	Fort Worth, TX 76119-1835 DS	17	17
Salutation	Dear Mrs. McNeil DS	20	20
Body	The new holiday season is just around the corner, and we invite	13	33
	you to beat the rush and visit our exciting Gallery of Gifts.	26	45
	Gift-giving can be a snap this year because of our vast array of	38	58
	gifts "for kids from one to ninety-two." DS	47	67
	What's more, many of our gifts are prewrapped for presentation.	64	80
1" LM	All can be packaged and shipped right here at the store. DS 1" RM	71	91
	A catalog of our hottest gift items and a schedule of holiday	84	104
	hours for special charge-card customers are enclosed. Please	96	117
	stop in and let us help you select that special gift, or call us	109	129
	if you wish to shop by phone. DS	115	135
	We wish you happy holidays and hope to see you soon. DS	126	146
Complimentary close	Cordially yours QS	3	149
	Carol J. Suess		
Writer's name and title	Ms. Carol J. Suess, Manager DS	9	155
Reference initials	rj DS	9	155
Enclosure notation	Enclosures	11	157

WordPerfect Users

To turn on the automatic hyphenation feature, do the following:

- Shift F8
- Line
- Hyphenation
- Yes
- Return
- Return

28D ◆ 14'

RESPONSE PATTERNS

1. Each pair of lines twice SS (slowly, then faster); DS between 4-line groups.
2. A 1' writing on line 2 and on line 4; find *gwam* on each writing.
3. Rekey the slower line.

letter response
1 face pump ever milk area jump vast only save upon safe union
2 As we were in a junk, we saw a rare loon feast on a crawdad.

word response
3 quay hand also body lend hang mane down envy risk corn whale
4 Tisha is to go to the lake with us if she is to do the work.

combination response
5 with only | they join | half safe | born free | firm look | goal rates
6 I sat on the airy lanai with my gaze on the sea to the east.

gwam 1' | 1 | 2 | 3 | 4 | 5 | 6 | 7 | 8 | 9 | 10 | 11 | 12 |

LESSON 29 — 7 AND 3

SM: 1" (or defaults); LS: SS

29A ◆ 6'

CONDITIONING PRACTICE

each line twice

alphabet 1 Gavin made a quick fall trip by jet to Zurich six weeks ago.
figures 2 Key 1 and 4 and 5 and 8 and 9 and 0 and 190 and 504 and 958.
easy 3 The man is to fix the big sign by the field for a city firm.

gwam 1' | 1 | 2 | 3 | 4 | 5 | 6 | 7 | 8 | 9 | 10 | 11 | 12 |

29B ◆ 18'

LEARN 7 AND 3

each line twice SS (slowly, then faster); DS between 4-line groups; practice each line again

7 *Right pointer* finger

3 *Left middle* finger

Learn 7

1 j j 7j 7j jj 77 j7j j7j 77j 77j Reach up for 7, 77, and 777.
2 Key the figures 7, 77, and 777. She checked Rooms 7 and 77.

Learn 3

3 d d 3d 3d dd 33 d3d d3d 33d 33d Reach up for 3, 33, and 333.
4 Add the figures 3, 33, and 333. Read pages 3 to 33 tonight.

Combine 7 and 3

5 Key 33, 37, 73, and 77. Just 37 of the 77 skiers have come.
6 Please order 7 Model 337 computers and 3 Model 737 printers.
7 On August 7, the 33 bikers left on a long trip of 377 miles.

LESSON 56 BUSINESS LETTERS/ADDRESSING ENVELOPES

56A ◆ CONDITIONING PRACTICE

each line twice

alphabet 1 Barth was given a big prize for completing six quick high jumps today.

figures 2 The inventory includes 96 pamphlets, 1,827 books, and 3,450 magazines.

fig/sym 3 The #329 item is sold by Janoch & Co. for $875.46 (less 10% for cash).

speed 4 The key to proficiency is to name the right goals, then work for them.

gwam 1' | 1 | 2 | 3 | 4 | 5 | 6 | 7 | 8 | 9 | 10 | 11 | 12 | 13 | 14 |

56B ◆ FORMAT LETTER PARTS

Drill 1

1. Begin return address on line 13 (2" top margin).
2. After keying the salutation, space down 14 lines to begin closing lines.

Drill 2

1. Study the business letter formatting guides on p. 94; check each placement point with the model letter on p. 106 and with the copy in Drill 2 at right.
2. Key the drill, inserting hard returns as shown.

Drill 1: Personal-Business Letter

3204 Mount Holly Road
Charlotte, NC 28216-3746
November 10, 19-- (Return 4 times)

Mrs. Juanita L. Ruiz
1859 Boston Road
Springfield, MA 01129-3467 DS

Dear Mrs. Ruiz DS

Space down 14 times (hard returns)

Cordially yours (Return 4 times)

Ms. Gloria C. Ainsley DS

Enclosure

Drill 2: Business Letter

November 10, 19-- (Return 4 times)

Attention Mr. Kevin J. Marx
Kendall Computers, Inc.
733 Marquette Avenue
Minneapolis, MN 55402-1736 DS

Ladies and Gentlemen DS

WORD PROCESSING EQUIPMENT ORDER DS

Space down 14 times (hard returns)

Sincerely yours (Return 4 times)

Evan L. Ritchey, Director
Word Processing Center DS

tbh DS

Enclosure DS

c Miss Mary E. Durbin

56C ◆ FORMAT BUSINESS LETTERS

File name: L56C

1. Format and key the letter shown on p. 106.
2. Proofread and correct errors before removing the document.
3. If time permits, take a 2' writing on the opening lines (date through subject line); then a 1' writing on the closing lines (complimentary close to the end).

29C ◆ 12'

TECHNIQUE: FIGURES

each line twice SS (slowly, then faster); DS between 2-line groups; practice each line again

3/7 1 Flights 337 and 377 will be replaced by Flights 733 and 737.
5/0 2 You had 500 books and 505 workbooks but returned 50 of each.

4/9 3 For the answer to Problem 94, see Unit 9, page 494, line 49.
1/8 4 Irv will be 18 on Tuesday, October 18; he weighs 181 pounds.

all figures learned 5 Key these figures as units: 18, 37, 49, 50, 73, 81 and 94.
6 We sold 18 spruce, 37 elms, 49 maples, and 50 choice shrubs.

29D ◆ 14'

CENTER LINES

1. Review *How to center manually* and, if applicable, *Get typewriter ready to center* in 27E, page 52.
2. Beginning on line 26, center each line of Problem 1. DS the lines.
3. Beginning on line 27, center the lines of Problem 2. DS the lines.

1

IMPORTANT TERMS

income tax

gross national product

balance of trade

consumer price index

national debt

social security

2

FBLA ANNOUNCES

NEW OFFICERS

Christopher Linden, President

Mary Ann Stokes, Vice President

ElVon Gibbs, Secretary

Carla Johnson, Treasurer

LESSON 30 6 AND 2

SM: 1" (or defaults); LS: SS

30A ◆ 6'

CONDITIONING PRACTICE

each line twice

alphabet 1 Jared helped Mazy quickly fix the big wood stove in the den.
figures 2 Bella lives at 1847 Oak Street; Jessi, at 5039 Duard Circle.
easy 3 They may make their goals if they work with the usual vigor.

gwam 1' | 1 | 2 | 3 | 4 | 5 | 6 | 7 | 8 | 9 | 10 | 11 | 12 |

30B ◆ 14'

CHECK TECHNIQUE

1. Key each of lines 1-10 twice SS as your teacher checks your keyboarding technique; DS between 4-line groups.
2. Take a 1' writing on line 11 and on line 12; find *gwam* on each writing.

finger reaches to top row 1 if 85 | am 17 | or 94 | me 737 | dot 395 | lap 910 | kept 8305 | corn 3947
2 In 1987, we had 305 workers; in 1991, we had a total of 403.

quiet hands and arms 3 Celia doubts if she can exceed her past record by very much.
4 Brian excels at softball, but many say he is best at soccer.

quick-snap keystrokes 5 Ella may go to the soap firm for title to all the lake land.
6 Did the bugle corps toot with the usual vigor for the queen?

down-and-in spacing 7 Coy is in the city to buy an oak chair he wants for his den.
8 Jan may go to town by bus to sign a work form for a new job.

out-and-down shifting 9 Robb and Ty are in Madrid to spend a week with Jae and Aldo.
10 Are you going in May or in June? Ellena is leaving in July.

easy sentences 11 Rick paid for both the visual aid and the sign for the firm.
12 Glena kept all the work forms on the shelf by the big chair.

gwam 1' | 1 | 2 | 3 | 4 | 5 | 6 | 7 | 8 | 9 | 10 | 11 | 12 |

55B ◆

SIMPLIFIED MEMORANDUMS

File name: L55B

1. Review the formatting guides for simplified memos on p. 94 and the model memo on p. 102.
2. Format and key the three memos at the right.
3. When no date is given, use the **current date**.
4. For Memo 3, use **Keyboarding Students** as the addressee.
5. Proofread and correct errors before removing from the machine.
6. Computer users should spell check the document and insert a page break between memos.

Memo 1 — words

November 4, 19-- 3

Accounting Department 8

SELECTION OF NEW ACCOUNTING DEPARTMENT MANAGER 17

As most of you have heard by now, last week Marsha Mobley announced her 32
intent to retire at the end of this year. In keeping with company policy, 47
President Norwood prefers to have the position filled by a current employee. 62

If you are interested in applying for the position, submit an updated resume 78
and letter of application to the personnel office before November 21. It is 93
our intent to have the position filled by December 1 so that the new man- 108
ager will have the opportunity of working with Ms. Mobley for a month be- 122
fore she retires. 126

Sophia Ramirez, Personnel 131

xx 132

Memo 2 — words

Adrian S. Comstock | OFFICE TECHNOLOGY SYMPOSIUM 12

Information on the "Fifth Annual Office Technology Symposium" is enclosed. 28
I attended last year's symposium and found it very beneficial. Since we 42
have been allocated money for upgrading the word processing department, I 57
plan to attend again this year. 64

There is enough money in the budget to pay the expenses for two people to 78
attend. Since you will be involved in upgrading the word processing center, 94
you may be interested in attending. If you are, please let me know before 109
the end of the month so I can make the necessary arrangements. 122

Harriet D. Steinman | xx | Enclosure 128/**137**

Memo 3 — words

opening lines 7

Proofreader's Marks

- ∧ = insert
- # = add space
- ∾ = transpose
- ℓ = delete
- ⁀ = close up
- ≡ = capitalize

```
AUTOMATICLY CONTROLLED RIGHT MARGINS                          15

Some machines have built in software that control right mar-  28
gin; others, such as computers, depend upona separate software 41
disk too control how the lines end.                           48

However the rihgt margin is controll though, you can override 61
the defaults  to change a line ending.  adding or dividing a  74
wrdd may make the right margin ragged.You must fol low the    87
proceedure in your user's guide to make line ending changes.  99

Liang Chih, Keyboarding Teacher                               106

xx                                                            106
```

30C ◆ 12'
CHECK SPEED

Take 1', 2', and 3' writings, following your teacher's directions.

1' *gwam* goals

- ▽ 21 = acceptable
- ⊡ 25 = average
- ⊙ 29 = good
- ◊ 33 = excellent

all letters used | E | 1.2 si | 5.1 awl | 90% hfw

	gwam 2'	3'
. 2 . 4 . 6 . 8 . 10 .		
Time and motion are major items in building our keying	6	4
12 . 14 . 16 . 18 . 20 ▽ 22 .		
power. As we make each move through space to a letter or a	12	8
24 ⊡ 26 . 28 ⊙ 30 . 32 ◊ 34 .		
figure, we use time. So we want to be sure that every move	18	12
36 . 38 . 40 . 42 . 44 . 46 .		
is quick and direct. We cut time and aid speed in this way.	24	16
. 2 . 4 . 6 . 8 . 10 .		
A good way to reduce motion and thus save time is just	29	19
12 . 14 . 16 . 18 . 20 ▽ 22 .		
to keep the hands in home position as you make the reach to	35	23
24 ⊡ 26 . 28 ⊙ 30 . 32 ◊ 34 .		
a letter or figure. Fix your gaze on the copy; then, reach	41	27
36 . 38 . 40 . 42 . 44 . 46 .		
to each key with a direct, low move at your very best speed.	47	31

gwam 2' | 1 | 2 | 3 | 4 | 5 | 6 |
gwam 3' | 1 | 2 | 3 | 4 |

30D ◆ 18'
LEARN 6 AND 2

each line twice SS (slowly, then faster); DS between 2-line groups; practice each line again

6 *Right pointer* finger

2 *Left ring* finger

Learn 6

1 j j 6j 6j jj 66 j6j j6j 66j 66j Reach up for 6, 66, and 666.
2 Key the figures 6, 66, and 666. Have only 6 of 66 finished?

Learn 2

3 s s 2s 2s ss 22 s2s s2s 22s 22s Reach up for 2, 22, and 222.
4 Add the figures 2, 22, and 222. Review pages 2 to 22 today.

Combine 6, 2, and other figures

5 Key 22, 26, 62, and 66. Just 22 of the 66 scouts were here.
6 Reach with the fingers to key 26 and 262 as well as 2 and 6.

7 Key figures as units: 18, 26, 37, 49, 50, 62, 162, and 268.
8 The proxy dated April 26, 1990, was vital in Case No. 37584.

54B ◆

SIMPLIFIED MEMORANDUMS

File name: L54B
SM: 1"
TM: 2"

1. Study the formatting guides for simplified memos on p. 94 and the model memo illustrating the simplified format on p. 102. Note the vertical and horizontal placement of memo parts.
2. Format and key a copy of the memo on p. 102. Correct your errors as you key. Center **TEENAGE DRUG ABUSE** as shown.
3. Computer users should spell check the document.
4. Proofread the memo before removing it.
5. Process Memos 2 and 3 (below) using the same procedure used to process Memo 1. Computer users should insert a page break between memos and save the memos under L54B.

Memo 2 — words

October 24, 19-- QS 3

All Seniors DS 6

CHOOSING A COLLEGE OR UNIVERSITY DS 12

A voluntary assembly for seniors is planned for 22
3 p.m. next Friday, November 5, in the cafete- 31
ria. The purpose is to give you information and 41
answer your questions about choosing and get- 50
ting into the college or university of your choice 60
upon graduation. DS 64

Each guest speaker will summarize entrance 72
requirements and opportunities at his or her 81
college or university. A question/answer period 91
will follow. You may direct your questions to 101
the person of your choice: Miss Micaela Stokes 110
of Central Community College, Dr. Louise 118
Bolan of Midland State University, or Mr. John 128
Hawkes of Metropolitan College of Business. DS 137

If you plan to attend, sign your name below. QS 146

Melissa Briggs, Senior Class President 154

Memo 3 — words

October 28, 19-- 3

Leon Deitz 6

FOREIGN EXCHANGE STUDY 10

On Thursday, November 15, Mr. Earl Bosma 18
of Rotary International will be here to discuss 28
the foreign study program with prospective 37
exchange students. 41

The meeting will be at 11:15 a.m. in Conference 50
Room A of Tredwell Library. After the general 60
session, Mr. Bosma will visit with each applicant 70
separately. Your appointment is at 2:30 p.m. 79

Please be prompt for these meetings and bring 88
all your application materials with you. 97

Eileen P. Roth, Assistant Principal 104

xx (Use your own initials for reference.) 104

LESSON 55 SIMPLIFIED MEMORANDUMS

55A ◆ CONDITIONING PRACTICE

each line twice

alphabet 1 Jacki saw five prime quail and two big foxes down by the old zoo lake.
figures 2 We had 36 work tables, 247 office chairs, and 85 office desks in 1990.
fig/sym 3 The bookcase (36" x 59" x 14 1/2") is on sale at the Mart for $178.50.
speed 4 The busy visitor may work with usual vigor to form a key social panel.

gwam 1' | 1 | 2 | 3 | 4 | 5 | 6 | 7 | 8 | 9 | 10 | 11 | 12 | 13 | 14 |

KEYBOARDING WORKSHOP

MASTER TECHNIQUE

Extensive practice

For a comprehensive review of many of the keystroking patterns you have learned, key each set of 3 lines once for daily practice.

Intensive practice

Key the first line of each 3-line set once and note the difficulty of the various lines. Note each line that slowed you down or caused hesitation; then key all 3 lines of its set 3 times: first, slowly; faster; then at an in-between rate to gain skill. Take 1' writings on selected lines.

figure reaches

1 4f 8k la 7j 5f 91 2s 6j 3d 0; Key 1, 50, 72, 84, 92, and 63.
2 lines 19 and 20 | pages 387 to 465 | Rooms 9 and 10 | May 29 or 30
3 The sum of 84 and 174 is 258; the sum of 106 and 196 is 302.

adjacent-key reaches

4 he was | ask her | pop art | top post | you were | few weeks | was quick
5 Over twenty people were at the shop before we opened at ten.
6 Opal said that over forty people asked to join the new club.

long-direct reaches

7 a gym | any ice | my deck | my lace | must curb | any doubt | zany dance
8 Myra doubts that many will want to ice dance at my ice rink.
9 Alec must curb any doubts he has about my new zany ice show.

word response

10 pair auto maps fuel sick born laid coal body duty land goals
11 by them | to wish | am paid | if they | it also | she kept | held it for
12 They paid the firm for the land to make a lake for the town.

letter response

13 date limp best hull card upon area join case pool ever kinky
14 in case | my card | no date | oil trade | you state | serve on my case
15 Kip set up a data card on my mill gas pump as you are aware.

combination response

16 also upon auto area hand ever owns data half only dial after
17 to eat | for only | the pump | due date | own data | and join | may test
18 The ink firm may join my panel to fix a toxic waste problem.

alphabet

19 Dezi will quickly bring me guava to have six pints of juice.
20 Jacques was to find her by six to have a big pizza and milk.
21 Zoe quickly made six jugs of punch to serve by the new pool.

gwam 1' | 1 | 2 | 3 | 4 | 5 | 6 | 7 | 8 | 9 | 10 | 11 | 12 |

CHECK/IMPROVE SPEED

Take 1' guided writings on each ¶ and 2' unguided writings on both ¶s.

Quarter-minute checkpoints

gwam	1/4'	1/2'	3/4'	Time
16	4	8	12	16
20	5	10	15	20
24	6	12	18	24
28	7	14	21	28
32	8	16	24	32
36	9	18	27	36
40	10	20	30	40

all letters used | E | 1.2 si | 5.1 awl | 90% hfw

gwam 2'

If you wish to keep moving up in skill, take some time 6
once in a while to analyze just how well you key. By doing 12
this you may find things you do less well than they must be 18
done right now. You can then work to improve those things. 23

To excel, you have to try to refine what you do pretty 29
well and correct what you may now do in a wrong way. It is 35
quite likely that you may try to read too far ahead in your 41
copy. Learn now to read at the same speed you can key. 46

gwam 2' | 1 | 2 | 3 | 4 | 5 | 6 |

LESSON 54 SIMPLIFIED MEMORANDUMS

54A ◆ CONDITIONING PRACTICE

each line twice

alphabet 1 Five excellent joggers pounded quickly along the beach in a warm haze.
figures 2 They replaced at cost 50 plates, 78 knives, 194 forks, and 362 spoons.
fig/sym 3 The Roe & Son check, dated May 17, should be $45.39 instead of $62.80.
speed 4 She may cycle to the city to go to the ancient chapel by the big lake.

gwam 1' | 1 | 2 | 3 | 4 | 5 | 6 | 7 | 8 | 9 | 10 | 11 | 12 | 13 | 14 |

		words in parts	total words
Date	October 29, 19-- QS 2" TM (Line 13)	3	3
1" LM	1" RM		
Addressee	Student Leadership Program Committee DS	11	11
Subject	DALLAS JOHNSON TO ADDRESS ASSEMBLY DS	18	18
Body	Dr. Dallas T. Johnson telephoned to say that he will be pleased	13	31
	to address the special student assembly on March 10 on the topic DS	26	44
	TEENAGE DRUG ABUSE DS	30	47
	Dr. Johnson will use slides to present data on the incidence of	42	60
	drug use among teenagers. He will use a short film to highlight	55	73
	differences in attitudes and behavior before and after drug use.	69	86
	Finally, a young adult who has undergone treatment at the Drug Re-	82	100
	habilitation Center will tell us about her experiences with drugs. DS	95	113
	This assembly should be very interesting, but sobering. QS	106	125
	Juan F. Ramirez		
Writer	Juan F. Ramirez	3	128

Shown in 10-pitch (pica) type with 1" side margins, photo-reduced

Master Symbol-Key Operation

Learning Outcomes: After completing this unit, you will be able to

1. Key copy containing symbols, using proper technique with correct fingers.
2. Key script (handwritten) copy and copy containing figures at a high percentage of your straight-copy speed.

LESSON 31 / AND $

SM: 1" (or defaults); LS: SS

31A ◆ 6' CONDITIONING PRACTICE

each line twice SS; then a 1' writing on line 3; find *gwam*

alphabet 1 Di will buy from me as prizes the six unique diving jackets.
figures 2 The January 17 quiz of 25 points will test pages 389 to 460.
easy 3 Both of us may do the audit of the work of a big title firm.

gwam 1' | 1 | 2 | 3 | 4 | 5 | 6 | 7 | 8 | 9 | 10 | 11 | 12 |

31B ◆ 18' LEARN / AND $

each line twice SS (slowly, then faster); DS between 4-line groups; practice the lines again

Do not space between a figure and the / or the $ sign.

/ *Right little* finger

$ Shift; then *left pointer* finger

Learn / (diagonal)

1 ; ; /; /; ;; // ;/; ;/; 2/3 4/5 and/or We keyed 1/2 and 3/4.
2 Space between a whole number and a fraction: 7 2/3, 18 3/4.

Learn $ (dollar sign)

3 f f $f $f ff $$ f$f f$f $4 $4 for $4 Shift for $ and key $4.
4 A period separates dollars and cents: $4.50, $6.25, $19.50.

Combine / and $

5 I must shift for $ but not for /: Order 10 gal. at $16/gal.
6 Do not space on either side of /: 1/6, 3/10, 9 5/8, 4 7/12.
7 We sent 5 boxes of No. 6 3/4 envelopes at $11/box on June 2.
8 They can get 2 sets of disks at $49.85/set; 10 sets, $39.85.

53B ◆ (cont.)

1. Process Letters 2 and 3 as personal-business letters.
2. Before removing the letters from the typewriter or screen, proofread and correct any errors. Computer users should use the spell check feature after keying the documents and then proofread.

Letter 2 words

5209 W. Grand Avenue 4
Chicago, IL 60639-3372 9
October 23, 19-- 12

Dr. Dallas T. Johnson 17
Drug Rehabilitation Center 22
4056 W. Melrose Street 27
Chicago, IL 60641-2940 32

Dear Dr. Johnson 35

With the approval of the principal of Columbus 44
High School, the Student Leadership Club is 53
sponsoring a series of assembly programs this 62
year dealing with student problems in learn- 71
ing and life. One of these student assemblies 81
will address the serious problem of teenage drug 90
abuse. 92

As chair of the program committee, I would es- 101
pecially like you, or a member of your staff, to 111
talk to us on this timely topic. A presentation 121
similar to the one you made last year on local 130
TV would be ideal. 134

Can you give us 45 minutes of your time on 143
Friday, March 10, at 10:15 a.m. We need your 152
help, and we will appreciate it. If you prefer 162
to call, my telephone number (after 4 p.m.) is 171
555-2048. 173

Sincerely yours 176

Juan F. Ramirez 179

Letter 3 words

11300 Lower Azusa Road 5
El Monte, CA 91732-4725 10
October 24, 19-- 13

Ms. Laura J. Marsh 17
2274 Cogswell Road 21
El Monte, CA 91732-3846 26

Dear Ms. Marsh 29

How fortunate you are to have Dr. Mark C. 37
Gibson as a speaker for the November 18 meet- 46
ing of the El Monte PTA. If he speaks as well 55
as he writes, your meeting will be a success. 65

Because I strongly support the effort El Monte 74
schools are making to assure computer liter- 83
acy for all students, I would like to bring three 93
guests, not two, to the meeting. All three names 103
are listed on the enclosed card. If the limit is 113
two guests per member, please let me know. 122

We need parental support for the computer lit- 131
eracy program to be the success it should be. 140
You are to be commended for arranging this 149
informative program for us. 155

Cordially yours 158

Mrs. Alice M. Wiggins 162

Enclosure 164

31C ◆ 10'

MASTER SKILL

1. Key each set of lines twice: first slowly; then at a faster pace.
2. Take a 1' writing on line 6, then on line 8. Find *gwam* on each; then compare rates.
3. As time permits, key the slower line again.

figures
1 Keep your hands steady as you key 46, 57, 182, 193, and 750.
2 Ask for 16 men to work on Job 5749 at Pier 28 on January 30.

fig/sym
3 Space once between a whole number and a fraction: 8 1/2 oz.
4 I paid $195 for a 4 by 6 rug and $87 for 3 vases on June 20.

word response
5 jay aid oak the may she and but fix both fish also when make
6 Jemal may go to the lake dock with eight of the men to fish.

combination response
7 own was men saw hay are did pen get form were hand jump duty
8 Jane keeps a set of cards in a box on a shelf in the garage.

gwam 1' | 1 | 2 | 3 | 4 | 5 | 6 | 7 | 8 | 9 | 10 | 11 | 12 |

31D ◆ 16'

MASTER TECHNIQUE

1. Beginning on line 10, center each of lines 1-5 using the center feature or manual centering (see 27E, p. 52); DS.
2. QS and key each of lines 6-11 once SS; DS between 2-line groups.
3. Rekey the drill.

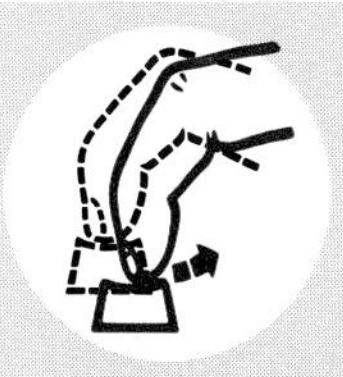

Quick-snap keystroke

center lines
1 WORD PROCESSING TERMS
2 automatic centering
3 delete and insert
4 store and retrieve
5 global search and replace

space bar
6 by us of an am to go by an urn of elm to pay she may and jam
7 Karen is to pay the man for any of the elm you buy from him.

CAPS LOCK
8 They are to see the musical play INTO THE WOODS on Saturday.
9 HBO will show THE KING AND I on Monday, May 13, at 8:30 a.m.

alphabet
10 Sprague is amazed at just how quickly he fixed the blue van.

figures
11 Invoice No. 2749 totals $163.85 plus $4.20 shipping charges.

gwam 1' | 1 | 2 | 3 | 4 | 5 | 6 | 7 | 8 | 9 | 10 | 11 | 12 |

LESSON 32 % AND -

SM: 1" (or defaults); LS: SS

32A ◆ 6'

CONDITIONING PRACTICE

each line twice

alphabet 1 Lopez knew our squad could just slip by the next five games.
figures 2 Check Numbers 267, 298, 304, and 315 were still outstanding.
easy 3 Dixie works with vigor to make the theory work for a profit.

gwam 1' | 1 | 2 | 3 | 4 | 5 | 6 | 7 | 8 | 9 | 10 | 11 | 12 |

32B ◆ 16'

MASTER TECHNIQUE

1. Key lines 1-11 of 31D, above, once each as shown.
2. Take a 1' writing on line 7 and on line 10 of 31D.

Goals:
- to refine technique
- to increase speed

53B ◆

PERSONAL-BUSINESS LETTERS

SM: default or 1"
Save as L53B (file name)

Letter 1

1. Format and key the handwritten copy as a personal-business letter in block style.
2. The return address and date:
   3988 Bancroft Court
   Roswell, GA 30075-9082
   March 15, 19--
3. The letter address:
   Mr. Martin Fehr
   Fehr Computer Products
   829 Silverwood Drive
   Atlanta, GA 30349-4217
4. Use **your name** in the closing lines and supply an **Enclosure** notation.

words

Dear Mr. Fehr 31
¶ Last week when I was in Atlanta, I purchased the 41
"Quality System" software package from your store. When 52
I tried to use the software, I found that there was 62
no user's manual. 66
¶ Please send me the manual as soon as possible so 76
that I will be able to install the software. I've 86
enclosed a copy of the receipt which contains the 96
identification numbers for the software. 104
Sincerely yours 107

Computer users: Review the procedures outlined below for your software for using the spell check. Use the spell check to find any errors you may have missed while keying the document. You will still need to proofread the document; the spell check only checks for the spelling of words, not content. If you keyed *you* instead of *your*, for example, the spell check would not detect the error.

Typewriter users: Proofread your document and correct any errors before removing from the machine.

Spell Check. Spell check is a feature in a word processing program that checks text for misspelled words.

WORDPERFECT

1. **Ctrl F2**
2. Select Option: 1—Word
   2—Page
   3—Document
3. If highlighted word is spelled correctly, either depress 1 Skip once or 2 Skip. If highlighted word is incorrectly spelled, either key the letter preceding the correct word from those offered or depress 4 and *Edit* the spelling of the highlighted word. (To exit in the middle of the spell check program, depress **F1** three times.)

WORKS DOS

1. Move cursor to the location where you want to start spell check.
2. Depress **Alt, O**
3. Strike **S**
4. If highlighted word is spelled correctly, depress **Alt I** or strike Return. If highlighted word is incorrectly spelled, either depress **Alt S** to get suggestions for the correct spelling (↓ to highlight; strike Return) or key the correct spelling of the highlighted word and strike Return. (Replacement word appears beneath Replace with.)
5. Strike Return to exit spell check.

Note: When a word, such as a proper name or technical term, appears several times in a document, depress **Alt G** to instruct spell check to ignore that word each time.

WORKS MAC

1. ~ **Spell** and drag to **Correct Spelling**.
2. If highlighted word is spelled correctly, ~ **Skip**. If highlighted word is incorrectly spelled, either select replacement word from dictionary listing by ~~ on correct spelling *or* key correct spelling of highlighted text and depress Return key. (Replacement text will appear in Replace with box as you key corrected spelling of highlighted word.)

(continued, p. 101)

32C ◆ 18'

LEARN % AND -

each line twice SS (slowly, then faster); DS between 4-line groups; practice the lines again

Do not space between a figure and the %, nor before or after - or -- (dash) used as punctuation.

% Shift; then *left pointer* finger

- *Right little* finger

Learn % (percent sign)

1 f f %f %f ff %% f%f f%f 5% 5% Shift for the % in 5% and 15%.
2 Do not space between a number and %: 5%, 75%, 85%, and 95%.

Learn - (hyphen)

3 ; ; -; -; ;; -- ;-; ;-; 4-ply I use a 2-ply tire on my bike.
4 I gave each film a 1-star, 2-star, 3-star, or 4-star rating.

Combine % and -

5 He can send the parcel by fourth-class mail at a 50% saving.
6 A dash is two unspaced hyphens--no space before or after it.
7 The new prime rate is 12%--but you have no interest in that.
8 You need 60 signatures--51% of the members--on the petition.

32D ◆ 10'

BUILD SKILL TRANSFER

Take 1' writings on each ¶; find and compare *gwam*. Try for a higher *gwam* on additional writings.

To find *gwam*, use the 1' *gwam* for partial lines in ¶s 1 and 2, but *count* the standard words (5 characters/spaces) in a partial line in ¶ 3.

all letters/figures used | LA | 1.4 si | 5.4 awl | 85% hfw |

gwam 1'

You should try now to transfer to other types of copy 11
as much of your straight-copy speed as you can. Handwritten 23
copy and copy in which figures appear tend to slow you down. 35
You can increase speed on these, however, with extra effort. 48

An immediate goal for handwritten copy is at least 90% 11
of the straight-copy rate; for copy with figures, at least 23
75%. Try to speed up balanced-hand figures such as 26, 84, 35
and 163. Key harder ones such as 452 and 890 more slowly. 47

Copy that is written by hand is often not legible, and 11
the spelling of words may be puzzling. So give major atten- 23
tion to unclear words. Question and correct the spacing used 35
with a comma or period. You can do this even as you key. 47

gwam 1' | 1 | 2 | 3 | 4 | 5 | 6 | 7 | 8 | 9 | 10 | 11 | 12 |

52C ◆ PERSONAL-BUSINESS LETTERS

SM: Default or 1"
Save under L52C

Document 1

Format the material at the right as a personal-business letter from **Willis R. Lowenstein**.

Computer users: After you key Document 1, insert a page break and key Document 2.

Document 2

1. Format and key the handwritten copy (below, right) as a personal-business letter in block style.
2. Use **your own return address**; date the letter **October 25** of the **current year**.
3. Address the letter to: **Shutterbug Shops, Inc. 812 Olive Street St. Louis, MO 63101-4460**
4. Use **your name** in the closing lines.

Document 3

Rekey Document 1 with these changes:

1. Use **November 20, 19--** as the date.
2. Address the letter to: **Mr. Charlton Schmidt 5489 Snow Road Cleveland, OH 44122-7117**
3. Bold **Congratulations** at the end of ¶1.
4. Underline serious in ¶2.

words

22149 West chester Road 5
Cleveland, OH 44122-3756 10
November 15, 19-- 13
QS

Mr. Trevor L. DeLong 18
5202 Regency Drive 21
Cleveland, OH 44129-2756 27

Dear Trevor 29

never
A news item inthe Shaker Haeights Gazette says that you are 42
to be graduated from Case Western Reserve at midyear. 53
with honors no less. Congratulations. High, 61
When you were a student at Woodmere I worried that you 73
might not put your potential to work in a serious way. But 86
evidently you have been able to continue your athletic 97
goals and at the same time pursue an academic major suc- 108
cessfully. I am glad you have done credit to us at Wood- 119
mere. We are quiet proud of you. 126

What are your plans after graduation? Whatever they are 138
your former teachers at Woodmere wish you well. I would 149
enjoy a note from you which I would share with the others. 161

Cordiallly yours 165

words

opening lines 25

Ladies and Gentlemen 29

The enclosed copy of my credit card statement shows that you 42
have not yet issued a credit for the Lycon Camera (Catalog 53
#C288) that I returned to you more than three weeks ago. 65
Will you please check to see whether a credit of $137.95 has 77
now been issued; and, if not, see that it is issued promptly. 90
I wish to pay the invoice less the appropriate credit. 101
Sincerely yours / Enclosure 106

LESSON 53 PERSONAL-BUSINESS LETTERS

53A ◆ CONDITIONING PRACTICE

each line twice

alphabet 1 The blitz vexed the famous quarterback whose game plan just went awry.
figures 2 Today we keyed 40 letters, 15 reports, 369 orders, and 278 statements.
fig/sym 3 Make finger reaches (hands quiet) to key 303#, 126.95%, and $1,475.98.
speed 4 He may hand me the clay and then go to the shelf for the die and form.

gwam 1' | 1 | 2 | 3 | 4 | 5 | 6 | 7 | 8 | 9 | 10 | 11 | 12 | 13 | 14 |

LESSON 33 # AND &

SM: 1" (or defaults); LS: SS

33A ◆ 6' CONDITIONING PRACTICE

each line twice

alphabet 1 Racquel just put back five azure gems next to my gold watch.
figures 2 Joel used a comma in 1,203 and 2,946 but not in 583 and 750.
easy 3 The auto firm owns the big signs by the downtown civic hall.

gwam 1' | 1 | 2 | 3 | 4 | 5 | 6 | 7 | 8 | 9 | 10 | 11 | 12 |

33B ◆ 10' MASTER ALPHANUMERIC COPY

Key the ¶ once at an easy pace with particular attention to figures and symbols. Take 2' and 3' writings.

	gwam 2'	3'
In one class of 16 students, 100% reached a speed of 28	6	4
words a minute or higher on a 3-minute writing by the middle	12	8
of December. The worst speed was 28, the best 64, the class	18	12
average 39.5. The error range was 0-6 with an average of 3.	24	16
Students could use the backspace/erase key to correct errors	30	20
as they keyed. Over 79% of the students earned an A or a B.	36	24

33C ◆ 18' LEARN # AND &

each set of lines twice SS (slowly, then faster); DS between groups; practice the lines again

= number/pounds
& = ampersand (and)

Do not space between # and a figure; space once before and after & used to join names.

Shift; then *left middle* finger

& Shift; then *right pointer* finger

Learn # (number/pounds)

1 d d #d #d dd ## d#d d#d 3# 3# Shift for # as you enter #33d.
2 Do not space between a number and #: 3# of #633 at $9.35/#.

Learn & (ampersand)

3 j j &j &j jj && j&j j&j 7& 7& Have you written to Poe & Son?
4 Do not space before or after & in initials; i.e., CG&E, B&O.

Combine # and &

5 Shift for # and &. Recall: # stands for number and pounds.
6 Names joined by & require spaces; a # sign alone does, also.
7 Letters joined by & are keyed solid: List Stock #3 as C&NW.
8 I bought 20# of #830 grass seed from Locke & Uhl on March 4.

52B ♦

REVIEW WORD PROCESSING FEATURES

SM: Default or 1"

Document Retrieval. After a file has been saved, the document can be displayed again. Once a file is retrieved, any of the word processing features learned may be used to change the document. The edited document may be saved under the same file name or a different one.

WORDPERFECT

1. **Shift F10**
2. Key name of document to be retrieved: WIGGINS
3. Return

Alternate Retrieval Method

1. **F5**, Return (If the correct drive is not displayed, key the letter of the desired drive, followed by a colon [C:] and strike the Return key.)
2. Use cursor keys to highlight file name (WIGGINS)
3. Depress **1** or **R**(etrieve)

WORKS DOS

1. **Alt, F**
2. Open Existing File
3. File to open: WIGGINS

You can key in the file name or you can use the up and down arrow keys to scroll the Files List. When using the Files List, depress the return key once you have the desired file name highlighted.

Note: If you are using a computer with a hard disk drive, you may have to change disk drives by depressing **Alt I** and using the up and down arrow keys to highlight desired drive. Depress the Return key to select highlighted drive.

WORKS MAC

1. ⌘ **O**
2. ~~ on the file you want to retrieve (WIGGINS).

If you don't see the file you want to retrieve in the file listings, use up and down arrow keys to move to the file name. File names are listed alphabetically. Once you have the desired file name highlighted, ~~ on it to retrieve file.

Note: If you are using a computer with a hard disk, you may have to click on Drive to change disk drives.

Typewriter users: Rekey the letter on p. 96 to Wiggins with the changes shown.

Computer users: Retrieve the letter to Wiggins that you keyed in Lesson 51, p. 96, and make the changes outlined to the right. WordPerfect users should save the letter under the file name GALEN. When you save the document under GALEN, you will have two files. The WIGGINS file will remain as it was before you made the changes; the GALEN file will be the document with the changes made.

Works DOS and Works MAC users should use **Save as** command when resaving the document. If the **Save** command is used, the letter to Wiggins will be replaced by the letter to Galen.

Change the letter address to:

Mr. Jon Galen
Silverbay Avenue
El Monte, CA 91732-6782

Paragraph 1:

bold **El Monte PTA**
change *Computer Literacy* to **Teenage Drug Abuse**
change *November 18* to **January 25**
underline 7 p.m.

Paragraph 2:

change *Dr. Mark C. Gibson* to **Dr. Rebecca Linton**
change *he* to **she**
change *Personal Computer* to **Teen Talk**
change *His* to **Her**

Paragraph 3:

change *Dr. Gibson* to **Dr. Linton**
underline two parents
change *November 1* to **January 3**

Page Break. Your software program will automatically insert a page break when the amount of text exceeds a page. You can manually insert a page break to force the software to start a new page. For example, if you were going to key two letters and save them in the same file—as you will do in 52C—a page break would be used to separate the two letters in the file.

WORDPERFECT

Ctrl Return

WORKS DOS

Ctrl Return

WORKS MAC

~ **Format**; drag to **Insert Page Break**

33D ◆ 16'

BUILD SKILL TRANSFER

Take 1' writings on each ¶ and compare *gwam* on straight copy and statistical copy.

Goal: To transfer at least 75% of your straight-copy speed to statistical copy.

To determine % of transfer:
¶2 *gwam* ÷ ¶1 *gwam*

all letters/figures used | LA | 1.4 si | 5.4 awl | 85% hfw

Figures appear often in personal and business documents. It is vital, therefore, that you learn to key them rapidly. If you will just keep your hands in position and reach with your fingers, you will soon be amazed at your ability to key all figures with ease.

Learn to read and key figures in distinct groups. For example, read 165 as one sixty-five and key it that way. Tackle the longer sequences in like manner. Read 1078 as ten seventy-eight and handle it as 2 units. Try this trick for 2493, also.

LESSON 34 (AND)

34A ◆ 6'

CONDITIONING PRACTICE

each line twice

SM: 1" (or defaults); LS: SS

alphabet 1 **Jacques could win a prize for eight more dives by next week.**
figures 2 **In 1987, Sam had only 150 computers; as of 1993, he had 264.**
easy 3 **The girls paid for the eight antique urns with their profit.**

gwam 1' | 1 | 2 | 3 | 4 | 5 | 6 | 7 | 8 | 9 | 10 | 11 | 12 |

34B ◆ 12'

CHECK SKILL

Take 2' and 3' writings on both ¶s; find *gwam* and circle and count errors. Take another 3' writing:

0-6 errors—speed
7+ errors—control

gwam	1/4'	1/2'	3/4'	Time
20	5	10	15	20
24	6	12	18	24
28	7	14	21	28
32	8	16	24	32
36	9	18	27	36
40	10	20	30	40
44	11	22	33	44
48	12	24	36	48

all letters used | LA | 1.4 si | 5.4 awl | 85% hfw

	gwam 2'	3'
When you need to adjust to a new situation in which new	6	4
people are involved, be quick to recognize that at first it	12	8
is you who must adapt. This is especially true in an office	18	12
where the roles of workers have already been established. It	24	16
is your job to fit into the team structure with harmony.	30	20
Learn the rules of the game and who the key players are;	6	23
then play according to those rules at first. Do not expect	12	27
to have the rules modified to fit your concept of what the	18	31
team structure and your role in it should be. Only after you	24	36
become a valuable member should you suggest major changes.	30	39

gwam 2' | 1 | 2 | 3 | 4 | 5 | 6 |
gwam 3' | 1 | 2 | 3 | 4 |

51C ◆

PERSONAL-BUSINESS LETTERS

SM: Default or 1"

1. Study the formatting guides for letters on p. 94 and the model personal-business letter illustrating block format on p. 96. Note the vertical and horizontal placement of letter parts and the spacing between them.
2. Format and key a copy of the letter on p. 96. Correct your errors as you key. Typewriter users, proofread document and remove from machine. Computer users, proofread document on screen and use the view feature to check the format of the letter before saving the letter under the file name WIGGINS.
3. Format and key Letters 2 and 3 shown below. Computer users save Letter 2 under RYAN and Letter 3 under TUTOR.

Note: Typewriter users listen for bell to determine line endings; computer users use automatic word wrap feature.

Letter 2 — words

5802 Lehman Drive 4
Colorado Springs, CO 80918-1123 10
October 20, 19-- 14
QS
Ms. Lorna K. Ryan, Director 19
Placement Services, Inc. 24
350 E. Colfax Avenue 28
Denver, CO 80203-6285 33
DS
Dear Ms. Ryan 36
DS
Today's <u>Times Star</u> quotes you as saying in a 47
recent talk that "more workers fail as a result 56
of personal traits than because of weak techni- 66
cal skills." 67
DS
I want to quote this statement in a paper I am 78
writing titled "Why Beginning Workers Fail," 87
and I would like to know the research studies to 96
which you referred so that I can include them 106
in my reference list. 111
DS
If you will send me the research references you 120
used to support your statement, I shall be most 130
grateful. I am sure the references will be of 139
great help to me in preparing my paper. 147
DS
Sincerely yours 151
QS
Edward R. Shields 154

Letter 3 — words

2405 Siesta Avenue 4
Las Vegas, NV 89121-2683 9
October 22, 19-- 12

Learning Tutor, Inc. 17
752 S. Bascom Avenue 21
San Jose, CA 95128-3605 26

Ladies and Gentlemen 30

On October 8, I ordered from your fall catalog a 40
copy of MATH TUTOR IX (Catalog #A2937) de- 48
signed for use on the Eureka GS. I have had the 57
diskette a week. 61

I follow the booting instructions step-by-step 70
but am unable to boot the program on my 78
Eureka GS. I took the diskette to the store 87
where I bought my computer, but the manager 96
could not boot the program on the same model 105
computer. 106

Will you please check the booting instructions 117
in the User's Guide to see if they are correct. 127
If they are, please send a replacement diskette 136
and I will return the faulty one to you. 145

Sincerely yours 148

Miss Ellen M. Marcos 152

LESSON 52 PERSONAL-BUSINESS LETTERS

52A ◆

CONDITIONING PRACTICE

each line twice

alphabet 1 Jan was very quick to fix many broken zippers for the bright children.
figures 2 The shipment included 162 sofas, 179 lamps, 104 desks, and 385 chairs.
fig/sym 3 Order the roll-top desks (57" x 26" x 48") from Hermann's for $391.50.
speed 4 Rick may wish to go downtown by bus to pay a visit to a busy rug firm.

gwam 1' | 1 | 2 | 3 | 4 | 5 | 6 | 7 | 8 | 9 | 10 | 11 | 12 | 13 | 14 |

34C ◆ 18'

LEARN (AND)

each set of lines twice SS (slowly, then faster); DS between groups; practice the lines again

Do not space between ( ) and the copy they enclose.

(Shift; then *right ring* finger

) Shift; then *right little* finger

Learn ((left parenthesis)

use the letter "l"

1 l l (l (l ll ((l(l l(l 9(9(Shift for the (as you key (9.
2 As (is the shift of 9, use the l finger to key 9, (, or (9.

Learn) (right parenthesis)

3 ; ;);); ;;)) ;); ;); 0) 0) Shift for the) as you key 0).
4 As) is the shift of 0, use the ; finger to key 0,), or 0).

Combine (and)

5 Hints: (1) depress shift; (2) strike key; (3) release both.
6 Tab steps: (1) clear tabs; (2) set stops, and (3) tabulate.
7 Her new account (#495-3078) draws annual interest at 6 1/2%.

34D ◆ 14'

MASTER TECHNIQUE

1. Beginning on line 10, center each of lines 1-5 using the center feature or manual procedure (see 27E, p. 52); DS.
2. QS and key each of lines 6-13 once SS; DS between 2-line groups.
3. Rekey the drill.

center lines

1 Dental Services, Inc.
2 Announces New Dental Center
3 in
4 Eastwood Circle Mall
5 Opening the First of March

letter response

6 upon ever join save only best ploy gave pink edge pump facts
7 You acted on a phony tax case only after a union gave facts.

word response

8 visit risks their world field chair proxy throw right eighty
9 Lana may sign the form to pay for the giant map of the city.

combination response

10 also fast sign card maps only hand were pair link paid plump
11 To get to be a pro, react with zest and care as the pros do.

alphabet 12 Shep quickly coaxed eight avid fans away from the jazz band.

fig/sym 13 Of 370 students, only 35 (9.46%) failed to type 18-20 w.a.m.

WordPerfect Users

The default setting for justification is *full* (both left and right margin justified). To change the justification setting to left justified (as in the illustration), do the following:

Shift F8
Line
Justification
Left
Return
Return

		words in parts	total words
Return address	2274 Cogswell Road 2" TM (Line 13)	4	4
	El Monte, CA 91732-3846	9	9
Date	October 15, 19-- Quadruple-space (QS): strike return key 4 times	12	12
Letter address	Mrs. Alice M. Wiggins	17	17
	11300 Lower Azusa Road	21	21
	El Monte, CA 91732-4725 Double-space (DS): strike return key twice	26	26
Salutation	Dear Mrs. Wiggins DS	30	30
Body	The El Monte PTA is devoting its next meeting to the important	13	42
	topic "Computer Literacy." The meeting is on November 18 and	25	55
(1" LM)	begins at 7 p.m. DS (1" RM)	29	59
	Our speaker will be Dr. Mark C. Gibson. For the past several	41	71
	years, he has written the "Personal Computer" column in the	53	83
	Los Angeles Post. His talk will combine wisdom and wit. DS	68	98
	To assure Dr. Gibson a large audience, we are asking selected	80	110
	members to bring as guests two parents who are not active mem-	93	123
	bers of our group. Please use the enclosed return card to	105	134
	give me the names of your guests by November 1. DS	114	144
	I shall appreciate your assistance. DS	121	152
Complimentary close	Cordially yours QS	3	155
	Laura J. Marsh		
Writer	Ms. Laura J. Marsh DS	7	159
Enclosure notation	Enclosure	9	160

Letter Spacing Summary

Three blank line spaces (a quadruple space) separate date from address and complimentary close from keyed name of writer. A double space separates all other letter parts.

Shown in 10-pitch type (pica) with 1" side margins, photo-reduced

LESSON 35 ’ AND ”

SM: 1" (or defaults); LS: SS

35A ◆ 6' CONDITIONING PRACTICE

each line twice

alphabet 1 Bowman fixed prized clocks that seven judges say are unique.

figures 2 Only 1,470 of the 6,285 members were at the 1993 convention.

easy 3 She lent the field auditor a hand with the work of the firm.

gwam 1' | 1 | 2 | 3 | 4 | 5 | 6 | 7 | 8 | 9 | 10 | 11 | 12 |

35B ◆ 20'

LEARN ’ (APOSTROPHE) AND ” (QUOTATION MARK)

Apostrophe: The ’ is to the right of ; and is controlled by the *right little finger*. (On some keyboards, the ’ is the shift of the 8.*)

Quotation mark: Key ” (the shift of ’) with the *right little finger*. Remember to depress the left shift before striking ”. (On some keyboards, the ” is the shift of the 2.*)

Learning procedure

1. Locate new symbol on appropriate chart above. Read the reach technique given below the chart.
2. Key twice SS the appropriate pair of lines given at right; DS between pairs. *If this statement describes your keyboard, go to *Alternative practice* at the bottom of the page.
3. Repeat Steps 1 and 2 for the other new symbol.
4. Key twice SS lines 5-8.
5. Rekey the lines with which you had difficulty.

Capitalization note: Capitalize the first and all important words in titles of publications.

Learn ’ (apostrophe)

1 ; ; ’; ’; ;; ’’ ;’; ;’; it’s he’s I’m I’ve It’s hers, I see.

2 I’m not sure if it’s Hal’s; but if it’s his, I’ll return it.

Learn ” (quotation mark)

3 ; ; ”; ”; ;; ””” ;”; ;”; “Keep on,” she said, but I had quit.

4 I read “Ode on a Grecian Urn,” “The Last Leaf,” and “Trees.”

Combine ’ and ”

5 “If it’s Jan’s or Al’s,” she said, “I’ll bring it to class.”

6 “Its” is an adjective; “it’s” is the contraction of “it is.”

7 Miss Uhl said, “To make numbers plural, add ’s: 8’s, 10’s.”

8 O’Shea said, “Use ’ (apostrophe) to shorten phrases: I’ll.”

Alternative practice

On some keyboards, ’ is the shift of 8 and ” is the shift of 2. If these are the locations of ’ and ” on your keyboard, key each set of lines at right twice SS; then key each of lines 5-8 above right twice SS.

apostrophe

1 k k ’k ’k kk ’’ k’k k’k Is this tie Ike’s? No, it’s Dick’s.

2 On Vic’s keyboard the ’ is on 8; on Lei’s, it’s in home row.

quotation mark

3 s s ”s ”s ss ””” s”s s”s 2” 2” “Go for a high goal,” he said.

4 Did Mrs. Negron use “there” for “their” and “two” for “too”?

LESSON 51 PERSONAL-BUSINESS LETTERS

51A ◆ CONDITIONING PRACTICE

each line twice SS; DS between 2-line groups; then three 1' writings on line 4; find *gwam*

alphabet 1 With quick jabs and deft parries, a young boxer amazed several people.

figures 2 Yuki keyed 51 letters, 84 envelopes, 37 tags, 92 labels, and 60 cards.

fig/sym 3 He's given me the numbers and prices: #16392, $48.30; #14593, $75.95.

speed 4 It is their duty to sign the amendment if he is to handle the problem.

gwam 1' | 1 | 2 | 3 | 4 | 5 | 6 | 7 | 8 | 9 | 10 | 11 | 12 | 13 | 14 |

51B ◆ (optional) WORD PROCESSING FEATURES

1. Study the specific commands for the software you are using.
2. Use the view feature to look at the full-page layout of the conditioning practice that you keyed for 51A.

Document View/Print Preview. The view/preview feature allows you to see the document format of a page or pages before printing the document.

WORDPERFECT

Shift F7

6—View Document

F7 (to return to input screen)

Options
1—100%
2—200%
3—Full page
4—Facing Pages

Cursor keys can be used to move around the view document screen. Striking the PgDn key allows you to view the next page of the document.

WORKS DOS

Alt, P

PreView

Alt P

Options
Strike PgUp or PgDn for previous or next page.

Depress Esc to return to input screen.

WORKS MAC

⌘P

~ print preview if not on. (When print preview is on, you print from the print preview screen. When it is not on, you print from the print screen.)
~ print.

Options
Cancel—to return to input screen
Previous—to go to previous page
Next—to go to next page
Print—to print document

~ the magnifying glass once to enlarge copy; ~~ to return to print preview screen.

Remove the text (51A) from the screen (clear screen).

Clear Screen. The clear screen feature allows you to remove text from the input screen without saving it.

WORDPERFECT

F7

N(o)

N(o)

WORKS DOS

Alt

F(ile)

C(lose)

N(o)

N(ew)

Ne**(w)** (Return after w for Version 3.0)

WORKS MAC

~ File

~ Close

No

~~ WP

35C ◆ 10'

FIGURES/ SYMBOLS

1. Key lines 1-10 at a slow but steady pace.
2. Key each line again; try to speed up the keying of figures and figure/symbol groups.

Figure review

1 I became 18 last month. I have a brother 8 and a sister 11.
2 Of the 98 test problems, she got 84 right and only 14 wrong.
3 She said to key 19, 48, and 50 quickly but 45 and 89 slowly.
4 On May 30, 58 boys came to camp; by July 19, we had only 47.
5 Of 20 persons, 9 keyed 38 or more; 6, 35 to 37; 5, 31 to 34.

Symbol review

6 Use / to make fractions: 1/2, 1/4; $ for dollars: $5, $10.
7 We offer discounts of 20% and 30% on our 2- and 4-ply tires.
8 Poe & Sons bought #1748 and #2936 L&M siding for Site #5026.
9 The railway sign said to (1) Stop, (2) Look, and (3) Listen.
10 Mr. Ho said: "It's your goal; don't stop 'til you make it."

35D ◆ 14'

MASTER TECHNIQUE

1. Key each pair of lines once as shown: SS with a DS between pairs.
2. Take two 1' writings on line 11 and on line 12; find *gwam* on each writing.
3. Rekey the slower line.

Technique goals

- curved, upright fingers
- quick-snap keystrokes
- quiet hands and arms

shift-key sentences
1 He and Vi crossed the English Channel from Hove to Le Havre.
2 J. W. Posner has left Madrid for Turin for some Alps skiing.

fig/sym sentences
3 I signed a 20-year note--$67,495 (at 13.8%)--with Coe & Han.
4 Order #29105 reads: "16 sets of Cat. #4718A at $36.25/set."

adjacent-key sentences
5 We spent a quiet week at the shore prior to the open season.
6 If we buy her coffee shop, should we buy the gift shop, too?

long-reach sentences
7 My niece has a chance to bring the bronze trophy back to us.
8 Ced once had many mussels but not since the recent harvests.

alphabetic sentences
9 Pam was quickly given the bronze trophy by six fussy judges.
10 Quent got six big jigsaw puzzles from the very dapper clerk.

easy sentences
11 Did he rush the rotor of the giant robot to the island firm?
12 The busy girl works with a fury to fix the signals by eight.

gwam 1' | 1 | 2 | 3 | 4 | 5 | 6 | 7 | 8 | 9 | 10 | 11 | 12 |

LESSON 36 _ AND *

SM: 1" (or defaults); LS: SS

36A ◆ 6'

CONDITIONING PRACTICE

each line twice

alphabet 1 Quig was just amazed by the next five blocks of his players.
figures 2 On October 20, 1993, the 187 members met from 5 to 6:45 p.m.
easy 3 Keith may hang the sign by the antique door of the big hall.

gwam 1' | 1 | 2 | 3 | 4 | 5 | 6 | 7 | 8 | 9 | 10 | 11 | 12 |

36B ◆ 14'

MASTER TECHNIQUE

1. Key lines 1-12 of 35D, above, once SS as shown; DS between pairs.
2. Take two 1' writings on line 11 and one on line 12; find *gwam* on each writing.

Goals:
- to refine technique
- to increase speed

Master Correspondence Format

Learning Outcomes: After completing this unit, you will be able to

1. Format personal-business letters in block style.
2. Format simplified memos in block style.
3. Format business letters in block style.

FORMATTING GUIDES:

Parts of a Letter

The parts of a letter are illustrated in the block format models shown on pp. 96 (personal-business letter) and 106 (business letter). Block format (style) means that all lines of a letter (or memorandum) begin at the left margin (LM). The parts are described below in order of their occurrence.

All parts described are not required for every letter. The subject line, reference initials, enclosure notations, and copy notations are special letter parts that may or may not be part of a letter. Regardless of which special letter parts are used, key them in the order given with a DS above and below.

Return address. The return address consists of a line for the street address and one for the city, state, and ZIP Code. Key the street address (or post office box or route number) on line 13 (2" top margin) from the top edge of the sheet; key the city, state abbreviation, and ZIP Code on line 14. No return address is keyed for business letters since they are keyed on letterhead which includes the company name and address.

Date. Key the date (month, day, and year) a single space (SS) below the last line of the return address. For *business letters* place the date on line 13 (2" top margin). If letterhead is used and is too deep for keying the date on line 13, place the date a DS below the letterhead.

Letter address. Begin the letter address on the fourth line space (QS) below the date.

Salutation. Key the salutation a double space (DS) below the letter address. The models (pp. 96 and 106) are keyed with *open punctuation;* no punctuation follows the salutation.

Subject line. A subject line (optional) identifies the topic of the letter. It is placed a DS below the salutation in ALL CAPS.

Body. Begin the letter body a DS below the salutation or a DS below the subject line when a subject line is used. Block the paragraphs of the body and SS them with a DS between paragraphs.

Complimentary close. Key the complimentary close a DS below the last line of the body. With open punctuation, no punctuation follows the complimentary close.

Name of writer. Key the name of the writer of the message a QS below the complimentary close. The name may be preceded by a personal title such as Miss, Mrs., or Ms. to indicate how a female prefers to be addressed in a response. For business letters, the writer's business title may follow the name on the same line, preceded by a comma, or may be placed on the next line.

Reference initials. If the keyboard operator is not the writer of the message, the operator's initials (lowercase) are keyed a DS below the writer's name or title.

Enclosure notation. An enclosure notation indicates that something other than the letter is included in the envelope. When appropriate, key the word *Enclosure* or *Enclosures* a DS below the reference initials (if used) or a DS below the name of the writer.

Copy notation. If a copy of the letter is to be sent to someone other than the addressee, the letter c, followed by a space and the recipient's name, is placed a DS below the enclosure notation. If two people are to receive copies, both names are placed on the same line with a comma and space between them or aligned vertically.

FORMATTING GUIDES:

Parts of a Simplified Memo

Simplified memorandums are often used as a quick and easy means of written communication. (See model memorandum on p. 102.) The parts of simplified memorandums are described below in order of their occurrence.

Date. Key the date (month, day, and year) on line 13. If letterhead is used and is too deep for keying the date on line 13, place the date a DS below the letterhead.

Name of addressee. Key the name(s) of recipients a QS below the date. No personal title(s) should be used before the name(s), but an official title (such as Principal or President) may follow a name, preceded by a comma.

Subject. The subject line specifies the topic discussed in the memo. Key the subject line in ALL CAPS a DS below the name of the addressee.

Body. Block the paragraphs in the body a DS below the subject line. SS the paragraphs with a DS between them.

Name of writer. Key the name of the writer a QS below the last line of the body. A personal title does not precede the name, but an official title may follow it, preceded by a comma.

Reference initials. If the keyboard operator is not the writer of the message, key the operator's initials (lowercase) a DS below the name of the writer.

Attachment/enclosure notation. If a supporting document is attached to the memo, key the word *Attachment* a DS below the name of the writer (or below the reference initials, if any). If the enclosure is not attached to the memo, use the word *Enclosure* rather than *Attachment.*

36C ◆ 18'

LEARN _ (UNDERLINE) AND * (ASTERISK)

Underline: Key _ (the shift of -) with the *right little finger.* Remember to depress the left shift before striking _.

Asterisk: Key * (the shift of 8) with the *right pointer finger.* Remember to depress the left shift before striking *.

Learning procedure

1. Locate new key on appropriate chart above. Read the reach technique given below the chart.
2. Key twice SS the appropriate pair of lines given at right; DS between pairs.
3. Repeat Steps 1 and 2 for the other new key.
4. Key twice SS lines 5-6.
5. Rekey the lines with which you had difficulty.

Computer: Use the Underline feature (22C, p. 42) to underline words as you key.

Electric typewriter: Key the word; backspace to beginning to underline it.

Electronic typewriter: Depress the automatic underline key before keying the word; strike that key after keying the word.

Learn __ (underline)

1 ; ; _; _; ;; __ ;_; ;_; We are to underline ready and begin.
2 To succeed, you should plan the work and then work the plan.

Learn * (asterisk)

3 k k *k *k kk ** k*k k*k She used * for a single source note.
4 All discounted items show an *, thus: 48K*, 588*, and 618*.

Combine _ and *

5 Use an * to mark often-confused words such as then and than.
6 *Note: Book titles (like Lorna Doone) are often underlined.

36D ◆ 12'

CHECK/IMPROVE SKILL

Take 1', 2', and 3' writings as directed by your teacher.

1' *gwam* goals

- ▽ 25 = acceptable
- ⊡ 29 = average
- ⊙ 33 = good
- ◊ 37 = excellent

all letters used | LA | 1.4 si | 5.4 awl | 85% hfw

	gwam 2'	3'
One reason we learn to key is to be able to apply that	6	4
skill as we format personal and business documents--letters,	12	8
reports, and tables, for example. Your next major goal will	18	12
be to learn the rules that govern how we arrange, place, and	24	16
space the most commonly used documents.	28	18
In one way or another, we must memorize the features	33	22
that distinguish one style of letter or report from another.	39	26
Our ability to retain in our minds the vital details will	45	30
help us place and space documents quickly and avoid having	51	34
to look up such facts as we key letters or reports.	56	37

gwam 2' | 1 | 2 | 3 | 4 | 5 | 6 |
gwam 3' | 1 | 2 | 3 | 4 |

MODULE 3 Master Document Formatting

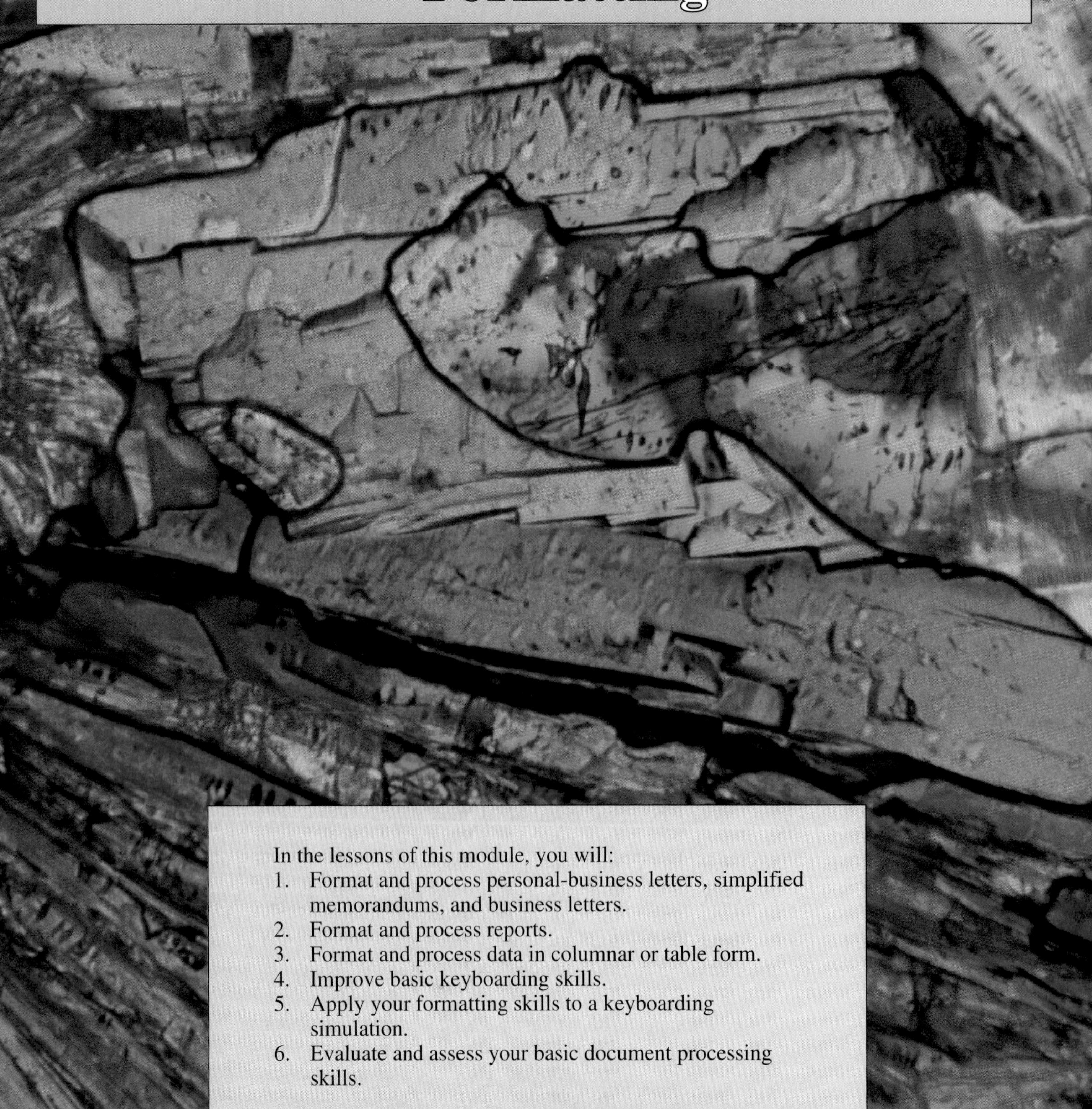

In the lessons of this module, you will:

1. Format and process personal-business letters, simplified memorandums, and business letters.
2. Format and process reports.
3. Format and process data in columnar or table form.
4. Improve basic keyboarding skills.
5. Apply your formatting skills to a keyboarding simulation.
6. Evaluate and assess your basic document processing skills.

KEYBOARDING WORKSHOP

TIMED WRITING: STRAIGHT COPY

Take 1' guided writings, reaching for your 1/4' goals; take 2' and 3' unguided writings.

gwam	1/4'	1/2'	3/4'	Time
20	5	10	15	20
24	6	12	18	24
28	7	14	21	28
32	8	16	24	32
36	9	18	27	36
40	10	20	30	40
44	11	22	33	44
48	12	24	36	48

all letters used | E | 1.2 si | 5.1 awl | 90% hfw

	gwam 2'	3'
When you try to do better something that you cannot do	6	4
as well as you wish, you practice. You do not just duplicate	12	8
your actions; or if you do, you do not improve. What you do	18	12
repeat, instead, is the general response but with some change.	24	16
So the next time you are asked to do a drill again, try	30	20
to do it in a better way. Think about making quick, exact	36	24
motions so that your mind can tell the fingers what to do.	42	28
Size up the problem and learn better methods of increasing	47	32
your speed and control.	50	33

gwam 2' | 1 | 2 | 3 | 4 | 5 | 6 |
gwam 3' | 1 | 2 | 3 | 4 |

TIMED WRITING: STATISTICAL COPY

Take 1', 2', and 3' writings and determine the % of transfer (3' *gwam* divided by 3' *gwam* on writing at top of page).

Goal: *At least* 75% transfer

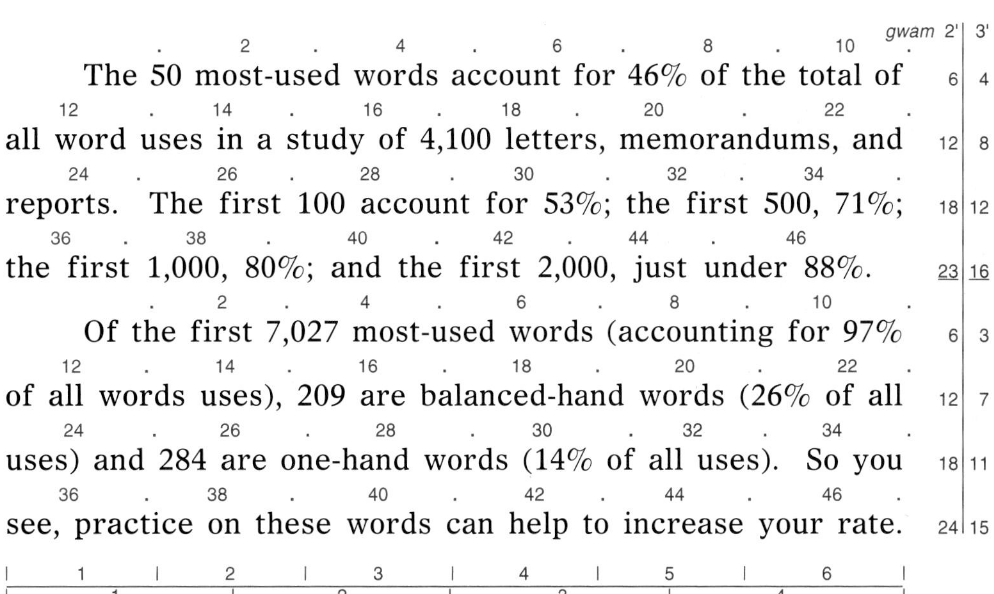

	gwam 2'	3'
The 50 most-used words account for 46% of the total of	6	4
all word uses in a study of 4,100 letters, memorandums, and	12	8
reports. The first 100 account for 53%; the first 500, 71%;	18	12
the first 1,000, 80%; and the first 2,000, just under 88%.	23	16
Of the first 7,027 most-used words (accounting for 97%	6	3
of all words uses), 209 are balanced-hand words (26% of all	12	7
uses) and 284 are one-hand words (14% of all uses). So you	18	11
see, practice on these words can help to increase your rate.	24	15

gwam 2' | 1 | 2 | 3 | 4 | 5 | 6 |
gwam 3' | 1 | 2 | 3 | 4 |

KEYBOARDING WORKSHOP

MASTER TECHNIQUE

1. Key each pair of lines twice SS: first, slowly; then faster. DS between 2-line groups.
2. Key a 1' writing on line 11, then on line 12; find *gwam* on each.

alphabetic sentences	1	Virg fixed a unique bronze sculpture he won at my junk shop.
	2	Vic was pleased with a quartz jewelry box Karen got for him.
figures/ symbols	3	Didn't she say Invoice #9480 was for $376 (plus 5 1/2% tax)?
	4	Ramo & Lo used * to identify "best buys": #17285*; #30496*.
long-direct reaches	5	Marilyn can carve many unique pieces out of onyx and marble.
	6	Herbie doubts if any of my dancers must bring bronze medals.
adjacent keys	7	Very few workers will try for a top spot in the local union.
	8	Over twenty people opted for a review to avoid a short quiz.
combination response	9	We got an award for the extra work we did on the stage sets.
	10	Handle the oil with care and test it when you get to a pump.
word response	11	Did the busy man rush the six bus panels to the firm by air?
	12	They wish to go to the city to visit the busy field auditor.

gwam 1' | 1 | 2 | 3 | 4 | 5 | 6 | 7 | 8 | 9 | 10 | 11 | 12 |

CHECK/IMPROVE SKILL

Take 3', 2', and 1' writings, following your teacher's directions. On 1' *guided* writings work to improve speed (increase goal rate) OR accuracy (reduce goal rate).

all letters used | A | 1.5 si | 5.7 awl | 80% hfw |

	gwam 2'	3'
. 2 . 4 . 6 . 8 . 10 .		
People who take part in activities like tennis, cards,	5	4
12 . 14 . 16 . 18 . 20 . 22 .		
golf, or ballet work to increase their skill. An excellent	11	8
24 . 26 . 28 . 30 . 32 . 34 .		
performance for many of them may be just as critical as the	17	12
36 . 38 . 40 . 42 . 44 . 46 .		
final score. So before their next game, they practice some	23	16
48 . 50 . 52 . 54 . 56 . 58 .		
tactics that may help to increase their acuity, fluency, or	29	20
60 . 62 . 64 . 66 . 68 .		
another facet. Many also do this in keyboarding.	34	23
. 2 . 4 . 6 . 8 . 10 .		
If you have developed a speed of thirty to forty words	40	27
12 . 14 . 16 . 18 . 20 . 22 .		
a minute with good technique and acceptable accuracy, begin	46	31
24 . 26 . 28 . 30 . 32 . 34 .		
a vigorous drive for speed. You have the potential for new	52	35
36 . 38 . 40 . 42 . 44 . 46 .		
growth; you should not be satisfied with your current level	58	39
48 . 50 . 52 . 54 . 56 . 58 .		
of developed speed. Good for now, it is merely a milestone	64	43
60 . 62 . 64 . 66 . 68 . 70		
to a level you will readily prize throughout your life.	69	46

gwam 2' | 1 | 2 | 3 | 4 | 5 | 6 |

gwam 3' | 1 | 2 | 3 | 4 |

Master Keying and Word Processing Skills

Learning Outcomes: After completing this unit, you will be able to

1. Demonstrate improved technique on alphanumeric copy.
2. Key rough-draft copy at acceptable levels of speed and control.
3. Computer users, demonstrate greater mastery of the word processing features you learned previously .

LESSON 37 KEYBOARDING/WORD PROCESSING SKILLS

SM: 1" (or defaults); LS: SS

37A ◆ 6' CONDITIONING PRACTICE

each line twice SS; then a 1' writing on line 3; find *gwam*

alphabet 1 Jarvis will take the next big prize for my old racquet club.
fig/sym 2 My income tax for 1993 was $5,274.60--up 8% over 1992's tax.
speed 3 A neighbor paid the girl to fix the turn signal of the auto.

gwam 1' | 1 | 2 | 3 | 4 | 5 | 6 | 7 | 8 | 9 | 10 | 11 | 12 |

37B ◆ 15' MASTER KEYBOARD CONTROL

1. Key line 1 at a brisk pace. Note the words that were awkward for you.
2. Key each of the awkward words three times at increasing speed.
3. Key line 2 at a steady fluent rate.
4. Key each of the other pairs of lines in the same way.

A/N
1 an and pan nap any nag ant man aunt land plan hand want sand
2 Ann and her aunt want to buy any land they can near the inn.

B/O
3 bow lob bog rob boy mob gob fob bob body robe boat born glob
4 Bobby bobbed in the bow of the boat as the boys came aboard.

C/P
5 cup cop cap pack copy cape cope pick pecks clips camps claps
6 Cap can clip a copy of the poem to his cape to read at camp.

D/Q
7 did quo quid ride quit road quiz paid aqua dude squid squads
8 The dude in an aqua shirt did quit the squad after the quiz.

E/R
9 or re ore per are her red peer here rent fore leer sore very
10 Vera read her book report to three of her friends at school.

F/S
11 if is fish fuss soft furs self fast fans sift surf fist fees
12 Floss said that fish on this shelf is for fast sale at half.

G/T
13 get got tag togs grit gilt gust tang right guilt fight ghost
14 Garth had the grit to go eight rounds in that fight tonight.

H/U
15 hue hut hub hurt shut shun huge hush brush truth shrug thugs
16 Hugh said four burly thugs hurled the man off the huge dock.

I/V
17 vie vim give view five vein dive vial vice vigor voice alive
18 Vivian made her five great dives with visible vim and vigor.

J/W
19 jay wow jet own jab town just will jest when joke what judge
20 Jewel jokes with your town judge about what and who is just.

K/X
21 oak fix kid fox know flax walk flex silk oxen park axle work
22 Knox fixed an oak axle on a flax cart for a kid in the park.

L/Y
23 lay sly try ply all pry lei ally only rely reply truly fully
24 Dolly truly felt that she could rely fully on only one ally.

M/Z
25 may zoo man zam zone make fuzz mama jazz maid jams game zoom
26 Zoe may make her mark in a jazz band jam session at the zoo.

50D ◆ 20'

CHECK WORD PROCESSING SKILL: REPORT

SM: 1"; LS: DS

PI: 5 spaces (0.5")

1. About 2" from top, center the heading MATURITY in ALL CAPS.
2. Quadruple-space (2 hard returns) and key the ¶s DS. Correct the marked errors and any errors you make as you key.
3. After completing the report, make the changes listed below.

Using the word processing features you have learned:

1. Bold the heading.
2. In ¶1, line 2, change *yet* to **but**.
3. In ¶2, line 1, change *attempt* to **try**.
4. In ¶2, line 5, underline flight and fight.
5. In ¶3, line 1, insert **As the song says**, before the quoted statement.
6. In ¶3, line 2, change *face up to* to **confront**.
7. In ¶3, last line, change *conflict* to **problems**.
8. Proofread your copy and correct any errors you find.
9. Change left margin to 1.5" and line spacing to SS; print a copy of your completed report.

MATURITY

Not all adults are mature. Some have grown up bodies and childish minds, yet it requires maturity to ajust to others with out expecting them to do all the adjusting. No one lives without choming in contact with others. So conflicts come and will keep on coming until all men realize that they have to work forthe solution of the problems instead of being the cheif cause of them.

Problems come to us eventually. How we attempt to solve it is a clue to our maturity or the lack of it. Wether we are young or old, our imaturity is showning when we try to solve problems through flight or fight. We may run from some problems and fight back at some critics, but this this is the immature way of handling dificulties.

"You can run, but you cannot hide." So begin learning to face up to problems and try to find ways to resolve conflict without flight or fight. Learn to communicate and reason with those who are in conflict with you. By a mature process of "give and take" comes the solutions to conflict.

37C ◆ 14'

IMPROVE KEYBOARDING SKILL

Take 1' guided writings and 2' and 3' unguided writings, following your teacher's directions. Save the copy for use in 37D. Computer users: Print the copy.

gwam	1/4'	1/2'	3/4'	1'
20	5	10	15	20
24	6	12	18	24
28	7	14	21	28
32	8	16	24	32
36	9	18	27	36
40	10	20	30	40
44	11	22	33	44
48	12	24	36	48
52	13	26	39	52
56	14	28	42	56

all letters used | LA | 1.4 si | 5.4 awl | 85% hfw

	gwam 2'	3'
What is it that makes one person succeed and another	5	4
fail when the two seem to have about equal ability? Some	11	7
have said that the difference is in the degree of motivation	17	11
and effort each brings to the job. Others have said that an	23	16
intent to become excellent is the main difference.	28	19
At least four items are likely to have a major effect	5	22
on our success: basic ability, a desire to excel, an aim	11	26
to succeed, and zestful effort. If any one of these is ab-	17	30
sent or at a low point, our chances for success are lessened.	23	34
These features, however, can be developed if we wish.	29	38

gwam 2' | 1 | 2 | 3 | 4 | 5 | 6 |
gwam 3' | 1 | 2 | 3 | 4 |

37D ◆ 15'

PROOFREAD YOUR COPY

1. Note the kind of errors marked in the ¶ at right.
2. Note how the proofreader's marks above the copy are used to make corrections in the ¶.
3. Proofread the copy you keyed in the 3' writing above and mark for correction each error you made.
4. Center FEATURES OF SUCCESS about 2" from the top of a clean sheet or clear screen.
5. QS and rekey the ¶s from your rough draft; correct all errors.

= space ^ = insert ⁀ = close up ℓ = delete ∿ = transpose (tr)

Line 1 Sucess does not mean thesame thing to every one.

Line 2 For some, it means to get the top att all costs: in

Line 3 power, in fame, and in incone. For others it means juts

Line 4 to fulfill thier basic needs or or wants with as little

Line 5 effort required.

Line 1	Line 2	Line 3	Line 4	Line 5
1 Omitted letter	1 Omitted word	1 Misstroke	1 Transposition	1 Omitted word
2 Failure to space	2 Added letter	2 Omitted comma	2 Added word	
3 Faulty spacing	3 Faulty spacing	3 Transposition		

COMPUTER on-screen changes

After completing Steps 1-5, make these on-screen changes:

1. In ¶1, line 3, change *degree* to **amount**.
2. In ¶2, line 1, change *major* to **vital** underlined.
3. In ¶2, line 4, change *point* to **level**.
4. Proofread your copy on screen and correct any errors you find.
5. Reset the right margin only at 1" and line spacing for SS.
6. Print a copy of the paragraph.

LESSON 50 ASSESS WORD PROCESSING SKILLS

SM: 1" (or defaults); LS: SS

50A ◆ 6' CONDITIONING PRACTICE

each line twice

alphabet 1 Jacki had won first place by solving my tax quiz in an hour.
fig/sym 2 Our 1993 profit was $58,764 (up 20% from the previous year).
speed 3 Roddy may sign the six forms and work with the city auditor.

gwam 1' | 1 | 2 | 3 | 4 | 5 | 6 | 7 | 8 | 9 | 10 | 11 | 12 |

50B ◆ 12' CHECK CENTERING

1. Beginning about 2" (approximately line 13) from top, center DS *each line* of Announcement 1 horizontally; correct errors as you key.
2. Space down 4 DS; then center SS *each line* of Announcement 2 horizontally; correct errors as you key.

Announcement 1

FUND-RAISING AUCTION
Student Activity Center
Central High School
Saturday, March 9
Catered Dinner at 6:30 p.m.
Auction at 8 p.m.
Reservation Required: 555-4027

Announcement 2

SENIOR CLASS OFFICERS DS

Ella Mae Flores, President
Shawn Bennett, Vice President
Kathryn Richardson, Treasurer
Cyril Jackson, Secretary
Rita Metz/Jon Hicks, Historians

50C ◆ 12' CHECK WORD PROCESSING SKILL

Using the word processing features you have learned, key the lines given at the right DS. Be guided by the numbered statements above the sentences.

Do not key the numbers or letters used to identify the sentences.

1 Key the following sentence as shown:

Angela will fly to Florida on Thursday.

2 Make the following changes using the insert mode.

Angela ^Childs will fly to ^Miami, Florida^, on Thursday, Veterans Day.

3 Make these additional changes using typeover mode as necessary.

^Dr. Angela Childs,^ our new principal, will fly to Miami, Florida, on ~~Thursday,~~ ^Monday, ~~Veterans~~ ^Labor Day.

4 Key the following sentences; **bold** and underline as you key.

a <u>As the Crow Flies</u>, by Jeffrey Archer, was published in 1991.

b She said that **don't** means <u>do not</u> and **doesn't** means <u>does not</u>.

c Ms. Lindsay said to **bold** and ALL CAP the heading EXCELLENCE.

d A book title may be shown in ALL CAPS <u>and</u> **bold** for emphasis.

e Key <u>Time</u>, a magazine, in cap and lowercase and <u>underline</u> it.

f Mr. Mendez said to center the talk title on a separate line:

WORD PROCESSING: KEY TO THE FUTURE

LESSON 38 KEYBOARDING/WORD PROCESSING SKILLS

SM: 1" (or defaults); LS: SS

38A ◆ 6' CONDITIONING PRACTICE

each line twice

alphabet 1 Bevis had quickly won top seed for the next games in Juarez.
fig/sym 2 THE DIAMOND CAPER (Parker & Sons, #274638) sells for $19.50.
speed 3 Shana may make a bid for the antique bottle for the auditor.

gwam 1' | 1 | 2 | 3 | 4 | 5 | 6 | 7 | 8 | 9 | 10 | 11 | 12 |

38B ◆ 12' MASTER KEYBOARDING TECHNIQUE

1. Each line twice SS; DS between 4-line groups.
2. Take a 1' writing on each of lines 6, 8, and 10; find *gwam* on each.
3. Rekey the two lines on which you had the lowest *gwam*.

shift keys
1 Jane and Robb go to a New Year's party with Donna and Spiro.
2 R. J. Appel was paid by the Apollo Insurance Co. of Jackson.

space bar
3 It is up to me to do my best in each try to make a new goal.
4 Andy may use his pen to sign the form for a job in the city.

letter response
5 A tax rate was set in my area only after we set a case date.
6 We are free only after we get him set up on a tax rate case.

combination response
7 I shall bid on the antique vase only if I regard it as rare.
8 You are to sign all of the artwork you turn in to be graded.

word response
9 He is to do the work for both of us, and she is to pay half.
10 The girl with the titian hair owns the title to the autobus.

gwam 1' | 1 | 2 | 3 | 4 | 5 | 6 | 7 | 8 | 9 | 10 | 11 | 12 |

38C ◆ 12' KEY FROM ROUGH-DRAFT

1. Read the two ¶s shown at the right; check the proofreader's marks using the key below.
2. Key the ¶s DS, correcting the errors marked in the copy. Computer users, go to corrections at bottom right.
3. Proofread your own copy, using proofreader's marks to indicate needed corrections.
4. Key the ¶s again from your own rough draft; correct all errors.

```
    Although the copy lines in the book are even at the
right margin they maynot be when you type them. The reason
for this is that type used by a printer is uniform in width
as is that on your machine.  Be sure to recognize this.
    Don't think that because your copy is even at the
right, it contains no erors.  To be certain that the work
is cor rect, you must check it to see taht each character
and space is a match with copy from which you key.
```

Proofreader's Marks

- delete (take out)
- insert
- add space
- close up
- transpose

Computer users

After you complete Steps 1 and 2 of the directions at the left, make these on-screen changes.

1. In ¶1, line 1, change *book* to **text** and underline it.
2. In ¶2, line 3, change *correct* to **perfect** and **bold** it.
3. Proofread your copy on screen and correct any errors you made.
4. Center 4 lines above your copy the heading VARIABLE VS. UNIFORM SPACING.
5. Reset side margins for 1.5", line spacing to SS.
6. Print; then mark corrections with proofreader's marks.

49C ◆ 12'

CHECK SKILL: SCRIPT

Take 2' and 3' writings, circling errors on 3' writings. Figure the percentage of your straight-copy skill transferred to script copy (divide 3' *gwam* on this writing by 3' *gwam* on 49B).

Goal: 90%

all letters used | LA | 1.4 si | 5.4 awl | 85% hfw

	gwam 2'	3'
Many workers fail to get ahead, yet they do not seem to	6	4
realize quite why this is so. They believe they should get	12	8
a promotion or salary increment simply because they are	17	11
next in line. What they fail to understand is that to deserve a	24	16
better job, competence counts more than being next in line.	30	20
As you get promoted, more will be required of you than	35	23
mere job competence, although that is vital. You must get	41	27
along with other people even when they may not desire to get	47	31
along with you. Working harmoniously with others is a major	53	35
test of leadership, so begin learning to do this right now.	59	39

49D ◆ 12'

CHECK SKILL: ROUGH DRAFT

Take 2' and 3' writings, circling errors on 3' writings. Figure the percentage of your straight-copy skill transferred to rough-draft copy (divide 3' *gwam* on this writing by 3' *gwam* on 49B).

Goal: 80%

all letters used | LA | 1.4 si | 5.4 awl | 85% hfw

	gwam 2'	3'
~~Set~~ Pick a definite time and place for studying ~~to study~~. ~~Arrange~~ Have all	5	4
books and paper s within easy ~~your~~ reach. You will understand and	12	8
recall better what you rea~~e~~d if you out line it or underline	17	12
each key ~~important~~ statement. Equally ~~I~~mportant is to read for meaning	24	16
and not ~~merely~~ just to cover so many pages in the book.	28	19
Many ~~Some~~ students have serious ~~grave~~ learning difficulties and do	34	22
not know why. # The fault may be that they do not use the proper	40	27
study habits. When they realize this, they should get help	46	31
in learning how to study. Doing so may help them acquire	52	35
exact study habits that can lead to ~~bring~~ good work and success.	58	38

38D ◆ 20'

CHECK/IMPROVE SKILL

1. Take 3', 2', and 1' writings as directed by your teacher. On 1' *guided* writings, try to improve either speed (increase goal rate) OR accuracy (reduce goal rate).
2. Center the heading PLANNING MESSAGES about 2" (PB about line 13) from the top of a sheet;* QS; then rekey the ¶s as a short report; correct all errors.

***Computer users:** Find the width of the default top margin. Subtract this number from the desired width of the top margin. The result indicates placement of the centered heading.

all letters used | LA | 1.4 si | 5.4 awl | 85% hfw

	gwam 2'	3'
Planning is the first step in composing a message. The	6	4
plan should include a goal, what you want to accomplish. It	12	8
also should include a list of the points you will use to con-	18	12
vince the reader of your point of view or of the action you	24	16
want taken. The list should be arranged in logical sequence.	30	20
Your goal is the major idea behind the topic sentence.	36	24
The topic sentence is often stated first, followed next by	41	28
facts and ideas that support it. You may instead decide to	47	32
work up to the main idea at the end. In either case, you	53	35
itemize the information and tie it to the main thought.	59	39

gwam 2' | 1 | 2 | 3 | 4 | 5 | 6 |
gwam 3' | 1 | 2 | 3 | 4 |

LESSON 39 KEYBOARDING/WORD PROCESSING SKILLS

SM: 1" (or defaults); LS: SS

39A ◆ 6'

CONDITIONING PRACTICE

each line twice

alphabet	1	Zoe quickly made six jugs of punch to serve by the new pool.
fig/sym	2	We got a discount of 10% on Invoice #1837; only 5% on #2946.
speed	3	They wish us to make a copy of an ancient map of the island.

gwam 1' | 1 | 2 | 3 | 4 | 5 | 6 | 7 | 8 | 9 | 10 | 11 | 12 |

39B ◆ 15'

MASTER KEYBOARDING TECHNIQUE

1. Key lines 1-7 twice each: first, slowly; then faster.
2. Take a 1' writing on each of lines 8, 9, and 10; find *gwam* on each.

figures	1	By May 25 in 1993 we had planted 475 trees and 1,608 shrubs.
fig/sym	2	Al asked, "How much is due by May 28 on Account #4039-1657?"
shift keys	3	Marla Appel and Pat Coe will play Nan Epps and Larry Sparks.
space bar	4	Any of you can go by the inn for a swim in the pool at noon.
one hand	5	My war on waste at a union mill was based upon minimum data.
long reach	6	Myna said I must curb at once my urge to glance at my hands.
adjacent key	7	Coila hoped for a new opal ring to wear to her next concert.
double letters	8	Bobby will sell the cookbook for a little less than it cost.
combination	9	He may join us for tea at the pool if he wishes to see them.
balanced hand	10	Did they make the right title forms for the eight big firms?

gwam 1' | 1 | 2 | 3 | 4 | 5 | 6 | 7 | 8 | 9 | 10 | 11 | 12 |

LESSON 49 ASSESS BASIC KEYBOARDING SKILLS

SM: 1" (or defaults); LS: SS

49A ◆ 6' CONDITIONING PRACTICE

each line twice

alphabet 1 Jake led a big blitz which saved the next play for my squad.
fig/sym 2 Beth has ordered 26 5/8 yards of #304 linen at $7.19 a yard.
speed 3 Good form is the key if all of us wish to make the big goal.

gwam 1' | 1 | 2 | 3 | 4 | 5 | 6 | 7 | 8 | 9 | 10 | 11 | 12 |

49B ◆ 20' CHECK SKILL

1. Take a 1' writing on each ¶; find *gwam* on each writing.
2. Take a 2' writing on ¶s 2-3 combined; find *gwam*.
3. Take two 3' writings on ¶s 1-3 combined; find *gwam* and circle errors on each.

Record your rate for use in later lessons.

If time permits, key the ¶s as a short report, centering the heading EXCELLENCE on line 13 from the top and inserting a QS below it. Correct all errors.

Computer users

1. As you center the title, boldface it.
2. In line 4 of ¶1, change *though* to **however**.
3. At the end of ¶1, change *sufficient* to **enough**.
4. Underline Really in line 4 of ¶2.
5. In line 1 of ¶3, change *all* to **those** and *the* to **a**.

all letters used | LA | 1.4 si | 5.4 awl | 85% hfw

	gwam 2'	3'
A desire to excel is a quality that forces us to try to	6	4
improve our own performance and to surpass that of others.	12	8
All our major achievements have been sparked by a desire to	18	12
improve. The desire, though, had to be turned into a series	24	16
of right actions. Desire alone was not sufficient.	29	20
An excellent performance shows the real concern of the	34	23
performer for the task. It gives one a feeling of personal	40	27
success and causes all as a matter of habit to do our best.	46	31
Really successful men and women take great delight in their	52	35
work and pursue it with a lot of satisfaction.	57	38
A factor common to all who succeed is the need to have	63	42
a good job recognized by others. If good work goes without	69	46
notice, the desire to excel will be reduced. Lucky, indeed,	75	50
are people who can study their own performance, recognize	80	54
its quality, and do what must be done to improve it.	87	57

gwam 2' | 1 | 2 | 3 | 4 | 5 | 6 |
gwam 3' | 1 | 2 | 3 | 4 |

39C ◆ 13'

CHECK KEY-BOARDING SKILL

Take 1', 2', and 3' writings, finding *gwam* and circling errors after each.

About 2" (about 12 lines) from the top of a sheet,* center TECHNIQUES AND SPEED (computer users key it in bold); QS; then key the ¶s as a short report; correct all errors.

***Computer users**, remember to include the default top margin when figuring which line to begin on. See * in 38D, p. 71.

all letters used | LA | 1.4 si | 5.4 awl | 85% hfw

	gwam 2'	3'
As you work for higher skill, remember that how well you	8	4
key fast is just as important as how fast you key. How well	12	8
you key at any speed depends in major ways upon the technique	18	12
or form you use. Bouncing hands and flying fingers lower the	24	16
speed, while quiet hands and low finger reaches increase speed.	31	20
Few of us ever reach what the experts believe is perfect	36	24
technique, but all of us should try to approach it. We must	42	28
realize that good form is the secret to higher speed with	48	32
fewer errors. We can then focus our practice on the improve-	54	36
ment of the features of good form that will bring success.	60	40

gwam 2' | 1 | 2 | 3 | 4 | 5 | 6 |
gwam 3' | 1 | 2 | 3 | 4 |

39D ◆ 6'

MASTER SKILL: ROUGH DRAFT

1. Key a 2' writing on the ¶, making the marked changes as you key.
2. Proofread your copy; circle errors; and find *gwam*.
3. Key another 2' writing; try to increase your speed.

∧ = insert
 = delete
= add space
∿ = transpose
⁀ = close up

all letters used | LA | 1.4 si | 5.4 awl | 85% hfw

	gwam 2'
When you key from marked copy, read just a litle ahead	6
of where your keying. Doing this will keep you from missing	12
changes that must be made. Learn to reconize quickly thee	18
correction simbols so that you don't have to reduce speed	24
or stop toread. Expcet to copy rough/draft at about eighty	30
five per cent of your straight copy speed.	35

39E ◆ 10'

COMPOSE (CREATE) AS YOU KEY

LS: DS; PB: line 13

1. Select a topic from those given at right.
2. Compose one or two ¶s giving your plans (or point of view) regarding the topic.
3. Edit your copy: add and delete words, phrases, and sentences until the ¶(s) says just what you want it to say.
4. Proofread your copy; mark corrections with proofreader's marks.
5. As time permits, prepare a final draft with errors corrected.

1 My future education plans
2 The job I want and why
3 Why I want to excel
4 Why I do not care to be No. 1
5 How to reduce teenage drinking
6 My plans for a future career
7 Why cheating is wrong
8 How to reduce teenage drug use
9 My plans for next summer
10 How I do my homework

Note: In later lessons, choose different topics and practice composing as you key.

48C ◆ 10'

CHECK/IMPROVE SKILL

Take a 1' writing on each ¶; find *gwam*. Try to key this *gwam* on a 2' writing (both ¶s). End with a 3' writing; find *gwam*; circle errors.

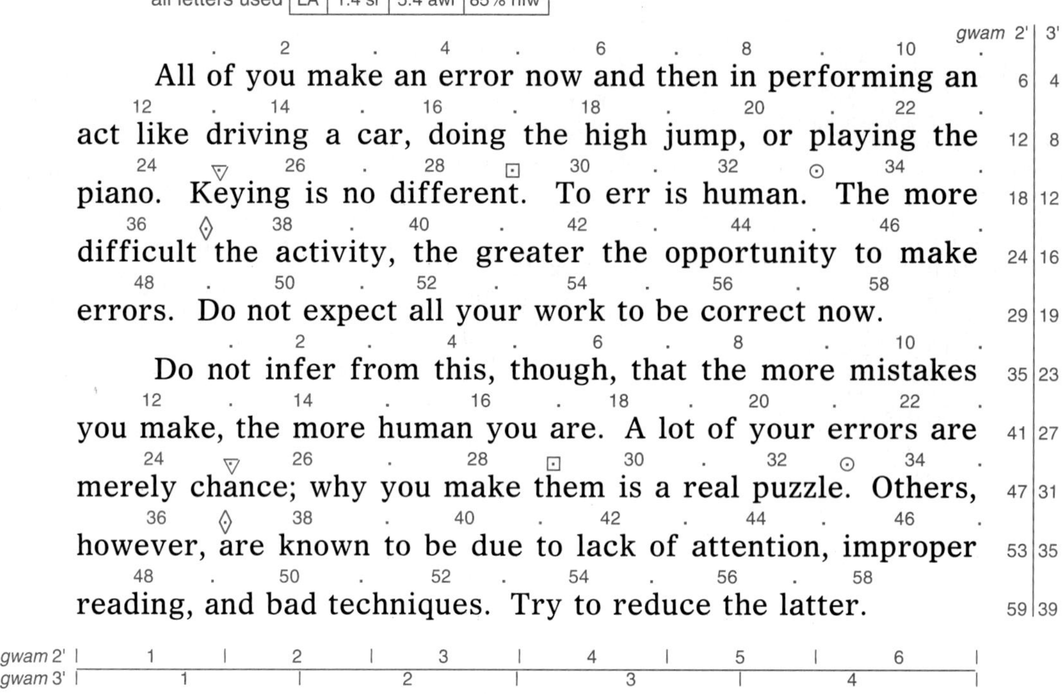

all letters used | LA | 1.4 si | 5.4 awl | 85% hfw

	gwam 2'	3'
All of you make an error now and then in performing an	6	4
act like driving a car, doing the high jump, or playing the	12	8
piano. Keying is no different. To err is human. The more	18	12
difficult the activity, the greater the opportunity to make	24	16
errors. Do not expect all your work to be correct now.	29	19
Do not infer from this, though, that the more mistakes	35	23
you make, the more human you are. A lot of your errors are	41	27
merely chance; why you make them is a real puzzle. Others,	47	31
however, are known to be due to lack of attention, improper	53	35
reading, and bad techniques. Try to reduce the latter.	59	39

gwam 2' | 1 | 2 | 3 | 4 | 5 | 6 |

gwam 3' | 1 | 2 | 3 | 4 |

48D ◆ 15'

SHORT REPORT

SM: 1.5"; LS: DS

PI: 5 spaces (0.5"); TM: 2" (PB line 13)*

1. Center the heading in ALL CAPS.
2. Key the report DS, correcting errors as you key.

*On a computer, remember to count lines in the default top margin; then insert enough hard returns for the heading to print about 2" (13 lines) from the top of the page.

Typewriter users

1. Proofread copy and mark any remaining errors for correction.
2. Rekey the report from your own rough draft, all errors corrected.

COMPUTER ETHICS QS (2 DS)

Ethics has been defined as a set of moral principles that are designed to guide human conduct. Dealing with what is good and bad, ethics represents a pattern of personal and group conduct that is acceptable to society.

If somebody in one business breaks into computer files of another company to seek information in order to obtain a competitive advantage, would you judge that to be moral conduct? If an employee of one firm gives privileged data to someone in another firm to give the latter firm an advantage, do you view that as being moral conduct? Your answer to both questions should be "No."

In a similar situation, a student who uses someone else's data disk to print a copy of assigned work as his or her own is not being ethical. Generally, one who breaks a rule of acceptable conduct, whether at work or at school, is guilty of violating the code of ethical behavior.

Computer users

Complete Steps 1-3 at right.

1. Proofread on screen and correct all errors you find.
2. Make the following changes:
   a. Bold **Ethics** in line 1.
   b. Underline No at the end of ¶2.
   c. Delete *and group* near the end of ¶1.
   d. Insert **or values** after *principles* in line 1, ¶1.
3. Key the report again from the text; SS.

Master Numeric Keypad Operation

Learning Outcomes: After completing this unit, you will be able to

1. Operate the keypad of a computer with proper technique: fingers well curved and upright over home keys.
2. Enter all-figure copy at acceptable speed with good control by touch (minimum of looking).

LESSON 40 4/5/6/0

40A ◆ GET ACQUAINTED WITH 10-KEY PAD

Figure keys 1-9 are in standard locations on numeric keypads of computers and 10-key calculators.

The zero (0 or Ø) key location may vary slightly from one keyboard to another.

The illustrations at the right show the location of the figure keys on selected computer keyboards.

Note: To use the keypad, the Num (number) Lock must be turned on.

Macintosh LCII numeric keypad

IBM PC

40B ◆ CORRECT OPERATING POSITION

1. Position yourself in front of the computer—body erect, both feet on floor for balance.
2. Place this textbook at the right of the keyboard.
3. Curve the fingers of the right hand and place them on the numeric keypad:
   - pointer finger on 4
   - middle finger on 5
   - ring finger on 6
   - thumb on 0

Assess Keyboarding/Word Processing Skills

Learning Outcomes:

1. Demonstrate correct technique and acceptable speed and control as you key straight copy, script, and rough-draft copy.
2. Demonstrate that you can center individual lines horizontally.
3. Demonstrate that you can proofread and correct errors in your copy.
4. Computer users: Demonstrate proper use of word processing features.

LESSON 48 PREPARE FOR ASSESSMENT

SM: 1" (or defaults); LS: SS

48A ◆ 6' CONDITIONING PRACTICE

each line twice SS; then a 1' writing on line 3; find *gwam*

alphabet	1	Jocko will place a high bid for my next prized antique vase.
fig/sym	2	Ora asked, "Wasn't R&N's check #285067 deposited on 1/4/93?"
speed	3	When did the field auditor sign the audit form for the city?

gwam 1' | 1 | 2 | 3 | 4 | 5 | 6 | 7 | 8 | 9 | 10 | 11 | 12 |

48B ◆ 19' CHECK/IMPROVE TECHNIQUE

1. Key lines 1-15 once SS; DS between 3-line groups.
2. Key a 1' writing on each of lines 16-21; find *gwam* on each writing.
3. Key another 1' writing on each of lines 19-21; find *gwam* on each writing.

	1	by man fry men boy jam may pan city slam body trim duty dorm
spacing	2	Clem is to stay for only a day or two at an inn on the quay.
	3	Many a boy wants to make the team, but only a few can do so.
	4	Mabel or Sophi; Martin or Tobias; Larry Epson or Janet Spahn.
shifting	5	Ms. Alexis Epworth said that she saw Jan Spinx in Nantucket.
	6	Coach Jason Parker will speak to the Gridiron Club in March.
	7	Buy the three silver coins we saw in the new shop yesterday.
adjacent keys	8	We hope to open a new pottery store in the square next week.
	9	Pop saw his sister swim into choppy water off Misty's Point.
	10	Myrna now doubts that anyone at my gym can outjump my niece.
long-direct reaches	11	Cecil must race for any medal to curb any doubts anyone had.
	12	Nyles is to serve a nice iced drink to my aunt and my niece.
	13	I went to work at #4956 Holt Road on January 27 at 8:30 a.m.
figures/ symbols	14	A 32-inch screen costs $760 while a 19-inch costs only $485.
	15	She said: "Buy 250 of J&B Preferred at $364.87 on June 19."
letter response	16	John was in a great act on my union stage after you saw him.
word response	17	I wish to pay the auditor for the good work he did for them.
combination	18	I gave the best grade to the girl with the best work of art.
letter	19	Jim was up at my mill after you saw him act on a union case.
word	20	The eight girls wish to pay for their half of the lake dock.
combination	21	Di may see my aunt at a bazaar to be held at the union hall.

gwam 1' | 1 | 2 | 3 | 4 | 5 | 6 | 7 | 8 | 9 | 10 | 11 | 12 |

40C ◆

ENTER DATA USING HOME KEYS: 4, 5, 6, 0

Complete the drills, as directed below, entering the numbers in columns, as shown, on your word processing software; but do not key the totals.

When you can operate the keypad by touch—Lesson 44 completed—determine whether your word processing software contains a calculator (math) function. If so, repeat Lessons 40-44 using the math function. Check your totals against the printed totals. Reenter the data whenever you do not get the correct total.

1. Turn equipment, including Num Lock, "on".
2. Curve the fingers of your right hand and place them upright on home keys:
   pointer finger on 4
   middle finger on 5
   ring finger on 6
   little finger on + bar
   thumb on 0 or Ø (zero)
3. Using the special Enter key to the right of the keypad, enter data in Drill 1a as follows:
   4 Enter
   4 Enter
   4 Enter
   Strike Enter

Note: Ignore any decimal (.) or comma (,) that may appear in an entry or total figure.

4. Enter and check columns b, c, d, e, and f in the same way.
5. Using the special Enter key to the right of the keypad, enter data in Drill 2a as follows:
   44 Enter
   44 Enter
   44 Enter
   Strike Enter
6. Continue Drill 2 and complete Drills 3-5 in a similar manner. In Drills 4 and 5, strike 0 (zero) with the *side* of your right thumb.

Technique cue

Strike each key with a quick, sharp stroke with the *tip* of the finger; release the key quickly. Keep the fingers curved and upright, the wrist low, relaxed, and steady.

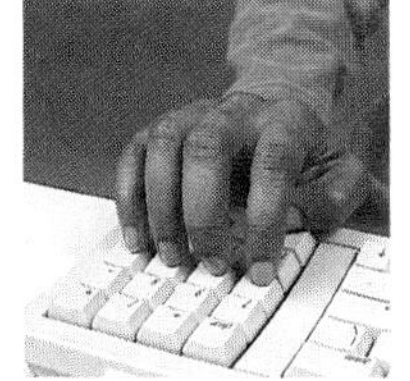

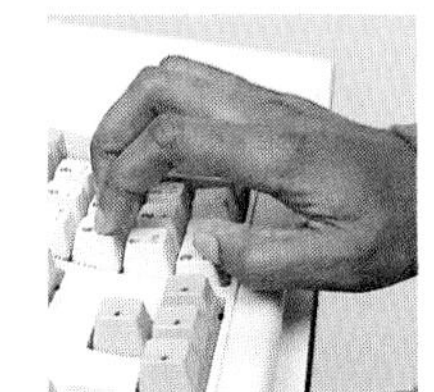

Drill 1

a	b	c	d	e	f
4	5	6	4	5	6
4	5	6	4	5	6
4	5	6	4	5	6
12	15	18	12	15	18

Drill 2

a	b	c	d	e	f
44	55	66	44	55	66
44	55	66	44	55	66
44	55	66	44	55	66
132	165	198	132	165	198

Drill 3

a	b	c	d	c	f
44	45	54	44	55	66
55	56	46	45	54	65
66	64	65	46	56	64
165	165	165	135	165	195

Drill 4

a	b	c	d	e	f
40	50	60	400	500	600
40	50	60	400	500	600
40	50	60	400	500	600
120	150	180	1,200	1,500	1,800

Drill 5

a	b	c	d	e	f
40	400	404	406	450	650
50	500	505	506	540	560
60	600	606	606	405	605
150	1,500	1,515	1,518	1,395	1,815

KEYBOARDING WORKSHOP

MASTER TECHNIQUE: SPACING

1. Key each pair of lines once SS; DS between pairs.
2. Check accuracy of spacing with punctuation marks.
3. Key each pair of lines again, spacing properly after each punctuation mark.

period/question
1 Why are they not here? The meeting is at 7. All know that.
2 I want a dozen roses. How much are they? May I mix colors?

comma
3 Ms. Reid, the store manager, asked Max, Flo, and me to help.
4 When roll was called, Hatch, Parker, and Ross were not here.

semicolon/colon
5 We made three stops: Tampa, FL; Key West, FL; San Juan, PR.
6 CLUB MEETING: date, May 19; time, 7:45 p.m.; place, Room 8.

abbreviations/initials
7 Drs. Rosa M. and Juan P. Ruiz begin house calls at 4:15 p.m.
8 Jean has a Ph.D. from Cornell; D. K., a D.B.A. from Indiana.

parentheses
9 Is the space after . following initials (a) 1, (b) 2, (c) 3?
10 Is the space after : in stating time (a) 0, (b) 1, or (c) 2?

hyphen
11 Words such as co-worker and self-service always require a -.
12 A compound adjective like 4-ply or 12-foot requires a - too.

gwam 1' | 1 | 2 | 3 | 4 | 5 | 6 | 7 | 8 | 9 | 10 | 11 | 12 |

CHECK/IMPROVE SKILL

1. Take 1' writings on each ¶ and 2' and 3' writings on both ¶s. Find *gwam*, circle errors for each writing.
2. For 1' guided writings, use the better 1' *gwam* in No. 1 as your base rate.

gwam	1/4'	1/2'	3/4'	Time
20	5	10	15	20
24	6	12	18	24
28	7	14	21	28
32	8	16	24	32
36	9	18	27	36
40	10	20	30	40
44	11	22	33	44
48	12	24	36	48
52	13	26	39	52

all letters used | A | 1.5 si | 5.7 awl | 80% hfw

	gwam 2'	3'
One of the great hazards in social and medical science	6	4
lies in pretending that we know exactly what is best for an	12	8
individual, a couple, or a group. People vary so much that	18	12
the utmost we can expect is a series of general or specific	24	17
guidelines that have been tested and proven quite effective	30	20
in careful research with large numbers of individuals.	35	23
Education is a social science, and teaching people how	40	30
to key is not an exception. Good teaching, like developing	46	31
solid learning material, depends upon a set of major guides	52	35
or rules that are based on the findings of careful research	58	40
into how learners acquire a skill most easily. This is why	64	43
a teacher knows best what and how a student should practice.	70	47

gwam 2' | 1 | 2 | 3 | 4 | 5 | 6 |
gwam 3' | 1 | 2 | 3 | 4 |

LESSON 41 7/8/9

41A ◆ IMPROVE HOME-KEY TECHNIQUE

Enter the columns of data listed at the right as directed in Steps 1-6 on p. 74.

a	b	c	d	e	f
4	44	400	404	440	450
5	55	500	505	550	560
6	66	600	606	660	456
15	165	1,500	1,515	1,650	1,466

41B ◆ LEARN NEW KEYS: 7, 8, 9

Learn reach to 7

1. Locate 7 (above 4) on the numeric keypad.
2. Watch your pointer finger move up to 7 and back to 4 a few times *without striking keys.*
3. Practice striking 74 a few times as you watch the finger.
4. With eyes on copy, enter the data in Drills 1a and 1b.

Learn reach to 8

1. Learn the middle-finger reach to 8 (above 5) as directed in Steps 1-3 above.
2. With eyes on copy, enter the data in Drills 1c and 1d.

Learn reach to 9

1. Learn the ring-finger reach to 9 (above 6) as directed above.
2. With eyes on copy, enter the data in Drills 1e and 1f.

Drills 2-4

Practice entering the columns of data in Drills 2-4 until you can do so accurately and quickly.

Drill 1

a	b	c	d	e	f
474	747	585	858	696	969
747	777	858	888	969	999
777	474	888	585	999	696
1,998	1,998	2,331	2,331	2,664	2,664

Drill 2

a	b	c	d	e	f
774	885	996	745	475	754
474	585	696	854	584	846
747	858	969	965	695	956
1,995	2,328	2,661	2,564	1,754	2,556

Drill 3

a	b	c	d	e	f
470	580	690	770	707	407
740	850	960	880	808	508
704	805	906	990	909	609
1,914	2,235	2,556	2,640	2,424	1,524

Drill 4

a	b	c	d	e	f
456	407	508	609	804	905
789	408	509	704	805	906
654	409	607	705	806	907
987	507	608	706	904	908
2,886	1,731	2,232	2,724	3,319	3,626

41C ◆ UNEQUAL DIGITS

Enter single, double, and triple digits in columns as shown, left to right. The computer will align the digits automatically.

a	b	c	d	e	f
4	90	79	4	740	860
56	87	64	56	64	70
78	68	97	78	960	900
90	54	64	60	89	67
4	6	5	98	8	80
232	305	309	296	1,861	1,977

47C ◆ (cont.)

Exercise 1

1. Key the listing of cities and states as shown at the right. Return twice after keying the last entry.
2. After you key the list, use the move feature to alphabetize the listing by city.
3. Use the copy feature to copy the list and place a copy of the list a double space below the first listing.
4. Use the move feature to alphabetize the second listing by state.

Boise, Idaho
Scottsdale, Arizona
Portland, Oregon
Logan, Utah
Los Angeles, California
Seattle, Washington
Reno, Nevada

Exercise 2

1. Key the ¶s at the right.
2. Use move feature to:
   a. move ¶1 to end.
   b. move ¶3 to beginning.
   c. move first sentence of ¶2 to end of ¶2.

¶1 If you have any questions about any of the furniture you looked at yesterday, please call me at 555-4829.

¶2 As I indicated, Wilson's Department Store is committed to customer satisfaction. In the meantime, you may be interested in looking over the brochures of furniture that are enclosed. If a set particularly interests you, we could order it. You would be under no obligation to buy the set if it does not meet your expectations when it arrives.

¶3 Discussing your furniture needs with you yesterday was enjoyable. I checked with the department manager, and the next shipment of furniture should arrive within a few weeks. Eight new styles of dining room sets were ordered. When the shipment arrives, I will call you.

47D ◆ 12'

CHECK/IMPROVE SPEED

Take 1' writings on each ¶ and 2' writings on both ¶s; find *gwam* on each writing.

all letters used | LA | 1.4 si | 5.4 awl | 85% hfw |

gwam 2'

It is okay to try and try again if your first efforts do 6
not bring the correct results. If you try but fail again and 12
again, however, it is foolish to plug along in the very same 18
manner. Rather, experiment with another way to accomplish the 24
task that may bring the skill or knowledge you seek. 30

If your first attempts do not yield success, do not quit 35
and merely let it go at that. Instead, begin again in a better 41
way to finish the work or develop more insight into your 47
difficulty. If you recognize why you must do more than just 54
try, try again, you will work with purpose to achieve success. 60

gwam 2' | 1 | 2 | 3 | 4 | 5 | 6 |

LESSON 42 1/2/3

42A ◆

REINFORCE REACH STROKES

Enter the columns of data listed at the right as directed in Steps 1-6 on p. 74.

a	b	c	d	e	f	g
44	74	740	996	704	990	477
55	85	850	885	805	880	588
66	96	960	774	906	770	699
165	255	2,550	2,655	2,415	2,640	1,764

42B ◆

LEARN NEW KEYS: 1, 2, 3

Learn reach to 1

1. Locate 1 (below 4) on the numeric keypad.
2. Watch your pointer finger move down to 1 and back to 4 a few times *without striking keys*.
3. Practice striking 14 a few times as you watch the finger.
4. With eyes on copy, enter the data in Drills 1a and 1b.

Learn reach to 2

1. Learn the middle-finger reach to 2 (below 5) as directed in Steps 1-3 above.
2. With eyes on copy, enter the data in Drills 1c and 1d.

Learn reach to 3

1. Learn the ring-finger reach to 3 (below 6) as directed above.
2. With eyes on copy, enter the data in Drills 1e, 1f, and 1g.

Drills 2-4

Practice entering the columns of data in Drills 2-4 until you can do so accurately and quickly.

Drill 1

a	b	c	d	e	f	g
414	141	525	252	636	363	174
141	111	252	222	363	333	285
111	414	222	525	333	636	396
666	666	999	999	1,332	1,332	855

Drill 2

a	b	c	d	e	f	g
114	225	336	175	415	184	174
411	522	633	284	524	276	258
141	252	363	395	635	359	369
666	999	1,332	854	1,574	819	801

Drill 3

a	b	c	d	e	f	g
417	528	639	110	171	471	714
147	280	369	220	282	582	850
174	285	396	330	393	693	936
738	1,093	1,404	660	846	1,746	2,500

Drill 4

a	b	c	d	e	f	g
77	71	401	107	417	147	174
88	82	502	208	528	258	825
99	93	603	309	639	369	396
264	246	1,506	624	1,584	774	1,395

42C ◆

ENTER DATA CONTAINING COMMAS

Enter the data in Columns a-g. (Even though number data often include commas to separate hundreds from thousands, do not enter them.)

a	b	c	d	e	f	g
14	25	36	17	28	39	174
174	285	396	197	228	339	285
1,014	2,025	3,036	9,074	1,785	9,096	1,736
1,740	2,850	3,960	4,714	8,259	6,976	3,982
7,414	8,250	9,636	1,417	2,528	3,639	2,803
753	951	321	283	173	357	196
1,474	2,585	3,696	4,974	5,285	6,398	1,974
2,785	3,896	4,914	8,795	6,836	7,100	8,200
15,368	20,867	25,995	29,471	25,122	33,944	19,350

46D ◆ (cont.)

1. Key lines 1-4 at the right. Do *not* bold or underline the copy as you key.
2. Use the block feature to bold and underline the copy as shown at the right. Center line 4.

1 **Jo's** birthday is on **Sunday**, May 2; mine is on **Monday**, May 3.

2 The next **FBLA** meeting is on **Thursday**, June 15, at 12:30 p.m.

3 The **Hixons** moved from 3748 Key Street to 1629 Vivian Street.

4 **Sandra Mackey, President**

LESSON 47 LEARN COPY AND MOVE

SM: defaults; LS: SS

47A ◆ 8' CONDITIONING PRACTICE

each line twice

alphabet 1 Jay knew Bix and Gavin had perfect papers on my weekly quiz.

fig/sym 2 The 6 deep-pile carpets (15' x 24 7/8') were sold at $1,039.

easy 3 Nancy is to handle all title forms for the eight auto firms.

gwam 1' | 1 | 2 | 3 | 4 | 5 | 6 | 7 | 8 | 9 | 10 | 11 | 12 |

47B ◆ 7' REVIEW FEATURES

Bold and underline existing text from the above conditioning practice as shown at the right.

1 **Jay** knew Bix and Gavin had **perfect papers** on my weekly quiz.

2 The 6 deep-pile carpets (**15' x 24 7/8'**) were sold at $1,039.

3 Nancy is to handle all **title forms** for the eight auto firms.

47C ◆ 23' LEARN FEATURES

Move. The move feature takes text from one location and places it in another.
Copy. The copy feature duplicates text from one location and places it in another.

WORDPERFECT

Move

1. Place cursor at beginning of text to be moved.
2. Depress **Alt F4** to turn block on; use arrow keys to highlight desired text.
3. Depress **Ctrl F4**.
4. Depress **B**(lock); depress **M**(ove).
5. Move cursor to new text position; strike Return.

Copy

1. Place cursor at beginning of text to be copied.
2. Depress **Alt F4** to turn block on; use cursor keys to highlight desired text.
3. Depress **Ctrl F4**; depress **B**(lock); depress **C**(opy).
4. Relocate cursor at position where you want copied text placed.
5. Strike Return.

WORKS DOS

Move

1. Move cursor to beginning of text to be moved.
2. Depress Shift key and use arrow keys to highlight text to be moved.
3. Depress **Alt**, **E**, **M**.
4. Position cursor at location where you want text moved to; strike Return.

Copy

1. Move cursor to beginning of text to be copied.
2. Depress Shift key and use arrow keys to highlight text to be copied.
3. Depress **Alt**, **E**, **C**.
4. Position cursor at location where you want copied text placed and strike Return.

WORKS MAC

Move

1. Move cursor to beginning of text to be moved.
2. Use I-beam to highlight text desired.
3. Use mouse to click on (~) **Edit**; drag (→) to **Cut** and release (or use ⌘**X**).
4. Position cursor at location where you want to place text.
5. Click (~) on **Edit**; drag (→) to **Paste** and release (or use ⌘**V**).

Copy

1. Move cursor to beginning of text to be copied; highlight text to be copied.
2. Click on **Edit**; drag to **Copy** and release (or use ⌘**C**).
3. Position cursor at location where you want copied text to be placed.
4. Click on **Edit**; drag to **Paste** and release (or use ⌘**V**).

LESSON 43 REVIEW/SKILL BUILDING

43A ◆

REVIEW KEY LOCATIONS

Enter the columns of data listed at the right as directed in Steps 1-6 on p. 74.

a	b	c	d	e	f	g
44	55	66	714	414	525	636
14	25	36	825	474	585	696
74	85	96	936	400	500	600
132	165	198	2,475	1,288	1,610	1,932

43B ◆

IMPROVE FACILITY

Enter the data listed in each column of Drills 1-3.

Note: If you are using the math function of your word processing software, remember to check your totals against the printed totals.

Drill 1

a	b	c	d	e	f	g
14	19	173	1,236	1,714	4,174	4,074
25	37	291	4,596	2,825	5,285	5,085
36	18	382	7,896	3,936	6,396	6,096
74	29	794	5,474	7,414	1,400	9,336
85	38	326	2,975	8,525	2,500	8,225
96	27	184	8,535	9,636	3,600	7,114
330	168	2,150	30,712	34,050	23,355	39,930

Drill 2

a	b	c	d	e	f	g
1	3	40	123	114	1,004	8,274
14	36	50	789	225	2,005	9,386
174	396	70	321	336	3,006	7,494
2	906	740	456	774	7,004	1,484
25	306	360	174	885	8,005	2,595
285	20	850	285	996	9,006	3,686
805	50	960	396	500	5,005	6,006
1,306	1,717	3,070	2,544	3,830	35,035	38,925

Drill 3

a	b	c	d	e	f	g
126	104	107	707	4,400	3,006	1,714
786	205	208	808	5,000	2,005	2,825
324	306	309	909	6,600	1,004	3,936
984	704	407	1,700	7,000	9,006	7,144
876	805	508	2,800	8,800	8,005	8,255
216	906	609	3,900	9,000	7,004	9,366
3,312	3,030	2,148	10,824	40,800	30,030	33,240

43C ◆

ENTER DATA WITH DECIMALS

Enter the data in Columns a-f, placing the decimals as shown in the copy.

a	b	c	d	e	f
1.40	17.10	47.17	174.11	1,477.01	10,704.50
2.50	28.20	58.28	285.22	2,588.02	17,815.70
3.60	39.30	69.39	396.33	3,996.03	20,808.75
4.70	74.70	17.10	417.14	4,174.07	26,909.65
5.80	85.80	28.20	528.25	5,285.08	30,906.25
6.90	96.90	39.30	639.36	6,396.06	34,259.90
24.90	342.00	259.44	2,440.41	23,916.27	141,404.75

46C ◆ 12'

CHECK/IMPROVE SPEED

Take 1' writings on each ¶ and 2' writings on both ¶s; find *gwam* on each writing.

all letters used | LA | 1.4 si | 5.4 awl | 85% hfw

gwam 2'

A major difference between an expert and the beginning 6
keyboard operator is that the former has put the act together, 12
but the latter is still trying to arrange the props. One keys 18
with speed and quiet control, while the other works with jerks 24
and pauses. Begin now to become an expert. 29

Like the pieces of a jigsaw puzzle, every movement as you 34
key must fit into its specific place. So if you want to get 41
your keying act together, study how you key and try to find a 47
quicker way of fitting all the pieces together. How well you 53
are able to do this is an index of your future success. 56

gwam 2' | 1 | 2 | 3 | 4 | 5 | 6 |

46D ◆ 20'

LEARN FEATURES

Bold and Underline Existing Text. Text can be bolded or underlined after it is keyed by using the block feature to highlight text and then using the specific software commands for underlining or bolding.

WORDPERFECT

1. Move cursor to beginning of text to be bolded or underlined.
2. Depress **Alt F4** to turn block on, use cursor keys to highlight text to be changed.
3. Depress **F6** to bold highlighted copy, or depress **F8** to underline highlighted copy.

WORKS DOS

1. Move cursor to beginning of text to be bolded or underlined.
2. Use Shift and arrow keys to highlight text to be changed.
3. Depress **Ctrl B** to bold highlighted copy, or depress **Ctrl U** to underline highlighted copy.

WORKS MAC

1. Move I-beam pointer to beginning of text to be bolded or underlined.
2. Click and drag (→↓ or ←↑) I-beam over the text you want changed.
3. Depress ⌘ **B** to bold highlighted copy, or depress ⌘ **U** to underline highlighted copy.

Center Existing Text. Existing text can be centered by using the specific software centering command.

WORDPERFECT

With the cursor at the beginning of text to be centered, depress **Shift F6**.

WORKS DOS

With the cursor positioned any place on the line to be centered, depress **Ctrl C**.

WORKS MAC

With the cursor positioned any place on the line to be centered, click on **Format**, drag (→) to **Justification**, drag (→) to **Center**, release.

Information at the right applies to WordPerfect only.

Reveal Codes. You can display on the screen the WordPerfect formatting codes by depressing the reveal codes keys (Alt F3). This will display where you have instructed the WordPerfect program to do such things as bold [BOLD], underline [UND], and center [CENTER]. Upper case shows the beginning of the code; lower case [bold] shows the ending of the code. Formatting features can be deleted by moving the cursor over the code and depressing the Del key.

LESSON 44 REVIEW/SKILL BUILDING

44A ◆

REVIEW KEY LOCATIONS

Enter the columns of data listed at the right.

a	b	c	d	e	f	g
477	588	707	107	41.6	141.4	936.6
417	528	808	205	52.9	252.5	825.6
717	825	909	309	63.3	393.3	719.4
1,611	1,941	2,424	621	157.8	787.2	2,481.6

44B ◆

IMPROVE FACILITY

Enter the data listed in each column of Drills 1-4.

Note: When using the math function, enter each column of data a second time (bottom to top). If you get the same total twice, you can "assume" it is correct. If you get a different total the second time, reenter the data until you get two totals that match.

Drill 1

a	b	c	d	e	f	g
5	77	114	5,808	1,936	9,300	6,936
46	89	225	3,997	2,825	8,250	3,896
3	78	336	9,408	3,796	10,475	7,140
17	85	725	5,650	8,625	7,125	4,874
28	98	825	3,714	9,436	12,740	2,515
9	69	936	2,825	8,514	12,850	8,360
10	97	704	6,796	4,174	9,674	1,794

Drill 2

a	b	c	d	e	f	g
99	795	1,581	1,881	2,642	4,573	2,185
67	657	1,691	1,991	2,772	4,683	3,274
88	234	1,339	2,202	2,992	5,477	9,396
96	359	1,221	2,432	3,743	6,409	4,585
84	762	1,101	3,303	3,853	6,886	5,872
100	485	1,144	4,650	4,714	7,936	6,903

Drill 3

a	b	c	d	e	f
1,077	3,006	5,208	7,104	1,774	7,417
1,400	3,609	5,502	8,205	2,885	8,528
1,700	3,900	5,205	9,303	3,996	9,639
2,008	4,107	6,309	7,407	4,174	3,936
2,500	4,400	6,600	8,508	5,285	5,828
2,805	1,704	6,900	9,609	6,396	4,717

Drill 4

a	b	c	d	e	f
1.4	14.00	170.40	1,714.70	7,410.95	1,147.74
2.5	17.00	170.43	2,825.80	8,520.55	2,258.88
3.6	25.00	250.90	3,936.90	9,630.65	3,369.93
7.4	28.00	288.50	4,747.17	10,585.78	7,144.74
8.5	36.00	369.63	5,878.25	11,474.85	8,255.85
9.6	39.00	390.69	6,969.39	12,696.95	9,366.63

Does your word processing software have a calculator function? If so, learn how to use it. Then complete Lessons 40-44 a second time using the calculator and checking your totals against the printed totals.

45C ◆ 12'

CHECK/IMPROVE SPEED

Take 1' writings on each ¶ and 2' writings on both ¶s; find *gwam* on each writing.

all letters used | LA | 1.4 si | 5.4 awl | 85% hfw

A vital difference exists between a job done right and one done just about right. One is given approval while the other is not. To receive full approval of the jobs you do, recognize that just about right is not adequate. Attempt now to do every task just right.

Before long you will try problems in which are applied the seemingly little things that are crucial in learning to key. Mastery of little things now is certain to make the big jobs easier to do just right a little later. Knowledge, skill, and purpose are the key to your success.

gwam 2' | 1 | 2 | 3 | 4 | 5 | 6 |

45D ◆ 10'

REVIEW WORD PROCESSING FEATURES

1. Rekey the two paragraphs of 45C.
2. Make the changes outlined at the right.

Line 1 Delete *vital*.
2 Change *just about* to **nearly**.
3 Change *of the work you do* to **of your work**.
4 & 5 Delete the final sentence of ¶1.

Line 6 & 7 Delete *in which are applied the seemingly little things*.
9 Delete *just right a little*.
9 & 10 Delete the final sentence of ¶2.
Undelete the final sentence of ¶2.

LESSON 46 BOLD, UNDERLINE, AND CENTER EXISTING TEXT

SM: defaults; LS: SS

46A ◆ 8' CONDITIONING PRACTICE

each line twice

alphabet 1 Jan Fox left my quiz show and gave back a prize she had won.
fig/sym 2 He signed a 36-month note for $1,740 (at 8.5%) on August 29.
easy 3 The city auditor may handle the penalty for the island firm.

gwam 1' | 1 | 2 | 3 | 4 | 5 | 6 | 7 | 8 | 9 | 10 | 11 | 12 |

46B ◆ 10'

REVIEW WORD PROCESSING FEATURES

Make the changes outlined at the right to the sentences you keyed for 46A.

~~Jan~~ [Tom] Fox left ~~my~~ [the] quiz show and gave back a prize ~~s~~he had won.
~~He~~ [I] signed a ~~36~~ [24]-month note for $~~1,740~~ [9,780] (at ~~8.5~~ [13.6]%) on ~~August 29~~ [October 5].
The ~~city~~ auditor may ~~handle~~ [reduce] the penalty for ~~the island firm~~ [Marsha's paying late].

KEYBOARDING WORKSHOP

SKILL BUILDING

1. Each line twice SS; DS between pairs.
2. A 1' writing on each even-numbered line.
3. Compare *gwam*; take 1' writings on three slowest lines.

word response	1	by with then worn they make corn pens them vigor their right
	2	I shall make a big name panel to hang by a door of the hall.
combination response	3	to my of him for you they were pale pink torn card goal rate
	4	The men are to fix a water pump for the big pool in the gym.
double letters	5	all ill odd ebb hall mass fizz sell cuff purr flee good need
	6	Ann will sell all her old school books at a good price, too.
adjacent keys	7	as top was open were ruin very tray coin mask soil rent port
	8	Jered was to open a coin shop in an old store at the square.
long-direct reaches	9	my gym fun mud ice sum run any curb nice must many hunt glum
	10	Ceci had much fun at the gym and the ice center this summer.
fig/sym	11	25% $483.10 #36790 PO #472-413859 Model #1600LS 2-floor plan
	12	She said: "You must keep your eyes on the copy as you key."

gwam 1' | 1 | 2 | 3 | 4 | 5 | 6 | 7 | 8 | 9 | 10 | 11 | 12 |

TIMED WRITING

Take 1' guided and 2' and 3' unguided writings.

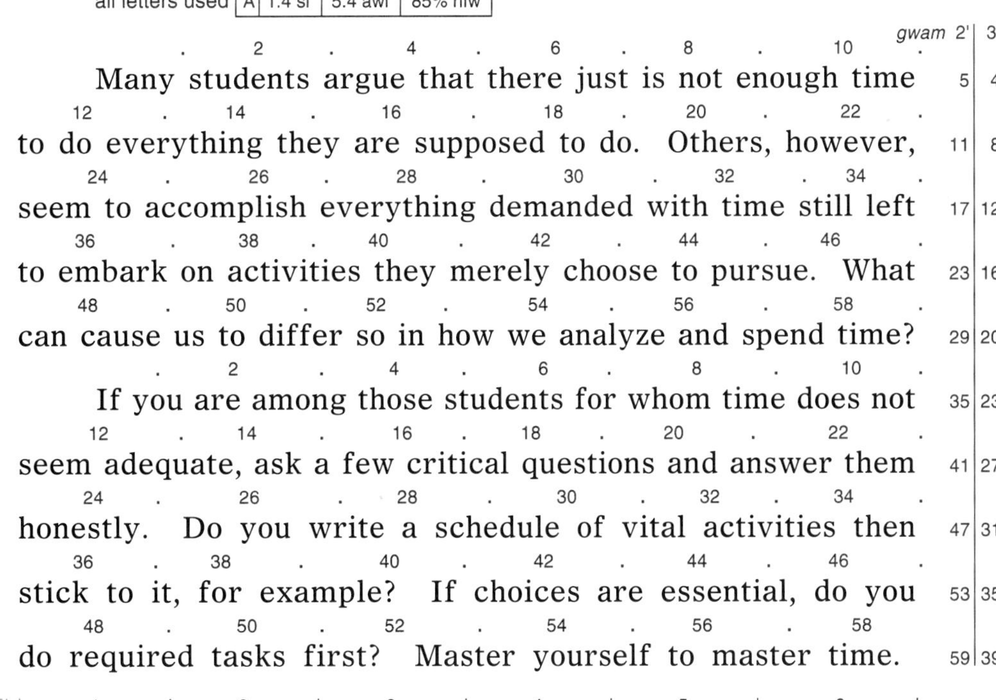

all letters used | A | 1.4 si | 5.4 awl | 85% hfw

	gwam 2'	3'
Many students argue that there just is not enough time	5	4
to do everything they are supposed to do. Others, however,	11	8
seem to accomplish everything demanded with time still left	17	12
to embark on activities they merely choose to pursue. What	23	16
can cause us to differ so in how we analyze and spend time?	29	20
If you are among those students for whom time does not	35	23
seem adequate, ask a few critical questions and answer them	41	27
honestly. Do you write a schedule of vital activities then	47	31
stick to it, for example? If choices are essential, do you	53	35
do required tasks first? Master yourself to master time.	59	39

gwam 2' | 1 | 2 | 3 | 4 | 5 | 6 |

gwam 3' | 1 | 2 | 3 | 4 |

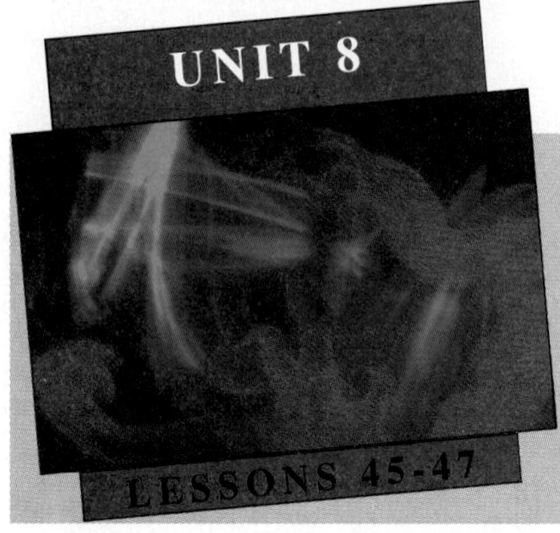

Master Word Processing Features

Learning Outcomes: After completing this unit, you will be able to

1. Use block and delete/undelete features.
2. Use bold, underline, and center features for existing text.
3. Use copy and move features.

LESSON 45 LEARN BLOCK AND DELETE/UNDELETE

SM: defaults; LS: SS

45A ◆ 8' CONDITIONING PRACTICE

each line twice SS; then three 1' writings on line 3; find *gwam*

alphabet 1 Cindy was pleased by the old quartz box Fran Majak gave her.
fig/sym 2 Brian asked, "Can't you touch-key 56, 73, $480, and 9 1/2%?"
easy 3 When did the field auditor sign the audit form for the city?

gwam 1' | 1 | 2 | 3 | 4 | 5 | 6 | 7 | 8 | 9 | 10 | 11 | 12 |

45B ◆ 20' LEARN WORD PROCESSING FEATURES

Delete/Undelete. Delete means to remove from text a segment of text such as a character or space, a word, a line, a sentence, or a defined block of text. Undelete means to restore deleted text.

Block. Block is a feature that defines a specific portion of text; used with the copy, move, and delete features. Cursor keys or mouse can be used to define (highlight) text to be deleted.

WORDPERFECT

character left of cursor	**Backspace**
character above cursor	**Del**
word	**Ctrl Backspace**
end of line	**Ctrl End**
end of page	**Ctrl PgDn**

To delete blocks of text, move cursor to beginning of text to be deleted. Depress **Alt F4** to turn block on; use arrow keys to highlight block of text to be deleted. Depress **Ctrl F4**, **B**(lock), **D**(elete). To undelete depress **F1**, **R**(estore).

WORKS DOS

character left of cursor	**Backspace**
character above cursor	**Del**
word	**Shift Ctrl →, Del**
end of line	**Shift End, Del**
end of page	**Shift Ctrl End, Del**

To delete blocks of text, move cursor to beginning of text to be deleted. Depress the shift key and strike the arrow keys to highlight the block of text to be deleted. Depress the Del key. To undelete, depress Alt Backspace.

WORKS MAC

character left of cursor	**Delete** (backspace)

To delete larger blocks of text, click (~) and drag (→↓ ←↑) the I-beam over the text to be deleted. Depress the **Delete** (backspace) key. To undelete, depress ⌘ **Z**.

1. Review the word processing features; study the specific commands for the software you are using.
2. Key the paragraph at the right; underline and bold text as shown.
3. Using the most efficient method, delete all text that is bolded or underlined.
4. Proofread paragraph and correct any keying errors.
5. Delete the entire paragraph.
6. Undelete or restore the paragraph.

Speaking before a group **of people** can cause a great deal of anxiety for an individual. This anxiety is so extensive <u>that</u> it was ranked as the greatest fear among adults in a **recent** survey. Such fear suggests that <u>many</u> people would rather perish than **go before the public to** give a talk. Much of this fear <u>actually</u> comes from a lack of experience and training in giving **public** speeches. <u>People who excel in the area of public speaking have developed this unique skill through hard work</u>.

Word Processing Feature	WORDPERFECT	WORKS DOS	WORKS MAC
Block (p. 80)	Alt F4, arrows	Shift, arrows	Click and drag
Bold (p. 42)	F6	Ctrl B (Ctrl Space Bar)	⌘B
Bold Existing Text (p. 82)	Block text to be bolded; F6	Block text to be bolded; Ctrl B	Block text to be bolded; ⌘B
Center (p. 42)	Shift F6	Ctrl C (Ctrl L)	Format, Justification, Center (Format, Justification, Left)
Center Existing Text (p. 82)	Place cursor at beginning of text to be centered; Shift F6	Move cursor to any place on line to be centered; Ctrl C	Move cursor to any place on line to be centered; click on Format; drag to Justification; drag to Center
Clear Screen (p. 95)	F7; N; N	Alt, F; C; N; N; W (on 3.0, Return)	File; Close; No; ~~ double click on WP
Copy (p. 83)	Block text to be copied; Ctrl F4; B; C; position cursor for placing text; Return	Block text to be copied; Alt, E; C; position cursor for placing text; Return	Block text to be copied; click on Edit; drag to Copy; position cursor for placing text; click on Edit; drag to Paste
Cursor Move (p. 40)			
Beginning of Line	Home, ⟵	Home	Drag I-beam pointer to desired location; click; release mouse
End of Line	Home, ⟶	End	
Top of Screen	Home, ↑	Ctrl PgUp	
Bottom of Screen	Home, ↓	Ctrl PgDn	
Right One Word	Ctrl, ⟶	Ctrl ⟶	
Left One Word	Ctrl, ⟵	Ctrl ⟵	
Delete (p. 80)			
Word	Ctrl Backspace	Shift Ctrl ⟶, Del	Block text to be deleted; depress delete key
End of Line	Ctrl End	Shift End, Del	
End of Page	Ctrl PgDn	Shift Ctrl End, Del	

Word Processing Feature	WORDPERFECT	WORKS DOS	WORKS MAC
Delete File (p. 107)	F5; Return; highlight file name; D; Y; F7	Alt, F; F; D; Return; highlight file name; Return; Return Esc	Select File; select Delete; click on file name; click on Delete; click on OK
Document Retrieval (p. 98)	Shift F10 OR F5; Return; highlight file name; R	Alt, F; O; key or highlight file name; Return	⌘O; double click on file name
Document View (p. 95)	Shift F7; 6	Alt, P; V; Alt P	⌘P; click on Print Preview
Indent from LM (p. 119)	F4	Alt, T; A; set indent; Return	Drag LM (and PI)
Line Spacing (p. 44)	Shift F8; L; S; 1 (SS) or 2 (DS); Return; F7	Ctrl 1 (SS); Ctrl 2 (DS)	Format; Spacing; Double (or Single)
Margins (p. 44)	Shift F8; L; M; #" (LM); Return; #" (RM); Return F7	Alt, P; M; Alt E; #" (LM); Alt R; #" (RM); Return	Click and drag triangles (◁,▷)
Move (p. 83)	Block text to be moved; Ctrl F4; B; M; move cursor to desired position; Return	Block text to be moved; Alt, E, M; move cursor to desired position; Return	Block text to be moved; click on Edit; drag to Cut; move cursor to desired position; click on Edit; drag to Paste
Page Break (p. 98)	Ctrl Return	Ctrl Return	Click on Format; drag to Insert Page Break
Rename File (p. 109)	F5; Return; highlight file; M; key new file name; Return; F7	Alt, F; F; R; Return; highlight file name; Return; key new file name and extension; Return; Esc	In File Menu, click on Save As; key new file name; click on Save
Reveal Codes (p. 82)	Alt F3 OR F11	None	None
Spell Check (p. 100)	Ctrl F2	Alt, O; S	Click on Spell; drag to correct spelling
Tabs (p. 124)	Shift F8; L; T; Home, Home, ←; Ctrl End Set: #" (from LM); Return; D(ecimal); R(ight); F7; F7	(Clear all tabs:) Alt, T; T; Alt A (Set:) # (tab position); Return; Alt L, Alt R, or Alt E; Return; Alt D	(Clear:) Drag tab into text (Set:) Click under ruler—once, left; twice, right; three times, decimal
Typeover Mode (p. 40)	Ins (Insert)	Block text to be replaced; key replacement text (on 3.0, Ins [Insert])	Block text to be replaced; key replacement text
Undelete (p. 80)	F1; R	Alt Backspace	⌘Z
Underline (p. 42)	F8	Ctrl U (Ctrl Space Bar)	⌘U
Underline Existing Text (p. 82)	Block text to be underlined; F8	Block text to be underlined; Ctrl U	Block text to be underlined; ⌘U